The DMA
Lead Generation
Handbook

The DMA Lead Generation Handbook

Ruth P. Stevens

Proven Techniques to Create Demand and Drive Sales

Direct Marketing Association

The Direct Marketing Association (The DMA) is the leading trade association for businesses interested in interactive and database marketing, with nearly 4,700 member companies from the United States and 53 other nations. Founded in 1917, its members include direct marketers from every business segment as well as the nonprofit and electronic marketing sectors. Included are catalogers, Internet retailers and service providers, financial services providers, book and magazine publishers, book and music clubs, retail stores, industrial manufacturers, and a host of other vertical segments, including the service industries that support them. According to a DMA-commissioned study, direct and interactive marketing sales in the United States exceeded $1.86 trillion in 2001, including $118 billion in catalog sales and $30 billion in sales generated by the Internet. The DMA's Web site is www.the-dma.org, and its consumer Web site is www.shopthenet.org.

ISBN: 0-931361-21-5

Printed in the United States of America

Preface

The concept behind *The DMA Lead Generation Handbook* grew out of the Direct Marketing Association's (The DMA's) desire to better serve the B-to-B direct marketing community. Our goal was to produce a resource that would serve as the cornerstone of The DMA's B-to-B program. Our objective was to produce a handbook that would teach B-to-B marketers the best techniques available in the lead generation process, to incorporate key industry statistics to assist managers in their budgeting efforts, and to compile a directory of the best suppliers serving the needs of the B-to-B marketplace. We believe that we've been successful in creating such a publication, which has put us well on our way toward reaching our broader goal of becoming the primary source of marketing and sales information for B-to-B marketers.

Generating leads, converting those leads to sales, and retaining those customers is the core job of every B-to-B marketer. Developing and applying a strong direct marketing skill set are the tools that business marketers need to be successful in the lead generation process. When Ruth Stevens signed on to be the author of *The DMA Lead Generation Handbook*, The DMA couldn't have been more pleased. Ruth draws on her lead generation and direct marketing expertise, and combines her experience with excellent teaching skills and a fun, easy-to-read writing style.

For those of you who are members of The DMA, you'll recognize this publication as one of the many steps The DMA has taken to improve its focus on serving the B-to-B marketplace. For those of you who are not members, we invite you to learn more about The DMA by visiting our Web site at www.the-dma.org/membership. You should also visit www.the-dma.org/b2b for additional up-to-date information on lead generation as well as other business marketing topics. And remember to make use of the Directory section of the book, which is packed with over 600 of the best suppliers of services to B-to-B marketers. Please note: The DMA has published this guide as a service to readers who want to implement lead generation programs and seek resources. No endorsement is implied by a company's inclusion as an example in the text section of this handbook.

We hope you enjoy *The DMA Lead Generation Handbook* and refer to it over and over again, as it helps you develop new business. Happy reading!

David Smith
Senior Vice President, Marketing and Business Development
Direct Marketing Association, Inc.

Acknowledgements

I am indebted to many colleagues and friends for their help, input, and advice, particularly Amy Africa, Terry Arnold, Jackie Ball, Bob Bly, Reggie Brady, Michael Brown, Larry Chase, John Coe, Perry Drake, Bill Furlong, Sandra Gassmann, Dick Goldsmith, Cyndi Greenglass, Bernice Grossman, Bob Hacker, Rich Hagle, Carolyn Hansen, Anne Holland, Russell Kern, Judy Kincaid, Brian Kirk, Mary Ann Kleinfelter, Laura McGuire, Bill McKay, Jim Obermayer, David Raab, Ellen Reid Smith, Judith Remondi, Alan Rosenspan, Simone Schoevaars, Rich Simms, Gary Skidmore, and Chad Slater.

I particularly want to thank Dave Smith, Susanne Sicilian, Ann Zeller, Jennifer Rice and Barbara Lewers of The DMA, who conceived this book's creation and shepherded it to publication. Thanks are also due to Marie Van Loan and Claire Coyne for their excellent copy editing and proofreading support.

My husband, Jim Spencer, claims he doesn't want to be acknowledged here. Since I rarely do what he wants anyway, I am not following this advice. Jim is my partner and great source of support, joy, and love, and I owe him everything.

Editorial note: Apologies to anyone who is offended by my consistent use of the masculine pronoun to refer to everyone in the business world. Frankly, the limitations of modern English usage overwhelm me. The rule is to either use the generic, but plural, "they" or craft each sentence to include he and she. So I've taken the easy — but politically indefensible — way out. I also apologize to those who view "data" as a plural noun. To me, it's become singular in modern usage, so I am taking the liberty of saying "data is" instead of "data are."

R.P.S.

Table of Contents

Introduction

Business marketing has evolved over the years from its early roots in "industrial marketing" to its more glamorous modern incarnation as "business-to-business" (B-to-B). Whatever its moniker, the objective of business marketers has always been to sell to other companies that are buying either raw materials to manufacture their own products, or services and supplies to run their businesses.

Much B-to-B marketing involves direct sales, whether via the telephone or face-to-face in the field, performed by in-house salespeople, manufacturer's reps, or resellers and distributors. The marketer's role traditionally has been to support the sales force, by providing them with the information, tools, and sales leads that will help identify the right prospective customers, get the sales rep in front of the customer, and let him close the sale.

Thus, in B-to-B, marketing is clearly a service role. It is a role that can chafe for a marketer who has been accustomed to profit and loss (P&L) responsibility. But there are consolations: business marketing is extremely complex, challenging, and fun, and the marketing role involves enormous variety, ranging from high-level strategy all the way down to selecting mailing lists.

At the most strategic level, the job of the marketer is to research and understand the needs of the market, and to select the most appropriate segments for the sales force to target. At the tactical end, the marketer's job is to build awareness, generate leads, and maximize the value of customer relationships. Marketers usually build awareness through traditional marketing communications, like advertising and publicity. You'll find marketers running seminars, developing collateral material, ordering T-shirts, and working booths at trade shows. When it comes to lead generation and customer retention, marketers turn to the powerful tools provided by direct marketing.

I. Direct marketing

Direct marketing comprises a set of marketing tools, approaches, and activities that are targeted, measurable, and driven by return on investment (ROI) considerations. Based on customer information captured and maintained in a database, and using a variety of analytical and communications techniques, direct marketing provides the underpinnings of some of today's most effective marketing approaches. These approaches include e-commerce, data mining, customer relationship management (CRM), and integrated marketing communications. The major contribution that direct marketing makes to the B-to-B marketing equation is generating leads for sales.

Lead generation can be defined as identifying prospective customers and qualifying their likelihood to buy, in advance of making a sales call. In short, it's about getting prospects to raise their hands.

The major contribution that direct marketing makes to the B-to-B marketing equation is generating leads for sales.

The DMA's annual report on market performance, *Economic Impact 2002*, estimates that, by the year 2006, direct marketing for lead generation will represent close to $878 billion in B-to-B sales and involve 5.3 million workers. Sales from lead generation are expected to grow at an annual compound rate of 8.8% through 2006. This is big business, in every sense of the word.

For salespeople, lead generation is the first part of a challenging process known as the sales cycle. Traditionally, B-to-B salespeople made cold calls, whether by physically knocking on office doors, or over the phone. They would hope to find enough qualified prospects among the population of cold calls they made to convert some of them, eventually, to buyers. After closing the sale, the salesperson would continue to call on the customer, to keep the relationship warm, and in the hope of selling something else or getting a referral to a new prospect. The entire end-to-end process, in the old days, was handled by the sales team.

In the modern business world, as the cost of using a field sales force has grown, many companies have broken this sales process into its component parts and delegated certain pieces of the process to lower-cost resources. Lead generation, qualification, and nurturing can be more efficiently handled by a direct marketing function that manages databases, direct response (DR) communications, and call centers. Once the direct marketers generate and qualify a lead, they hand it over to sales for closing. When the sale is closed, often the direct marketing function is again involved in the business of ongoing customer contact and relationship management.

A lead is little more than the name, contact information, and background information on a prospective buyer — preferably someone who has expressed some level of interest in your product, service, category, or company. A qualified lead represents a prospect who is ready to buy. The defining characteristics of "qualified" vary by industry, company, and salesperson. Typically, they involve criteria about the prospect's available budget, whether he has the authority to buy, his strength of need for the product or service, and the timing of his intended purchase. Lead generators must tailor their definitions of lead qualification to the requirements of the sales force they serve.

II. What a lead is not

It is important to distinguish a lead from an inquiry or from a mere list of names. Mailing lists or contact lists of business prospects are often presented as "lead lists"— a misnomer that sows much confusion and even ill will in the world of business marketing. Make no mistake: a passive list of prospects (or, more appropriately, suspects) does not deserve to be called a list of leads.

The same holds true for inquirers. Simply because someone has expressed a modicum of interest in you does not mean that he is ready, willing, or able to buy. But an inquirer has plenty of value. You can continue to communicate with him, nurture his interest, and keep a relationship going until he is closer to buying.

Marketers must deliver a lead to sales only when the lead is truly qualified, by criteria developed in consultation with the sales force. Consistent delivery of qualified leads that convert satisfyingly to sales and meet sales quotas is the hallmark of successful B-to-B direct marketing lead generation.

The process of lead generation is fairly straightforward. However, it involves a long and complex series of steps. You have to first establish a series of outbound and inbound contacts to generate the inquiry and qualify it as a lead; next, hand the lead over to sales; then, track the lead through conversion to sales revenue. The secret to success is in having a focus on business rules and process. Lead generation and management may be the less glamorous side of marketing because they involve developing the rules and refining them, testing, tracking, and continuous. However, the company with the best process, executed consistently, is the one with the true competitive advantage.

The company with the best process, executed consistently, is the one with the true competitive advantage.

If you are new to lead generation, and establishing a program for the first time, give yourself credit. This is as complex — and productive — a direct marketing application as exists anywhere. It can take several years to define, build, and fine-tune all the processes, so please be patient. The payoff will be huge.

There are many parties involved in the lead generation process, both internal to the company and external. Each has a role and each has a share in the credit for the results. To be successful in this kind of business environment, direct marketers must focus on elaborate planning and process development, regular consultation with sales, disciplined measurements and analysis, and constant communication with everyone.

Defining our terms

There often exists considerable confusion about the "right" meaning of various terms in lead generation. In fact, there is no right or wrong. Companies and cultures tend to create their own definitions, which are passed down internally from management, generation to generation. Usage also varies from industry to industry. For the record, here are the definitions of terms as they are used in this book:

- **Prospect:** An individual or company that is likely to need your product or service, but has not bought from you yet.

- **Customer:** An individual or company that has made a purchase from you.

- **Inquiry:** The first inbound contact from a prospective customer. An inquiry may come in "over the transom" or, more likely, from a campaign. It may also be from a current customer seeking a refill, replacement, upgrade, or new product or service.

- **Response rate:** The rate at which prospects or customers respond to an outbound campaign. It is calculated by dividing the number of responses by the number of prospects promoted. Once received, responses are called inquiries.

- **Lead (also called qualified lead):** An inquiry that has met the agreed-upon qualification criteria, such as having the right budget, decision-making authority, need for the product or service, and readiness to make the purchase in a suitable amount of time. Once an inquiry has become a qualified lead, it is ready to be worked by the sales force.

- **Qualification:** The process by which you establish whether the inquiry is qualified to become a lead.

- **Qualification rate:** The rate at which inquiries migrate to qualified leads. Calculated by dividing the number of qualified leads during a time period, or from a particular campaign, by the number of inquiries in the period, or from the campaign.

- **Nurturing:** The process of moving an unqualified inquiry to the point where it becomes qualified. Some inquiries qualify right away; many, however, need some nurturing via outbound communications until the prospect is entirely ready to be contacted by a salesperson.

- **Conversion:** When a lead becomes a sale.

- **Closed lead:** A lead that has converted to a sale.

- **Conversion rate:** The rate at which qualified leads convert to sales. It is calculated by dividing the number of closed leads by the number of qualified leads delivered to the sales force.

- **Retention:** The process of developing a customer, continuing to satisfy him, stimulating him to buy again and more frequently, and preventing him from defecting to the competition.

Please see Appendix III for additional B-to-B glossary terms.

III. How this book works

This book offers an overview of the lead generation function provided by direct marketers in the B-to-B world. It introduces the tools and techniques used in lead generation, covers how campaigns are developed, executed, and measured, and explains how campaign responses are managed and qualified for delivery to the sales function. The book then describes the sales conversion process and the role of direct marketing in the ongoing customer retention process.

You may wonder why customer retention is included in a discussion of leads. We have included retention in this book for two reasons. First, it's the job of B-to-B marketers both to acquire and to retain customers. To complete that job, marketers must find good prospective customers, convert them to buyers, and then keep them buying. It is far more profitable to retain current customers than to constantly find new ones. Second, direct marketing plays a leading role in both lead generation and customer retention — the two areas that comprise direct marketing's greatest contribution to the function and process of business marketing as a whole.

CHART 0.1
The lead generation process

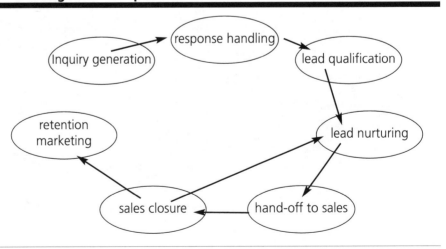

IV. Getting the most out of this book

This book is divided into five parts.

Part One reviews the elements of the lead generation tool kit. These are the databases and the communications media that direct marketers use to generate leads. In Part One, each tool is described in detail. There is also a discussion of how the tools can work together for maximum effect, and an introduction to some of the software that is now available to help in the lead generation and management process.

Part Two puts the tools to work. This section walks through the campaign process, from setting objectives, segmenting, and carrying out pre-campaign research, to developing and executing the campaign. There is also a discussion on testing — that critical DR discipline — and results analysis. Finally, we review budgeting and the roles of various functions in lead generation campaigning.

Part Three covers response management and lead conversion — how campaign responses are handled, qualified, and passed to the right sales resource, and how the sale is tracked to closure, reported on, and measured. With this section, the lead generation process comes full circle.

Part Four moves from customer acquisition to customer retention. Part Four covers retention strategies and tactics, providing you with the tools and techniques you need to keep your customers longer, ensure their satisfaction, sell them more, and improve your profits. At the end of Part Four, you will find several appendices: a list of resources for B-to-B direct marketers, a section of relevant statistics and data from The DMA, and a glossary of terms.

Part Five of this book is devoted to a directory of suppliers for B-to-B direct marketers involved in lead generation. It includes list companies, database service providers, DR agencies, production specialists, and other suppliers that specialize in business marketing. This section is arranged by function, so you can find the right suppliers quickly and easily.

1

Part One
The Lead Generation Tool Kit

Chapter 1

The marketing database

The marketing database is the essential element of the lead generation tool kit. It allows customer and prospect data to be gathered, maintained, and analyzed, for the purpose of having a deep understanding of customer value, customer needs, and business opportunity, as well as selecting the right targets for marketing communications and sales activities — the core of lead generation.

Databases of business customers are often smaller than consumer marketing databases, but they are considerably more complex. They contain data from a variety of otherwise incompatible sources, such as billing systems and sales contact management systems. They must maintain information on the various players involved in the purchase process. They are:

- **Specifiers:** the people who research and report on the specifications needed by the company.

- **Influencers:** the people who will be using the product or service to do their business and have a sizable influence on what's needed.

- **Decision-makers:** the people who have approval authority for the purchase.

■ **Purchasing agents:** the clerical people whose job it is to issue a purchase order.

Business marketing databases must also aggregate information from specific business addresses, known as "sites" or "locations," with the umbrella company or enterprise to which they belong. For some marketers, this complexity is enough to drive us back to the comforts of consumer marketing. For others, it is a stimulating and welcome challenge.

The core of a business marketing database is information about current customers and prospective customers with whom the company has already had some contact, such as inquirers. Some business marketers also maintain databases of prospects. However, most business marketers will rent information about prospects on an as-needed basis for campaigning, and will only invest in the expense of maintaining that information once the prospect has raised his hand and indicated some level of interest.

Some companies find it helpful to maintain a separate database specific to lead generation. A specialized inquiry or lead database may allow for easier management of the inquiry-to-conversion process. Other companies manage leads within their marketing database. In either case, an inquiry is a valuable new record for a company — an asset that can be nurtured and maximized for future profit.

I. Data sources

The following are key sources of data about current customers and prospects with which the company has some kind of business relationship. Keep in mind that business data is very difficult to gather and maintain accurately. Your internal data is likely to be in far worse shape than data you can get from external sources, but the payoff can be huge in both lead generation and business intelligence. When you take the plunge in gathering data internally and externally, it's a good idea to be patient, stay calm, and keep an eye on the long-term value of your efforts.

Internal data sources

1. Sales contacts

Sales contact files can range from paper Rolodexes owned by the sales staff to highly sophisticated sales force automation systems, like those from Siebel Systems and SalesLogix. A large enterprise with thousands of sales reps will have a system that can be easily set up to feed data regularly to a marketing database. Smaller companies may be using off-the-shelf tools like Act! or Goldmine, and these, too, port easily. Life gets interesting for small companies, whose sales contact data is just as likely to live in a black book, on an Excel spreadsheet, or in an Access database. Here is where patience and calm will come in handy!

Field sales and inside sales teams are likely to have the most accurate and current information about customers and prospects. This is an extremely valuable company asset. However, salespeople are often reluctant to give up this information to the marketing function. Persuading them requires some combination of carrot and stick strategies. One suggestion is to offer a proprietary newsletter, magazine, or other publication to the prospect base that salespeople perceive as valuable and won't want their accounts to miss. Another technique is to offer the sales reps themselves the chance to be included in the marketing messages to their customers. For example, their names might be used as the signatory in direct mail letters. No matter what technique you use, you'll need to undertake plenty of communication about the benefits of lead generation to both salespeople themselves and the company as a whole. Persuading sales to give up data is only the first step.

2. Billing systems

The marketing database can receive critically important data from accounting systems, primarily relating to purchase history. Billing systems can also tell you how, when, and if customers pay — data that gives valuable insight to account preferences and creditworthiness. While the transactions will relate accurately to the account, be careful of the contact data from these systems, which is likely to be from a person in an administrative function, rather than a decision-maker.

3. Operations and fulfillment systems

Similarly, operations systems may provide valuable data about a customer's channel preferences and communications needs. Whether the customer is most comfortable communicating by mail or phone, or through a sales resource like a field rep or a distributor, this is information that can predict behavior and indicate the best channels for campaign communications.

The customer's preference in shipping method may also be useful. For example, someone who consistently requests overnight delivery may be signaling some additional needs, not to mention providing an indicator of the cost to serve the account. Finally, operating systems supply frequency data, which can give insights into customers' purchase patterns and preferences.

4. Customer service systems

Information about problems and customer service contacts provides much value to the marketing database. Complaints are generally recorded by type, using a coding system; a complaint code may give insights into the nature of the customer and your relationship with him. Marketers are very likely to discover that a customer whose problem has been resolved will turn into a very loyal buyer.

5. Inquiry files

A prospect who has indicated interest in more information or perhaps a sales call is a prime prospect for further attention. Inquiry files are fed by marketing campaigns of all types, like direct mail or print advertising, trade shows and seminars, or Internet-sourced contacts.

External data sources

External data will be the most productive source of potential
new prospects.

1. Prospect lists

Prospect lists are typically rented through specialized brokers, such
as Merit Direct, or the B-to-B divisions of Direct Media, and
American List Counsel (ALC). There are hundreds of business lists
available for rent, at prices ranging from $50 per thousand ($50/M)
to more than $200/M. Business lists often focus more on the job
title or function than the individual person, and come in two general types: compiled files and response files. Other sources include
prospecting databases and e-mail lists.

▶ *Compiled files*

Compiled lists are those created from directories or other public and
private sources for the purpose of resale or rental to mailers. The
names on compiled files have some characteristics in common,
whether they are geographic or demographic, or related to industry,
job function, or product type. The two largest compilers of original
business data are Dun & Bradstreet (D&B) and InfoUSA.
Compiled data may be sorted, repackaged, and sold by other companies, like Experian and Acxiom. Compiled files are also available
via list brokers.

Compiled files tend to be rented at a relatively low rate, usually
$50/M to $100/M. They generally offer good ability to select variables, like SIC (Standard Industrial Classification) code, phone
number, and details about the location and its relation to a corporate entity. This data is often sourced from larger compilers and
appended as an enhancement to make the names more valuable to
list renters.

Often, compiled files offer only the job function, known as a
"title slug," without an actual person's name. On an older file, it
may be more productive to mail, from a response standpoint, by job
function or title instead of by individual name, since people change
jobs so often.

If you are looking for particular niches in the market, you are likely to find a compiled list of suitable prospects for just about any business category. For example, you can find lists of federal government buyers from Amtower & Company, lists of schoolteachers from Market Data Retrieval (a subsidiary of D&B), and computer installation data from Harte-Hanks Market Intelligence. CC3 Source offers specialized databases of professionals in technology, law, accounting, real estate, and health care.

Because compiled lists are created solely for the purpose of rental, it's important that they be researched carefully. Before you rent, ask a lot of questions about list source and recency.

You'll want to test your way into compiled files judiciously. For example, take small amounts of a list to mail before rolling out to the balance available. Also, check a number of selectable variables (known as "selects") in testable quantities to find out which ones are most powerful in your situation.

▶ Response files

Response lists are created as by-products of other businesses and industries, such as catalog sales, seminar enrollments, trade organization memberships, or magazine and newsletter subscriptions. Response files tend to be more accurate than compiled files, and usually contain some information about product or service interest or buying authority. The fact that these people have joined, subscribed, or otherwise taken an action in the business world indicates that they are "responsive," and may be better prospects for lead generation than someone whose name was copied from a directory. On the other hand, response files represent a self-selected group, and thus cannot be counted on to serve as complete universes of all the potential prospects in a category. Also, they are less likely to have additional data available for targeted selection.

Catalogs represent one of the largest categories of B-to B response lists on the market, with office supplies a major catalog sub-category. Companies like Viking Office Products, Quill, Staples, and Hello Direct rent and exchange their names regularly. Another large sub-category is computer catalogs like PC Connection and Global Computer. Business seminar providers that rent their files include National Seminars, the American Management Association, The DMA, and Padget Thompson.

Magazine and periodical subscription files comprise either paid subscribers or controlled circulation. Leaders in the paid subscription world are *The Wall Street Journal, Business Week, Fortune, Fast Company,* and *Forbes.* Controlled circulation means that the subscribers receive the publication gratis, but they fill out a sometimes lengthy form to prove that they are qualified readers. Some leading providers of controlled magazine subscription files are Cahners Business Lists, Penton, IDG, Miller Freeman, and Ziff-Davis.

Both magazine list types may have additional data appended for good selectability. Selects available with response lists are similar to those in the consumer world, for example, subscription recency, and acquisition source. But publication files often are able to offer other selects as well, such as title, function, company size, buying authority, and products or services purchased.

Response files are, not surprisingly, priced higher than compiled files. Response files range from $95/M to $150/M, with hi-tech industry lists priced at a premium, in the $175/M to $250/M range.

▶ Prospecting databases

In recent years, some mailers have experimented with prospecting databases as a way to lower costs and increase the list options available to them. Typically, a prospecting database will be built and maintained by your list broker or manager, using the rental lists that are most productive for you. The benefit to you is fast and convenient access to pre-de-duplicated names that have appropriate appended information in place, and with approvals already secured.

Large catalogers like PaperDirect and Day-Timers have built their own dedicated prospect databases, populated by scores of rental files, which are all appended and de-duplicated. Even if your operation is too small to justify the investment in building a proprietary prospecting database, you can pre-negotiate list rentals on a frequency basis, thereby saving considerable money versus a series of one-time rentals.

Abacus, a division of DoubleClick, runs a membership database of business buyers called the B-to-B Alliance. In order to use names in the database, you must agree to contribute your entire file to it. Open cooperative business databases have been built by large brokers such as MeritBase from MeritDirect, and Data Warehouse from Direct Media. These databases offer not only good selects, but also pre-approvals and data modeling services. They may be more appropriate for smaller mailers in narrower industry segments.

▶ E-mail lists

E-mail lists are increasingly available and are proving to be very productive for business mailers. However, good e-mail response files have been slow to come to market. Most list brokers include e-mail list recommendations among their offerings and serve as a useful one-stop shop for what's available in both postal mail lists and e-mail lists.

Some of the best e-mail response files available in B-to-B are from publications, such as files from Ziff-Davis, IDG, Miller Freeman, and Cahners Business Lists. Also popular are Web-generated files such as Tech Republic, NetCreations, and MyPoints. Pricing for e-mail lists is changing quickly, since the industry is so new. Prices now range from $200/M to around $300/M. Many list owners add another $100/M for delivery, but are under considerable pressure to moderate this practice. Due to the industry's immaturity and rapid evolution, you will want to negotiate prices aggressively.

Businesses can take advantage of several services that will append e-mail addresses to their house files. For instance, Thumbprints, a service of Direct Media, investigates the e-mail address conventions at major companies, and then imputes the likely e-mail addresses of employees. Another approach is used by Markets on Demand and eDirect, which have created large databases of e-mail and postal addresses, and will conduct a match against your house file. Both services are relatively new, but show promise.

The converse is also now available. BusinessEdentify, a service of Direct Media, will append to your e-mail address the company's SIC code and sales volume data for approximately $0.25 per match.

2. Appended information

The large business file owners will make their information available for appending to your house file. You can overlay your file with such important data fields as SIC code, title, phone number, credit rating, executive contacts, and company size at a very low cost, ranging from $0.15 to $6 per piece matched, depending on the data element required. Most data providers require a minimum investment of around $2,000, but this amount may cover the entire price for a small file. Cahners Business Lists, Acxiom's InfoBase, InfoUSA, D&B, and iMarket (a Dun & Bradstreet subsidiary) are among the larger append service providers. D&B also offers information about a company's affiliation with other business entities, like a corporate parent company.

Appended data can be very useful. It is rather inexpensive and readily available, and can be very predictive for profiling purposes. On the other hand, be skeptical of its complete accuracy, given the high degradation rates of business data.

You may also want to explore the availability of industry vertical appends. The circulation file of a trade magazine in your industry, for example, may provide useful information to append to your house file. There are many specialized files available in larger industries, such as technology, utilities, and chemicals. A good list manager or broker specializing in your industry will be able to introduce you to the available alternatives.

II. Data fields

The data fields in chart 1.1 are those typically maintained by business marketers. Each industry and company will adjust this list as applicable to its specific needs.

CHART 1.1
Data fields used in marketing databases

Contact information: Name, address, phone/fax numbers, and e-mail address.

Title: Frequently, the contact's title is captured, but it's also a good idea to identify his function from a standardized list. This practice forces uniformity in a world where titles can be so random as to be almost meaningless. You may also want to capture his role in the purchase decision (e.g., specifier, influencer, decision-maker, etc.).

Enterprise versus site: Contact information is typically gathered at the site level — that is, the business location of the individual or the group. But you need to allow for a field to capture the relationship between the site and its parent enterprise. Typically, you will use an enterprise ID number with a suffix to indicate the site location.

SIC or NAICS: The U.S. Government is currently in the process of migrating the four-digit SIC system, a relic from the 1930s, to a new six-digit system called NAICS, or North American Industry Classification System. NAICS was developed in cooperation with Canada and Mexico. Read all about it at http://www.census.gov/epcd/www/naics.html. NAICS is a more modern classification system, reflecting the new realities of how our information economy operates. The migration process is proving cumbersome to both businesses and data providers, so progress is slow, albeit steady. In the meantime, check into http://www.osha.gov/oshstats/sicser.html, where you can search for SIC codes by keyword, and vice versa. Note: some companies use their own internally defined industry indicator instead of SIC codes, or as a supplement to them.

Year started in business.

Public versus private.

Revenue or sales: In the case of a publicly traded firm, it is easy to find and record revenues. Record company revenue at either the site level or enterprise level, depending on what is more meaningful for your business.

Employee size: In the case of privately held companies, where revenue numbers are not available, the number of employees can be used as a very powerful substitute indicator of purchase propensity and buying process.

Purchase history: Capturing what the account has purchased in the past, the date, the dollar amount, the order placement method, the payment method, and the frequency provides information that is highly predictive of future purchase propensity.

Credit score: This is either an internally generated indicator or a commercially available score from a provider like Dun & Bradstreet or Experian.

Size of Yellow Pages advertising: As odd as it may seem, the extent to which a company actively promotes itself here can be a predictive variable for direct marketers in some industries.

Product history: This includes the price, category, stock-keeping unit (SKU) numbers, and product names of item(s) purchased. Also keep a record if the purchased product was later discontinued and removed or uninstalled.

Purchase preferences: It can be helpful to record details about how accounts like to buy, their preferred channels, their terms, and other information that may be predictive.

Qualification questions: If your company has developed standard qualification questions, such as budget, authority, need, and time frame, and has a scoring system in place, this data will be helpful for sorting and selecting campaign targets.

Survey questions: Information gathered by mail, phone, e-mail, or Web-based surveys, such as customer satisfaction, needs, capabilities, and interests.

Promotion history: The frequency, medium, offer code, cost, and type of your outbound contacts with the account can be helpful in two ways: as a predictor of purchase propensity and as part of a customer value analysis. Response history is also helpful here.

Service history: This documents the contacts the customer has had with your service center, such as inquiries, returns, and problems, plus their resolution.

Source code: This indicates where the first contact with this person originated. Some companies also record the most recent source of the contact, which serves as an indicator of campaign results.

Data hygiene

Business data tends to degrade quickly. Jobs change, departments are reorganized, and numerous forces conspire to make it tough for us to stay in contact with our customers and prospects. By some estimates, business files degrade at the rate of 3% per month, which means that over a third of your file each year may become undeliverable or give you false intelligence. Even worse, as companies are bought, sold, and merged in the normal course of expansion and contraction, your ability to maintain correct information on influencers, purchasing agents, and other factors in your customers' buying processes are regularly imperiled.

But business contacts tend to represent a lot of value, so it is both important and potentially profitable to invest in data hygiene. There are a number of ways to keep customer and prospect data fresh and up-to-date:

- Develop processes to capture all non-delivered mail and update the database accordingly. The best way to do this is to mail First-Class and state "Return Service Requested" on the outer envelope. You will need a separate process for e-mail. The key point is that the marketing organization must develop these processes carefully and monitor them with vigilance.

- Take regular statistical samples of the data and check it manually via outbound phone calls. Decide in advance the acceptable incidence of errors in the record. If that error rate is exceeded, then undertake an outbound communications program by phone and e-mail to update the records. You may want to segment the file, investing more in keeping up data about your best customers and less in those who have not bought from you regularly.

- Encourage your best customers to maintain their own data on your Web site. Build a password-protected area for them to use, and explain the value to them in maintaining contact with you, their supplier. You might even consider offering an incentive, whether it be better terms, a discount, or some other offer.

Database issues

1. What data not to collect

Give careful consideration to the data you want to gather and maintain. It's tempting to want it all. But there are significant costs in data acquisition and maintenance, so be sure your data fields request only information that will have solid business value.

The issue is not data storage, which is relatively inexpensive these days. The real expense results from data degradation. Inaccurate data is worse than no data at all. So before you decide to focus on a particular data element, make sure that it is available, that you can maintain its accuracy, and that using it will drive business results.

USPS recommendations: Data hygiene/standardization

B-to-B mailers have many more data elements to be concerned about than the simple three-line consumer address. There are various permutations of firm names, the use of prestige/vanity addresses, auxiliary company and personnel data, i.e., titles – personal/professional and departmental or division, etc. Moreover, company, contact, distribution, and delivery address information for businesses can be daunting. Therefore, for the B-to-B mailer, the scope of address standardization and list maintenance and correction is quite complex.

The following are data elements that could be included in a business-to-business address.

Company/contact information — typically for purposes of presentation and marketing impact

Name prefix
First name
Middle name or initial
Surname
Suffix title (Title, Jr., Sr., PhD, Dr., DDS, etc.)
Professional title
Functional title
Division/department name
Mailstop code

Distribution and delivery address information:

Street number
Pre-directional
Street name
Street suffix
Post directional
Secondary unit indicator
Secondary number
Company name
PO box number
City
State
ZIP code
ZIP+4 code
Carrier route code
Optional endorsement
Key line code
POSTNET barcode
POSTNET address block barcode

Distribution and delivery address data elements are the focus of USPS standardization recommendations.

The U.S. Postal Service (USPS) has worked with B-to-B mailers in developing guidelines/standards for address formatting, standard abbreviations, and address compression to help alleviate the following problems that can result in processing B-to-B lists: inefficiencies in the merge/purge process, poor address hygiene, missed opportunities for barcoding discounts, and ultimately non-deliverability.

Most B-to-B list maintenance companies have adopted the USPS standards as part of their processing procedures. For a quick and easy reference, visit the USPS Web site (www.usps.com) and search for Publication 28, *Postal Addressing Standards*. Chapter three in Publication 28 focuses on B-to-B addressing.

2. Merge/purge

As valuable as it is, business data can be a nightmare. Consumer data is hard enough to manage, but when the extra variable of "company" is introduced to a record, all kinds of things can happen. Business locations may vary within the same company. Company names can be misspelled on different records. Information is frequently missing or incorrect. You have to decide whether you want to manage duplicate contact records at the site level or at the enterprise level. For these reasons, matching a new record with an existing record becomes very difficult.

But merge/purge is critically important to data management. It allows a new record or new data elements to be introduced to the marketing database correctly, it allows you to keep track of the various contacts within a site that you want to influence, and it allows records to be selected for campaigns efficiently. Merge/purge is a specialized skill, and it benefits greatly from the help of an outside service provider with a lot of experience with business data. Such firms as InfoUSA, Creative Automation, Harte-Hanks, Anchor Computer, and Acxiom can assist.

When selecting a service provider, it's a good idea to inspect the results of their matching algorithms as they apply to your business. One method for testing their results is to send each vendor a sample of data from a limited area — a mid-sized city, for example — and ask them to provide a printout of the duplicates they identify. A close look at the eliminated records as well as the survivors will give you a good sense of which method is most appropriate for you.

3. Database modeling

Since business files tend to be small in number but complex within each record, many of the excellent data modeling techniques that have been developed in the high-volume consumer world have limited application in B-to-B.

The easiest and least expensive database modeling application in lead generation is penetration analysis, which involves comparing your file of accounts to the larger universe of existing companies, usually by four- or six-digit SIC code. A relatively high penetration percent in certain industry segments might indicate "low-hanging fruit" there for you to pursue.

When it comes to developing predictive models from house files, most business databases rely on cluster analysis and CHAID (an abbreviation for the Chi-Square Automatic Interaction Detector), which allows relatively rich insights to be extracted from a relatively small number of records. CHAID is a kind of "tree algorithm" that develops statistically significant groupings of records based on behaviors, such as response or payment.

Clustering finds groupings based on a variety of variables (e.g., company size, industry, and purchase patterns). These clusters can then be used to create segmented messages relevant to each group. A cluster analysis of your best customers can help identify the characteristics you should be looking for when prospecting.

4. Who owns/manages the database?

The direct marketing function is the primary user and beneficiary of the marketing database. But most of the responsibility for the database itself rests with the information technology (IT) function. This results in a fascinating symbiotic relationship, which may be the source of some tension, as the IT and marketing functions must work hand-in-hand with one another.

IT clearly has the skills, resources, experience, and responsibility for managing and operating technology in a company. Marketing must decide what customer data is to be collected, what service levels will be required to maintain the data, and how the data is to be used. In addition, there is good reason for marketing to own the database budget, so that company needs for speed and service levels are met.

One solution to this cross-functional issue is to create a dedicated IT group that services and supports the marketing group. Also, as database software and querying tools become increasingly easy to use, IT is becoming more comfortable with sharing data access with the marketing function.

III. Segmentation

Once data is gathered and cleaned, it becomes possible to figure out how to target the right prospects. Targeting involves identifying the best potential prospects and selecting the ones most appropriate to approach with marketing communications. The first step in targeting is to divide the prospective universe into groups, based on a number of defining characteristics. This process is known as segmentation.

There are two reasons for segmenting the universe. First, it offers a handy way to group campaign targets in order to create the right messages, use the right communications channels, and increase the likelihood of response. Second, it allows each segment to operate as a small universe on its own for testing and rollout. You can test your messages to a part of the segment and later expand the communication to the rest of the segment with confidence that it will respond similarly.

An infinite number of variables can be used to create marketing segments. The most meaningful segments will be a function of the characteristics of your industry and your go-to-market strategy.

But first, a word on segmentation criteria. As market data becomes more available and computing power lets us analyze markets with considerable precision, it's very important to be disciplined about creating segments that will be meaningful to the business. Your marketing segment needs to be large enough in its profit potential to justify the effort. It needs to be accessible, whether by current sales channels or new ones that can be established. It must be serviceable, which means that your company has the resources and processes in place to manage the relationship. There is no point in targeting market segments that can't be served profitably. You must also consider the inevitable trade-off between the targetability of narrow segments and the cost of analyzing and customizing programs for small groups.

The following is a list of segmentation variable criteria frequently used by business marketers:

- The relationship existing today between the company and the buyer
  - Customers vs. prospects
  - Cold prospects vs. inquirers
  - Repeat customers vs. first-time buyers
  - Frequent customers vs. occasional buyers
  - Sales coverage
  - Source from which the buyer responded (trade show, seminar, mail, Internet, customer service call, etc.)
  - Offer to which they responded

- Geographics
  - Region, state, metropolitan area, etc.
  - Climate
  - Proximity to distribution channels or competitors

- Demographics, sometimes known as "firmographics"
  - SIC code or NAICS
  - Sales volume
  - Number of employees
  - Credit rating
  - Buyer characteristics (gender, purchasing patterns, style, etc.)
  - Buying process and requirements
  - Year founded

- Purchase history
  - Product lines/services offered
  - Stage in the life cycle of the product or service
  - RFM (recency, frequency, and monetary value of purchases)
  - Competitive purchases

Once the market is segmented, the campaign planner can make some critical decisions:

- Which segments to target in this campaign?

- How much customization of the campaign messaging or communication medium is required by segment?

- Which segments indicate the need for new products/services or new offers to be developed?

IV. Profiling

One of the easiest ways to select the right segments is to extract indicators from your current customer base. Characterizing your best and worst customers in a process known as profiling will offer some solid direction on new customers to pursue or avoid. Profiling can be done on a cocktail napkin or by building a statistical model. Briefly, it involves identifying the key characteristics of a group and using those characteristics to identify look-alikes in a prospect universe. Predictive characteristics are likely to include industry, company size (using number of employees as a proxy), company revenues, and geographic territory.

Characterizing your best and worst customers in a process known as profiling will offer some solid direction on new customers to pursue or avoid.

Profiling is an excellent step beyond simple segmentation by the variables discussed above because it allows you to identify prospects who are very similar to your best customers, and thus very likely to want to do business with you. However, it is not always possible to identify prospect pools by the actual characteristics of your best customers. For example, say your best customers turn out to be those who prefer to buy through a certain class of distributors. Knowing that will set you toward a marketing strategy of maximizing your relationships with that kind of distributor. But it's unlikely that you will be able to find media channels, such as mailing lists, that deliver buyers with that particular distribution channel preference per se.

Chapter 2

Direct response communications used in lead generation

After the database, the most important element in the lead generation tool kit is direct response (DR) communications — namely, outbound messages that ask for some kind of action or response from the recipient. DR communications act as a substitute for a sales force's face-to-face effort. In order to get people's attention and overcome their inertia, DR communications usually contain an offer or an incentive, as well as a specific call to action.

In the lead generation process, DR communications are the engine for gaining prospects' interest and for nurturing that interest, along the sales cycle toward closure. In complex buying situations, it's likely that a series of ongoing DR communications will be needed to get to the point where a lead is qualified enough to hand over to a salesperson.

I. Direct mail

The workhorse of DR communications for lead generation is direct mail. Addressable, intrusive, and flexible, direct mail has served us well for decades.

Direct mail formats

Business mailers generally prefer enveloped mail, whether it is inside #10 business size envelopes or 6 x 9 inch or larger packages. The standard elements of a consumer direct mail package (outer envelope, letter, brochure, reply form, business reply envelope [BRE]) work solidly for lead generation. If you plan to send an enveloped communication, do not succumb to the temptation to combine elements within the package. In a misguided attempt to save money, business mailers sometimes make the mistake of collapsing the letter and response device into the brochure. The result is nothing more than a self-mailer in an envelope, which is in itself unproductive and wasteful.

If you are looking for ways to save money on what to include in the envelope, insert the letter only. Business marketers often get away with just a well-written letter, as long as it contains a response device — i.e., a fax number, an 800 number, an e-mail address, or a URL. Letters are particularly effective when they are used to deliver a hard offer, such as asking for an appointment or paving the way for a phone follow-up.

Since business mail universes are small, your objective should be to penetrate them as deeply as possible. This means using every trick in the direct mail tool kit that lifts response. One of the most powerful among these is personalization. The incremental cost of laser personalization today is negligible, and personalization has become a de facto standard in B-to-B direct mail. New technologies for personalization are coming into the market at a rapid pace. Digital variable printing, for example, lets the personalization go beyond mere black-and-white lasered letters to customization of the entire message, art, and copy, in four colors, for each recipient. Software from suppliers like Xmpie enables customized communications in multiple media, which makes one-to-one communications faster and easier to produce.

1. Self-mailers

Business mailers also have great success with the self-mailer format. Self-mailers are widely used to promote seminars and trade shows.

The main advantages of self-mailers are their low cost and the fact that they are more likely than enveloped pieces to be passed along from one in-box to another within an office. There is still considerable debate about which is better for lead generation campaigns — a self-mailer or a package. Of course, the only answer to that question is to test.

2. Postcards

Postcards are also widely used in lead generation — typically oversized ones that announce a new product feature, service, or an upcoming seminar. This type of communication serves the need to stay in touch with a prospect, but does not require much detailed explanation or content. Postcards appeal to marketers because of their low cost, and to recipients because they can be skimmed and absorbed quickly.

3. Dimensional mail

Another format that business mailers use regularly is so-called dimensional packages. These are oversized, cleverly designed, and typically very expensive pieces that are intended to cut through the clutter of an administrative person's in-box, and actually get past the gatekeeper and onto the desk of a decision-maker. They often contain a physical premium: a video, gift, or some item that someone in the office thinks the boss will want to see. These packages can be quite effective in business marketing because they prove to be affordable. Samples of award-winning dimensional mail pieces can be found on the Echo Awards CD that is produced by The DMA: www.the-dma.org/industryawards/echo.shtml.

4. Catalogs

Catalogs are an important and versatile B-to-B tool, bridging both the sales and marketing functions. They can be used to sell, or as a mail order channel, or they can serve as collateral material, providing an easily referenced and long-lasting source of detailed product or service information for customers.

Postage: First-Class vs other classes

Business mailers tend to use First-Class Mail with good reason. For one thing, their universes are small and frequently do not qualify for bulk mail presort discounts. Also, business mailers are unwilling to accommodate any level of undeliverability, since each prospect has such a high potential value.

Business mailers that enjoy large volumes, notably catalogers and seminar or conference providers, may choose other classes of mail that allow presorting discounts. Many catalogers put their catalogs in envelopes in order to look more like First-Class, and move more smoothly through the corporate mail room. Other tricks in this vein include metering, or using live stamps or pre-cancelled stamps. Some companies do not use First-Class Mail for heavier mailing pieces, like fulfillment packages or dimensionals, but it is a good idea to test your way into this strategy in order to be sure the postage savings are not completely offset by lower delivery rates.

Postal rates are always changing. For the latest prices for various mail classes, visit www.usps.com.

Catalogs may be an expensive vehicle for prospecting. For this purpose, many mail-order companies develop an abbreviated catalog that they can mail more cheaply. Larger, comprehensive product-line catalogs are more likely to be viewed as a retention tool, allowing current customers to buy more when they need new or replacement products.

It makes sense to develop plans for using a catalog at various stages of the contact stream. Your catalog can serve as either an inquiry fulfillment piece or an effective second touch after the fulfillment package has been sent. New editions of your catalog will be productive during the nurturing process, as a way to provide value and keep in touch with the prospect.

Here are some principles to guide you in using catalogs for lead generation:

- Decide clearly in advance whether the catalog is intended to sell or to support face-to-face sales. If it is intended to sell, be sure to follow the tried-and-true principles of mail order cataloging.

- Just because you are promoting a business product, do not ignore the power of promotional language and graphics. Stress the benefits in both headlines and body copy. Technical specifications, which often are important to the buyer, can be detailed on your Web site. In the printed catalog, however, use lively, jargon-free copy.

- Supplement your print catalog with a Web-based catalog, where you can take advantage of search engines, limitless product depth, and inexpensive updating capabilities.

- Don't be afraid to use some of the classic consumer techniques — even in a business catalog: make promotional offers, use testimonials and guarantees, and humanize the catalog with people's photos.

- Feature your most popular products and hard-to-get items.

- Avoid offering low-priced merchandise in catalogs that will be used for lead generation. Creating multiple small orders will not endear you to the sales team.

Circulation levels for B-to-B catalogs are significantly lower than consumer and hybrid (see Chart 2.1). However, B-to-B books are significantly larger, feature 10 times as many products, and generate twice as much revenue as consumer or hybrid catalogs.

CHART 2.1
Circulation statistics for flagship b-to-b catalogs

Circulation statistics	B-to-B
Median annual circulation	1,500,000
Median number mailings per year	9
Median number pages per catalog	90
Median number products per catalog	4,500
Median order size	$252.00
Median number of items per order	2.7
Median net sales per catalog	$5.34
Median number of orders per year	128,000
Median number of pages circulated in '00	90,000,000
Percentage of catalogs represented by flagship	100.0%
Median cost per book - house file	$0.93
Median cost per book - prospecting	$0.98

Source: The DMA State of the Catalog/Interactive Industry Report, 2001.

II. Telephone

Traditionally, the telephone has been a very productive tool for lead generation. The beauty of the telephone is that it is flexible, personal, and cost-effective, and supports both inbound and outbound communications. Outbound phone calls are usually used in lead generation as a substitute for — or a supplement to — direct mail. This function is typically known as telemarketing, and its power lies in its ability to penetrate small universes effectively. Inbound, the phone is frequently used as a response device, meaning one of several options for prospects to express their interest if they prefer the phone to the Web or to a BRC.

But the phone has many other uses in generating leads. It is effective in response qualification, either inbound or outbound, when the operator poses a series of questions to evaluate the prospect's likelihood to buy. The phone is also productive for lead nurturing, when the prospect is not ready to buy, but the marketer wants to keep in touch, continue the relationship, and be there when the time is right for the prospect to see a salesperson.

Here are some tips on using the telephone to generate, qualify, and nurture leads:

- Cold calling to generate inquiries can be very effective if the list is targeted. One technique to increase the likeli-

---

Tips on telephone scripting

- Treat each business call as a conversation, not a sales pitch.

- Because B-to-B contact rates are lower than consumer rates, your script needs to be developed so it is more persuasive when you do get the prospect on the phone.

- Breakthrough creativity is not the key ingredient in successful telemarketing scripts. It is even more important to follow the established formula: gain the customer's attention, establish credibility, qualify the customer, and then move to the offer and the call to action.

- To gain credibility, have the caller state his name, title, company, and reason for the call.

- Personalize each script so that it is relevant to the customer's situation. Position features as benefits. Discuss what's in it for the customer.

- Scripts should include an explanation of the reason for the call, such as "Thanks for visiting our Web site," or to learn the prospect's reactions to the materials he reviewed.

- Ask for and record your customers' preferred contact methods — then honor their preferences.

- Far more important than the script itself are the research and preparation that should precede the call. Encourage your reps to find out, in advance, everything they can about the prospect and his needs. Visit the prospect's Web site, check the financial and trade press for articles about him, and, most obviously, review any information maintained internally on him.

hood of success is to select lists with characteristics similar to those of your best customers.

■ Calling for inquiry generation is best performed as a follow-up to a relevant event, such as an outbound marketing communications contact, a seminar or trade show visit, or a news article in the trade press. This way, the content of the call has a meaningful reference point and is no longer simply "cold."

■ Link the telephone function to the marketing database. With a "live" link, phone reps can take advantage of useful background about the prospect, and update the database record with information gathered via phone.

> ### In-house versus outsource
>
> *When to outsource your telephone functions:*
>
> • Your scripts are clear and consistent.
>
> • You experience peaks and valleys in your call volume requirements.
>
> • The function is simple, like order taking or event registration.
>
> *When to keep your telephone functions in-house:*
>
> • The conversation is complex and unpredictable.
>
> • For sales management of large accounts.
>
> • Customers expect empowered operators to solve their problems.

■ Outbound contact rates for business telephone calls are generally half those of consumer telemarketing, since business prospects are often screened by gatekeepers and voice mail. Delay discussing the nature of the call until the prospect himself is on the phone. Do not talk about the issue at hand with an assistant or leave a detailed voice mail message for the contact.

■ If you are using various offers in different media channels, be sure to apply your best offer to the phone. A prospect who knows of a better offer elsewhere will respond unfavorably to a weaker offer over the phone.

■ Many companies have sprung up to provide outsourced telemarketing services that are specific to B-to-B lead generation. LeadMasters, for example, specializes in setting up appointments for sales reps. The Sutherland Group specializes in sales lead generation via outbound telemarketing.

- Your company must decide for itself how many phone contacts you are willing to impose on customers and prospects. Outbound telemarketers usually set limits ranging from 90 days at a minimum to as long as 6 months.

- Use the very best phone reps you can afford. The telephone is a highly personal medium. If you are represented by someone with poor grammar, a bad attitude, or an incomprehensible accent, your business reputation will suffer.

- Consider using one of the industry-specific outbound telemarketing firms now available. Many of them are staffed with retired professionals who have solid industry knowledge, plus the skills and presence to conduct a high-quality conversation with a decision-maker.

Telephone script example, courtesy of Harte-Hanks Response Management

Lead Generation Program Call Script

INTRO: Hello, my name is <INSERT NAME> calling XYZ Company. We provide data storage, management, and protection solutions for companies looking to optimize their data availability. <PROSPECT NAME>, are you the person who is responsible for your company's data storage, management, or protection?
    YES   Continue to Q2
    NO   Continue to Q1

Q1. Who is responsible for this area within your company?
    RECORD NAME AND PHONE NUMBER
    EDIT EXISTING RECORD WITH NEW PERSON
    ATTEMPT TO CONTACT THIS NEW PERSON
    REVERT TO INTRO AND CONFIRM THEY ARE RESPONSIBLE FOR THIS AREA OF
    THEIR BUSINESS

Q2. In working with our customers, we've found that people in your position are expecting a great deal of pressure to provide a reliable and scalable solution for data storage, protection, and management. I suspect you too are feeling the pressure as well. (PAUSE…LET PROSPECT RESPOND)

Q3. What is some of the uniqueness in your business that is contributing to the challenges you are expecting? (*Allow prospect to freely discuss their issues. Prod only if needed.*)

> BUSINESS GROWTH (what percentage)
> MULTIPLE PLATFORMS (which ones)
> DISTRIBUTED ACCESS ISSUES (internet/intranet, lan, wan, remote users)
> BACK-UP ISSUES (what media are they using)
> OTHER (record a short description)

Q4. Have you developed formal plans for dealing with some of these issues?

> YES   Continue to Q5
> NO   Continue to Q6

Q5. What kinds of things are you considering?

> CAPTURE FREE FORM RESPONSE

Q6. XYZ works with companies like Qualcomm and Sony to deliver reliable solutions for issues that are similar to those you've also mentioned. In working with our customers, we've found that assessing their storage needs and recommending the right solutions has made a significant impact in their business. These types of assessments are usually offered for a consulting fee, but we are launching a new service to help customers such as you deal with these challenging issues.

Q7. *TRAIL CLOSE:* Many have found this free assessment to be a valuable step toward identifying some reliable solutions. Would you find this helpful for your business? (PAUSE…ALLOW PROSPECT TO RESPOND)

> YES   Continue to Q10
> NO   Continue to Q8

Q8. *REBUTTAL:* You mentioned earlier that <Response to Q3> was something uniquely challenging at this time and that you planned to deal with it by <Response to Q4>, is that still the case? Given the fact that several of those solutions will eventually cost money, wouldn't a free assessment present less risk at this stage of the game? (PAUSE…ALLOW PROSPECT TO RESPOND)

> YES   Continue to Q10
> NO   Continue to Q9

Q9. 2nd REBUTTAL: Okay, we understand. However, since you've indicated you will have to eventually deal with some of these challenges, I'd like to check back with you in a couple of weeks, would that be okay?

> YES   SCHEDULE SPECIFIC RECONTACT DATE
>   Continue to Close 1
> NO   Continue to Close 2

Q10. That's great, I'd like to have one of our consultants contact you to schedule/confirm a specific date and time for that assessment. Let's schedule something tentative right now. What does your schedule look like next week?
    RECORD SPECIFIC TIME AND DATE

CLOSE 1: Thank you for your time today. I really appreciate the opportunity to speak with you about XYZ and the solutions we provide. Have a nice day. Goodbye.

CLOSE 2: Thank you for your time today. Hopefully we can assist you in the future. Goodbye.

III. Internet

Many business marketers believe that, when it comes to lead generation, the Internet offers boundless opportunities. Indeed, the Internet performs many of the same functions of direct mail and the telephone, *and* is quicker, and — on a variable-cost basis — cheaper. In addition, the Internet is prized for its versatility and flexibility. It is rapidly being integrated into the lead generation process, replacing some media, while adding strength to other media, and generally proving itself to be an extremely valuable element in the lead generation tool kit.

Businesses were early adopters of the Internet as a business tool. Most business buyers today have e-mail addresses. And many of them use the Internet as a valuable procurement tool, whether searching for and evaluating new suppliers, or negotiating and completing transactions with current vendors.

Let us review the key components of the Internet marketing tool kit as they apply to lead generation.

Web site

By now, nearly every business has its own Web site, which has become the standard piece of collateral material and advertising presence in use today. Web sites allow companies to have global reach, universal access, and daily updating as the market and the products change. The Web site is such a powerful and flexible tool that many companies have abandoned printed collateral material altogether.

The Web site also can be designed to contribute to the lead generation process in a number of significant ways, as discussed immediately below.

1. Online registration

A corporate Web site that was originally designed as little more than an online brochure can easily be converted into a lead generation tool with the addition of a registration area that is accessible from the company's home page. These registration forms can be such a powerful generator of leads that it makes sense to put them on other pages throughout the site as well.

Deploy solid DR principles to make your registration area as attractive and powerful a lead generator as possible. The registration area should be described in welcoming, benefit-oriented copy, and supported with an offer, such as a white paper or a free consultation. The registration form should be short and easy to complete. It is also important to establish a process whereby registered visitors are speedily contacted for follow-up, whether by a marketer for qualification purposes or by a salesperson.

2. Online fulfillment

The Web site is also ideal as a fulfillment tool for lead generation campaigns. Instead of sending out printed collateral material or white papers, invite responders to download the material from your Web site. This lets you regularly update the material and avoid the carrying costs of warehousing printed brochures. You can also make the materials customizable before download, so the prospect only receives what matters most to him.

3. Web response forms

As a substitute for, or supplement to, a BRC, Web response forms invite targets to visit a particular URL to respond to your campaign. Sometimes called "splash pages," "jump pages," or "landing pages," these forms offer numerous advantages. Instantaneous and highly convenient, their response mechanism appeals to business buyers. They also permit campaign tracking and measurement via the assigned URL. There is plenty of room within the Web response form for additional detail, demos, downloads, seminar invitations — whatever other material will move the prospect along the buying curve.

The Web response form should continue the "look and feel" of the campaign, so that it is recognizable to respondents. Be sure it contains the standard qualification questions used in the campaign and asks for the key code from the original outbound communication. Finally, the form should explicitly request permission for follow-up communications via e-mail. It is also a good idea to program the form to pop up a thank-you message when completed, as well as trigger an e-mailed thank-you and confirmation note.

> **Web site design tips**
>
> - The user experience should be paramount in your design of site graphics and navigation pattern.
>
> - Avoid Flash introductions. Make page load times as fast as possible.
>
> - Lay out the site to support your objective, whether it's delivering product/service or company information, lead generation, inquiry fulfillment, or e-commerce.
>
> - Keep your copy brief and use type that's easy to read.
>
> - Break up the copy with clear, succinct headlines.

4. Mini-sites

A mini-site is something like a combined Web response form and Web site. Frequently used as a landing page for an outbound campaign, mini-sites are often created to support new product introductions, limited-time deals, or some other offering that deserves special highlighting. Mini-sites can be populated with contests, demos, downloads, cross-sell offers, or whatever makes sense. They should always contain a form to collect contact information for follow-up.

5. Online subscription sign-up

The company Web site is an ideal resource for inexpensively gathering subscribers to e-mail or print newsletters, or to corporate-sponsored magazines. You then can use the subscription lists as an ongoing resource for lead generation campaigns. Leading Web marketers find that the top right-hand corner of the home page is the best location for subscription offers. It also makes sense to repeat these offers on other pages deeper within the Web site.

6. Extranets

Companies that have extensive selling and buying relationships with large corporate customers often build dedicated Web sites known as extranets behind their top customers' firewalls. These extranets allow for purchasing and inquiries to be conducted at any time of the day, from sites all over the corporation, using the special terms and conditions pre-negotiated between supplier and customer. Like the corporate Web site, dedicated extranets can include registrations, subscription sign-up, links to the sales team covering the account, and other lead generation techniques.

E-mail

E-mail is proving to be a powerful medium for lead generation, qualification, and nurturing, not to mention customer relationship management, up-selling, and a host of other business marketing applications. Because most business buyers are connected to e-mail and comfortable with it, e-mail can provide a very fast and inexpensive supplement to direct mail and the telephone.

Here are some tips on the best ways to put e-mail to use in the lead generation process:

- Your first approach to developing an e-mail strategy can be as simple as integrating e-mail as a medium into your current communications stream. Examine the inbound and outbound communications you have in place today and substitute e-mail for as many as you can.

- Gather e-mail addresses and permission to use them, from customers and prospects at every point of contact. E-mail is generally welcome in business correspondence. Because it is so cheap and fast, it also makes sense to invest in gathering and maintaining as close to 100% e-mail penetration of your customer base as possible.

- Here are two ways to fill in any holes in your e-mail files: (1) conduct outbound communications via mail or phone to request e-mail addresses, or (2) consider using one of the e-mail append services available to business marketers today, such as Thumbprint, iMatcher, or eDirect.

- When you need a very targeted list of specific buyers, try commissioning custom e-mail list creation from a service like PerfectLeads from NuOS Corporation.

- Practice good e-mail etiquette. Ask permission to communicate via e-mail, offer recipients the option to "opt out" of continuing to receive e-mails, and honor those requests faithfully.

- Apply the basic rules of direct marketing in your e-mail communications. Test regularly. Use friendly, benefit-oriented copy. Make compelling offers. Ask for the action frequently within the copy. One e-mail exception to the direct marketing rules: short copy usually works better than long copy in this medium.

- Make sure your communication is relevant and of value to the recipient. If it isn't, he will quickly perceive it as junk and delete it.

- Be prepared for fast responses. E-mail replies come in quickly (usually within 48 hours or less) and responders expect a reaction from you just as quickly. Be sure you have response and fulfillment processes in place.

- Invite Web visitors to contact you via e-mail, with an address such as info@yourcompany.com. Be sure you have procedures in place to handle inbound e-mail quickly and appropriately.

Such inquiries can become one of your strongest sources of sales leads.

■ Set up Web response forms that relate to the e-mail message. For example, when a recipient clicks from within the e-mail, he is transported to a page that looks and feels relevant and consistent with your message.

■ Look into the automated e-mail marketing systems available today from such e-mail service providers as MarketFirst and e2 Communications. This technology lets you pre-program a series of e-mail messages that are sent in response to some "trigger" in the relationship between you and your customer. For example, pre-programmed e-mail is perfect for the automatic acknowledgment of an inquiry. It can be set up to ask useful qualifying questions and to nurture the continuing relationship.

Electronic newsletters

Electronic newsletters are an excellent tool for keeping in touch with customers and prospects at little cost. While primarily seen as a relationship management tool, they can also serve as a way to generate new leads with the addition of a "viral," or pass-along, component. Some tips for successful use of newsletters follow:

■ Place a subscription sign-up offer in the upper right-hand corner of your home page, and publish the newsletter semimonthly or monthly, determining its frequency by the amount of good-quality content available.

■ Make sure the content is of real value to the recipient, and not just sales pitches for your products or services.

■ Add a pass-along message within the newsletter, inviting readers to forward it to their friends and colleagues. Be sure to embed a subscription link, so those recipients can then subscribe easily themselves.

- Convert new subscribers to leads by putting in place an outbound contact strategy to qualify their interest and move them into the regular lead flow.

- If you decide not to publish a newsletter yourself, the medium can still be a productive lead generator for you. Advertise in, or sponsor, newsletters from publishers whose readership matches your prospective audience.

Banners

Even though Web banner ads have disappointed some consumer marketers with falling response rates, they are still viable as a vehicle for business marketers. The difference lies in targeting, and in the nature of business buyers. Business people need information in order to do their jobs properly, and they are likely to frequent Web sites where that information is available. So, highly targeted banner advertising can be an excellent medium for lead generation.

Here are some suggestions for successful banner use:

- Select your media carefully. The best place to start is the Web sites of the trade publications where you already advertise. You may be able to negotiate free banner placement as part of the "merchandising" deals available within your print media purchase. Also look at professional associations in your target industry, and at the sites of your business partners. Get help with media selection and negotiation from a broker such as B2BWorks or DoubleClick.

- Direct marketing fundamentals apply. Make a solid offer, test, and refine your offer and creative, and be sure your fulfillment is speedy.

- Add a "house ad" banner to your own Web site, to connect with an ongoing campaign or a special offer.

- As with other media, be sure you have a relevant landing page for those who click through.

- Banner ad rates are highly negotiable. You may want to explore exchange arrangements with other business marketers who are trying to reach a similar audience.

- Remember: as with e-mail, banner advertising is still an infant medium. Be open to try new ideas and new technologies, but use common sense.

Webinars

Web-based seminars, sometimes called "webinars," are quickly growing in popularity, because they combine the rich content of a traditional face-to-face seminar with the wide reach, flexibility, and low cost of the Internet. Webinars play the same role in lead generation as the traditional seminar — namely, they provide qualified prospects with detailed product or service information, case studies, and demonstrations.

The new webinar technologies, from such providers as Centra and PlaceWare, have improved greatly in recent years. However, it is still critically important to do a test run with a variety of browsers and computer hardware types to eliminate potential glitches.

Webinars, which can be scheduled live, pre-recorded, or provided on-demand, are often accompanied by a concurrent teleconference. Because the medium is still quite new, marketers may want to take advantage of the experience of agencies like B2B Web Marketing Solutions and Kern Direct to help plan a Webinar program. Online seminar service providers include WebEx, eInterCall, Present Online, and Raindance.

Incentive programs

The Internet is ideally suited to support contests, sweepstakes, scavenger hunts, coupons, and other incentive programs designed to stimulate an action. Numerous companies, such as MyPoints, GiftCertificates.com, and Promotions.com, are available to help you set up this type of program. Incentives are very likely to increase response rates and can serve as a source for e-mail address acquisition. However, there may be a decline in response quality.

Some of the best applications for incentive programs are:

- For product lines or service offerings with characteristics similar to those of a consumer marketer, such as office supplies.

- For building databases made up of inquirers for later conversion to qualified leads.

- When the incentive is tightly linked to the company's other products or overall message.

- When the incentive is combined with novel, eye-catching media types such as skyscraper-sized banners or other new formats.

- In combination with offline programs. A postcard, for example, can refer a recipient to a Web-based contest, where response information is gathered and the inquiry is qualified.

Affiliate programs

Many Web marketers find success in placing an offer on someone else's Web site, and then compensating the other site owner for any traffic it generates. Business marketers can benefit by setting up such deals with all kinds of relevant sites: business partners, trade associations — anywhere prospects are likely to visit. These informal deals often involve reciprocal links in lieu of compensation. If you select partners who attract the right visitors, links can be a very powerful source of new inquiries. On a more formal level, there are several well-established companies that will set up affiliate marketing programs for you, by introducing you to partners and administering the fee payments. LinkShare, Be Free, and Commission Junction are among the larger services in this field.

Search engine optimization

Internet search engines can direct interested inquirers to your site at a rapid clip, but it may take you some time to understand and manage them. To achieve high ranking results, you must submit your site to the top search engines and apply optimizing techniques. This can absorb the attention of a full-time staffer or the expertise of a service provider like Grantastic, ZenHits, or Intrapromote.

Another approach is to pay for certain keywords relevant to your product/service or company to pop up at the top of the search engine list whenever prospects undertake a search on the Internet. Overture, formerly known as GoTo, allows you to bid on the keywords of your choice, and a fee is charged only when visitors click on your keyword.

There are substantial benefits with search engine optimization. Most marketing efforts involve paying for outbound media contact to motivate potential buyers to raise their hands. This can involve a lot of expense and a lot of waste. Search engine optimization, however, allows you to reach the prospect when he has initiated a search. Not only is he eager to find information, chances are he is in buying mode.

IV. Print advertising

DR advertising in trade, industry vertical, and business publications can provide a steady, reliable stream of new prospective sales leads. Print can also serve as a way to reach high-level decision-makers whose names may not appear on the usual mailing lists.

The main issue faced by lead generators that use print advertising is conflicting goals within the company relating to brand awareness versus generating a response. Print advertising can be very powerful in generating awareness and building brand recognition and positive attitudes. But if your objective is to get leads, your ads must be created for response.

Here are some tips for successful lead generation using print advertising:

- Stress benefits and the offer in every possible element of the ad (the headline, body copy, design, and response device).

- Add an offer and a response device to all brand advertising. You'll be pleasantly surprised, and the sales force will be pleased with the results.

- The most responsive position in trade publications is placement directly opposite the table of contents.

- Do not permit your lead generation advertising to conflict with your brand image. All of your communications must support and enhance your brand. Do nothing to harm it. In fact, you can gain leverage for lead generation from the brand awareness conveyed in your advertising.

- Test all kinds of publications: Begin with industry verticals like *Supermarket News*, and functional horizontal trade publications like *Purchasing Magazine*. Once you find success in this market, move on to general business publications like *Fortune* and *The Wall Street Journal.*

V. Bingo cards and card decks

For years now, trade publications have been including reader service, or "bingo," cards as a value-added service to advertisers . These cards have generated untold numbers of inquiries, many of them frivolous. As a result, some marketers choose to ignore them. However, bingo cards can be productive if managed carefully. If you do participate in a readers service program with a print publication, however, implement a fulfillment process to serve legitimate inquirers quickly and efficiently. Also establish a method for sorting through and qualifying the inquiries before they land on the desk of a salesperson. If you still find that the qualification rates are too low to justify the expense, inform your print media supplier that you do not wish to participate in the readers service program.

Some trade publications offer additional access to their subscribers by publishing card decks, which are mailed separately to the subscriber base. While this approach can be a productive source of inquiries, a card often doesn't have enough space to describe the value proposition in depth. As a result, many responders are unqualified. So it is important to have a solid qualification process in place to deal with card deck inquiries.

VI. Broadcast advertising

Broadcast advertising is not widely used in business marketing. When it is, however, it is likely to be used for building awareness versus generating response. Due to the high costs of broadcast ad preparation and media buying, this form of advertising may lend itself better to national or global brand use than to typical industrial products.

There are, however, some exceptions. For product lines or service offerings that have a small office/home office appeal, or a crossover to consumer markets, television and radio can be excellent tools for lead generation. Office supplies and computers come to mind. In some local markets, radio can be inexpensive enough to work for even traditional business marketers.

VII. Trade shows

Exhibiting at trade shows and conferences is a time-honored way to get in front of customers and prospects in a focused, concentrated manner. Attendees are often highly qualified, their minds are on business at the show, and they are seeking solutions to business problems. Regrettably, marketers often squander opportunities to use trade shows to their best advantage in lead generation.

Here are some suggestions on how to optimize trade shows and conferences, and generate good quality leads:

- If your main objective is to generate qualified leads, then focus all of your show activity accordingly.

- Make sure the signage at your booth states clearly what your company does and how it benefits the customer. Remember that passers-by will give you only a few seconds to get your message across.

- Practice good boothmanship. Dress well, stand tall, look friendly and expectant, and don't eat or drink. Don't be shy. Move out of the booth and work the floor.

- Train your booth staff in good boothmanship and in meeting your objectives for the show.

- Insert one or two qualification questions into your inquiry-gathering process by attaching a short form to the prospect's business card or by using an electronic swipe tool provided by show organizers.

- Remember that there is an inverse relationship between give-aways and inquiry qualification levels. In a highly qualified environment — i.e., a show where most attendees are already solid prospects — an incentive can be an excellent traffic generator. But go slowly when the audience is more broadly based.

- Put in place a process to qualify the leads or arrange to have them contacted by a salesperson immediately on your return from the show.

Trade show managers are constantly seeking ways to help their exhibitors be more successful. New tools arrive on the market regularly. LEADLink from CompuSystems, for example, helps qualify trade show inquiries with survey questions, and captures them directly into your PC. RippleWare is another company that helps automate the trade show lead process.

VIII. Referral marketing

Business buyers are very good sources of referral business for two reasons. First, they are likely to know their counterparts in other companies via their own professional networking. Second, they are often happy to introduce a solution to a colleague as part of nurturing their web of business relationships. From a marketer's point of view, referrals are an outstanding source of new business. Recommendations from a colleague have great credibility, so not only is the referred prospect likely to be qualified, he is also likely to be motivated. The only downside of referral marketing is that the total volume of referred business you can ever hope to get is rarely enough to sustain your needs for growth.

With the arrival of the Internet, the perfectly respectable term of "referral marketing" has morphed into the rather loathsome expression "viral marketing." Nevertheless, because of its speed and informality, the Internet lends itself well to referral practices.

Some points to keep in mind when applying referral marketing to the lead generation process:

- Review all your marketing communications and add a referral request where appropriate.

- Conduct regular referral-request campaigns to your current customer base. You may want to offer an incentive to both the referrer and the referred to increase response.

- Place a pass-along request at the bottom of your e-mails — especially those that contain valuable information or an offer.

- Consider using a specialized company, like Takira or L90, that supports referral marketing with technology and services to make the procedures, tracking, and reporting easier.

Chapter 3

Other tools for lead generation

I. Integrated marketing communications

A valuable lead generation component of a business marketer's tool kit, integrated marketing communications involves the use of two or more media channels in a DR campaign. Print advertising, telephone, direct mail, and collateral materials are all communications media channels that can be put to good use in lead generation.

Integrated marketing has become a very hot topic in recent years, as media outlets proliferate and marketers struggle to be heard over the din. Marketing communications need to be well coordinated for two reasons. First, customers expect a consistent message from their vendors, and an inconsistent customer experience causes confusion and erodes the value of the brand. Second, each medium needs to be applied to its best possible use and pull its own weight within the entire mix. Therefore, coordinated communications are critically important.

However, integrating marketing communications is not easy. "Functional silos" in marketing communications have arisen — all with their own vocabularies, cultures, budgets, and objectives. Pulling all of this together requires tenacity, a maniacal focus on the customer experience, and support from senior management.

From a lead generation perspective, there are two key lessons to be learned in integrated marketing communications.

The first is to have a consistent brand message. All marketing communications, including those for lead generation, qualification, and nurturing, plus those intended to sustain an ongoing relationship with customers, must fit consistently beneath the brand umbrella. Messages that are inconsistent with the brand's image will confuse customers and, in the long term, reduce the power of the communication as a whole.

Second, lead generators should seek to gain leverage from the rest of the marketing communications function. All outbound contacts with customers, whether they be brand communications, customer service messages, or even billing-related messages, can potentially be harnessed for the lead effort. The simplest way to do this is to put the company Web site URL, which has a registration offer prominently placed on the home page, on all messages received by the customer. The same principle applies to customer touch points that are less obviously part of marketing communications, such as packaging, point of purchase displays, and billing statements: make sure the company Web site URL, with the registration offer, appears everywhere the customer comes in contact with the product or service.

Similarly, with a little effort, some marketing communications can do even more to support lead generation. Here are some tips:

- Include a white paper offer with response instructions, such as an 800 number or a Web response URL, in every press release.

- Ensure that all brand awareness advertising includes an offer, a call to action, and a response device.

- When your executives give speeches, invite customers and prospects to attend.

If you put your mind to it, you will come up with an endless stream of good ideas for harnessing the entire marketing function for lead generation. The best way to approach this effort is to systematically review everything in your company that "touches" customers and prospects, and to consider ways to convert the touch point into an actionable inquiry.

CHART 3.1
Outbound campaign media types

Medium	Strengths	Weaknesses	Best Applications
Mail	Many formats available Can adjust to support the need	Expensive/piece Long planning cycle	Inquiry generation Response handling Lead nurturing Retention
Telephone	Intrusive Universally available	Recipient is often unreachable Expensive	Response handling Lead qualification Lead nurturing
E-mail	Fast turnaround and results Inexpensive	Permission required Limited creative options Limited address availability	Lead qualification Lead nurturing
Print advertising	Broad reach Efficient/M	Less targeted	Inquiry generation Brand awareness
Banner advertising	Fast turnaround and results Deals available	Limited workable outlets Small creative space	Inquiry generation Brand awareness
Catalogs	Inexpensive (vs. field sales) Valued by customers as a reference	Expensive (vs. e-commerce) Prone to obsolescence	Retention Sales
Trade shows	Qualified reach	Limited reach Expensive/M	Inquiry generation Brand awareness
Seminars	Conveys deep product/ service information Develops personal relationships	Inefficient/M Limited reach	Lead nurturing Retention
Webinars	Broad reach Inexpensive/M	Imperfect technology	Lead nurturing Retention
Newsletters (print)	Inexpensive/M High perceived value	Difficult to sustain editorial quality	Lead nurturing Retention
Newsletters (e-mail)	Inexpensive/M High pass-along propensity	Difficult to sustain editorial quality	Inquiry generation Retention
Web site	Easy to update Multipurpose applicability Holds in-depth product/ service information	Passive, nonintrusive	Brand awareness Inquiry generation Response handling Retention

II. Call center/contact center

Traditionally, business marketers have operated in-house call centers, where customer service handled inbound calls while sales and marketing made outbound calls. In recent years, though, with the arrival of the Internet, these call centers are rapidly being converted to "contact centers" that handle inbound and outbound communications through a variety of media channels, among them telephone, fax, and e-mail.

Contact centers play a key role in the lead generation process. They handle inbound inquiries, qualify and nurture leads, and maintain ongoing contact with customers. Ideally, contact center personnel are equipped with current information about customers and prospects, which is fed to them from the marketing database. Armed with that kind of information, contact centers are in an excellent position to probe customer needs and identify sales opportunities that can then be pursued by the sales force.

Contact centers may also be used for outbound campaign execution. There is some controversy, however, about the wisdom of applying service-oriented people to a sales function. Some marketers believe that these functions require different personalities, training, and tools, and they recommend that they be kept separate. Yet, others have found success in combining these roles, for example, by motivating a service rep to conclude a call with an up-sell or cross-sell offer. Other marketers have their idle service personnel make outbound tele-qualifying calls to inquirers.

Here are some tips on how to mobilize your call center for lead generation:

- **Stay in close touch with your contact center**. Contact center personnel are often neglected by marketers, and are too often viewed simply as a utility. However, these reps are closer to the market than nearly everyone, and have valuable intelligence to share. Furthermore, they naturally produce more when marketers take the time to demonstrate their interest, share plans and objectives, and keep them informed.

What is CRM?

There is much controversy about the real definition of customer relationship management (CRM). Some people lump CRM in with customer service. In other companies, CRM means current customer marketing. Still others have broadened the term to include just about any kind of sales and marketing activity. When broadly defined to encompass sales, marketing, and customer service, CRM covers all the components of lead generation and customer retention, which are the subjects of this book. So, you might say that this book falls under the umbrella of CRM.

By most definitions, CRM is a philosophy that attempts to put the customer in the center of all business activity. CRM can be enabled by new software tools that automate the sales, marketing, and customer service functions, and connect those functions to real-time marketing databases. Software vendors such as E.piphany and Vantive have made a name for themselves in the world of CRM. However we define this term, CRM is clearly central to the job of acquiring and retaining customers profitably — the core of any business.

■ **Motivate call center personnel properly to support the lead mission by offering them an incentive**. Just as it's critical for marketers to be familiar with the goals of the sales force, call center teams need to understand and share in the mission of lead generators. So, communicate frequently and make sure that call center personnel include marketing's goals in their own incentive plans.

■ **Outsource functions where appropriate**. Many contact center functions can be outsourced — to suppliers such as Harte-Hanks and E-commerce Support Centers, Inc. — to shave overhead costs, or to adjust for peaks and valley in work flow.

III. Customer service

In some respects, the lines between sales, marketing, and customer service are beginning to blur. No longer is customer service expected simply to solve a customer's problem and be done with it. The function is now being seen as critically important to a company's success in a number of areas, including lead generation. Philosophically, we could say that a company that does not serve and satisfy its customers at all stages of the relationship will not be able to retain its customers' loyalty, at great risk to its profitability.

So where does customer service enter the lead generation picture? For one thing, customer service manages the contact center, which includes many aspects of inquiry management and lead qualification. But, perhaps the key contribution to lead generation by customer service is the process of up-selling and cross-selling. Customer service reps can enhance their usual function of solving problems and providing support by becoming alert to, and identifying, sales opportunities.

However, this can be difficult to engineer. One approach is to integrate customer information across the company, so that customer service personnel have access to up-to-date account data and previous interactions. While it's tricky to convert service reps to the sales function, it can be done with the right tools, training, and incentives.

IV. Lead generation and management software tools

In recent years, many excellent new software tools have become available to help marketers generate, manage, and track leads. This software ranges from campaign management and sales force automation systems to full-blown multichannel CRM solutions. Many solutions overlap with one another. Also, many of the products do not live up to their claims, so shop carefully: there's a lot of hype out there.

The easiest-to-use, and lowest-cost, set of tools would be a simple spreadsheet to capture and maintain a record of the campaign leads, combined with e-mail to distribute the leads to a salesperson, and the capability to follow up with him during the conversion process.

Some software focuses on certain discrete functions, like lead qualification, assignment, and tracking. Many of these tools take advantage of the universal communicative power and speed of the Internet. The more powerful tools, from such companies as Siebel, Oracle, and PeopleSoft, support the entire campaign process with software.

New software is constantly coming to the market. See Chart 3.2 for some of the applications available today. It is by no means a comprehensive list. Also, be warned: it does not include traditional sales force automation tools and contact managers, such as sales-force.com, SalesLogix, and Goldmine, which have a legitimate claim to providing lead generation and management automation, but are generally selected and supported by a company's sales function, versus the marketing function.

CHART 3.2

Currently available software tools

Function	Description	Some service providers/suppliers
Campaign management	Generates leads through multiple media channels	Sales Lead Generation by Amergent; TRACKWeb by Soffront Software; MarketFirst; Aprimo
Response capture	Automates lead collection from your Web site and transfers leads to the database without human intervention	TRACKWeb Leads by Soffront Software
Lead qualification	Converts raw contacts into qualified opportunities	Intelligent Optimization by deuxo
Lead assignment	Automates decision rules for distributing leads to the right sales resource	Lead Assignment by ChannelWave; InfoNow by deuxo; eLeads by MarketSoft
Lead tracking	Chooses the right distribution channel for leads and and tracks them to closure	Closed Loop Lead Distribution and Tracking by ChannelWave
Sales lead management	Automates sales force's handling of sales leads	Sales Tracker by GE, DirectSynergy
Multifunction	Manages several functions across lead generation, distribution, and tracking	DemandMore Leads by MarketSoft; Webridge Leads Manager; LEADTRACK; Sales Lead Management System by DirectSynergy; TactiCom
Comprehensive CRM	Automates the entire customer relationship management process	Clientele by Epicor; PeopleSoft/Vantive; E.Piphany; Siebel Systems; Oracle; SAP; Kana
Partner relationship management	Manages relationships with resellers and distribution partners, including lead management and tracking	Channel Advantage by Channel Automation; Siebel eChannel; ChannelWave; Partnerware; Allegis

2

Part Two
Lead Generation Strategies

Chapter 4

Campaign planning

Sometimes leads are received "over the transom," meaning they come to your company through the normal course of business, without any deliberate investment in outbound marketing activity. These lucky sales leads might be from a current customer who needs to buy a product upgrade, or from a prospect who is looking for a solution to a business problem and, through his own research, discovers your products. Or, they might come from a referral source — i.e., a buyer with a need who asked around and was shown to your door.

Over-the-transom leads are wonderful — when they happen. They cost you nothing, and tend to convert to sales at a very high rate. The only problem is that they don't happen often enough! It is very difficult to grow a business based solely on leads that come in over the transom. It is possible, but rather rare. So, how is it possible to encourage such apparently random and uncontrollable — yet extremely profitable — events? The best way is to be very good at what you do. The better you are in business, the more such over-the-transom leads will come to you naturally. They are a matter of luck, to be sure. Moreover, they are a matter of superior product quality, excellent service, and satisfied customers.

But it isn't possible to count on these blessed events to sustain your company's need for growth. You must generate leads deliberately via outbound campaigns. Fortunately, lead generation is a very engaging process. It can be a lot of fun. So let us now dive into the details of campaign planning and execution for lead generation.

I. Setting campaign objectives

The first step in campaign planning should be to set campaign objectives. Without them, it is impossible to recognize success when you see it.

Campaign objectives will typically cover:

- Number of leads expected

- Their degree of qualification

- Time frame during which they will arrive

- Cost per lead

- Lead-to-sales conversion ratio

- Revenue per lead

- Campaign ROI, or expense-to-revenue ratio

There are other, more refined objectives you may want to consider:

- Number of leads by sales territory

- Number of leads by industry or market segment

- Leads into new accounts

- Account penetration (i.e., new contacts within an existing account)

- Leads into competitive accounts

The most important aspect of developing a marketing campaign is to *plan* it before making a single investment. Be realistic. Make sure it is possible to generate — at the right cost — the number of qualified leads needed by your sales organization. Plan your fulfillment material up front, during the outbound campaign process; don't leave it until later. And make sure that your interim steps — the processes and people that capture, qualify, nurture, and fulfill the inquiries — are in place, with the capacity to handle the flow you intend to create.

Lead flow planning

The mission of lead generation marketing is to generate enough qualified leads so that each sales territory is optimally busy, productive, and fulfilling its quota. Marketing needs to deliver the right number of qualified leads to support sales objectives. Each rep wants enough leads to fulfill his sales quota, but he also has only a certain capacity to follow up on leads in his territory.

So, lead flow planning will stem from the needs of the sales force. Discuss their requirements with sales management and selected sales reps. Read their sales plan and consider their compensation plan in order to understand their business and personal objectives. Only then will you have the input needed to map your campaign strategies.

You'll find that each rep is likely to want a certain number of qualified leads per day, week, or month, based on specific requests by product category, industry, sales territory, or whatever else is defining his quota. Details like this will make your planning more complex, but will ultimately help you both be successful. So, gather as many details as you can.

It is the natural characteristic of salespeople to seek control of their territory and to want access to every communication within their set of accounts. Some of them, therefore, will ask you to send them every inquiry, claiming they will qualify it and handle it themselves. Others will ask you to send them all qualified leads — regardless of whether they can follow them up. However, do not tell them that you can or will send them "everything." Succumbing to these kinds of requests is a recipe for disaster, as reps "cherry pick" the leads they like, toss the unqualified inquiries, and quickly lose any appreciation for the value of the lead generation program as a whole. Even more tragically, customers who had a business need, a real business problem to solve, may go unsatisfied — or buy from the competition.

Calculating lead flow requirements

One way to figure out how many leads to generate is to ask the sales reps for their preferences. Another is to obtain their sales quotas and do some quick calculations yourself, backing your way into the number of leads required by figuring out their sales productivity per lead. This approach will serve as a useful point of validation for your conversations with the sales team.

To do this calculation, you will need several numbers from sales and finance: the average revenue quota per rep, and the average revenue per order. You will also need an additional number: the percent of revenue that the salespeople generate without the help of leads — i.e., repeat sales or deeper penetration within the account, as well as referrals within the sales arena to new business. In other words, this is the amount of self-generated sales that would have naturally occurred in the territory without the involvement of a lead generation program. It may be tough to pin this number down, but skilled and experienced salespeople and sales managers will be able to come up with a working figure.

Let's see how the calculation might work with some hypothetical numbers (see Chart 4.1).

Chart 4.1
Lead requirements worksheet

Revenue quota per rep	$3,000,000
Percent of quota self-generated	40%
Quota requiring lead support ($3 million × 1-.40)	$1,800,000
Revenue per order	$10,000
No. of converting leads required ($1.8 million ÷ $10M)	180
Conversion rate	30%
No. of qualified leads required per rep (180 ÷.30)	600

So, in this example, each rep will need 600 qualified leads to make his quota.

Some additional tips on lead flow planning:

- Most sales teams prefer a smooth, steady flow of leads, so plot your expected lead flow from month to month. Peaks and valleys will result from the output of your various campaigns, so plan additional efforts to smooth things over. For example, use tactics with short planning horizons, like a direct response print ad, banner ads, outbound telemarketing, or e-mail.

- Check with product management and sales management to plan lead requirements for special events like new product introductions or end-of-fiscal-year sales pushes.

- Hard-offer leads — for example, "Have a sales rep call me" — will convert faster and come in handy when you are under time pressures at the end of fiscal periods, or when you don't have a large enough staff or budget to nurture a prospect pool.

- Plan for resources in the middle of the process as well. Never overload your response/inquiry handlers and qualifiers, but do keep them busy. Overloading taxes these people, and worse, annoys customers. So, space out your campaigns whenever possible to smooth over both your marketing operations and your lead delivery.

- Secure buy-in to the campaign plan from both sales and the people involved in the inquiry process, whether it's the call center, a segment of the marketing department, or an outsourced service. Everyone needs to approve, and "own," the plan. The best way to get cooperation is to include these people in the planning process. You also need to communicate to them continuously — explaining and re-explaining the benefits of your activities.

Budgeting

Budgeting is like going to the dentist. You know you have to do it. There's a part of you that finds it useful. But often, it's something you would rather "have done," than actually "do." Whatever your attitude toward this matter, campaign budgets need to be set in

---

Calculating campaign volume requirements

Your objective is to set up campaigns that will provide a predictable, relevant, and timely lead flow. Here is a simple process to figure out how much campaigning is required to generate a month of leads for a sales team.

1. Estimate the number of qualified leads each salesperson can reasonably be expected to follow up on for a month.

2. Multiply that number by the number of reps in a geographic territory.

3. Divide the number by the qualification rate you expect for your campaign inquiries.

4. Divide the result again by the expected response rate on the campaign. The final number will be your campaign volume needed to support that one territory for a month. In mail campaigns, you can control the lead flow within the territory by selecting ZIP Codes for each volume required. In other media, you may end up with some peaks and valleys that can be smoothed over with tactical campaign efforts such as telemarketing.

5. Continue the process for each territory and add up the results. You will have total numbers for your qualified leads, inquiries, and campaign volumes for the month.

---

some form or other in advance of a campaign's execution. Some companies create detailed budgets as an early step, and others create them later in the process.

In this book, the detailed discussion of campaign budgeting comes later, because an overview of the lead generation strategic process is a prerequisite to the ability to plan numbers in a meaningful way. When you are ready to tackle budgeting, please refer to Chapter 6, beginning on page 97.

II. Analyzing the buying process

In making early campaign planning decisions, you must develop the right campaign for each chosen market segment being targeted. The simplest — and, at the same time, most sophisticated — approach toward being on-target is to analyze the buying process for each of these segments.

Initially, analyze how customers and prospects arrive at their buying decisions by answering these four questions:

- Who is involved? (See "Gatekeepers and other parties" on page 71.)

- What information do they need?

- Where do they usually buy?

- How long is their buying process?

Why go through this exercise? Because understanding each part of the buyer's buying process allows you to implement programs that can influence his buying process to your advantage. The more you know about how your customers and prospects buy, the more you can seek to persuade them to buy your product or service versus that of your competitors.

The buying process in many companies is fairly well defined, especially for major purchases. It also is often codified and followed precisely.

Here are some advantages to knowing about the buying process of prospects and customers:

- If you know that they make their final decisions by committee, then your campaign needs to speak to all the members of that committee, not just to the regular contact person.

- If you know they send out requests for bids once a month, then institute a monthly outbound call to reconfirm details and due dates.

- If you know that they need to examine a lot of information before they make a decision about a product like yours, you'll have a good idea about the collateral materials you will need. You'll make sure you help them get answers to their questions, easily and conveniently, right at the time when they are asking.

Once you analyze your prospects and customers' buying process in detail — who, where, what, and when — you can begin strategizing how to influence the process in your favor. Marketing is very complex, because people are multifaceted — to say nothing of their needs and preferences! Analyzing your prospects and customers as described in this chapter allows you to get a handle on the complexity, break it down, and manage it without missing a great business opportunity — or driving yourself nuts.

In summary, marketers map their marketing process to the buyer's buying process. They are two sides of the same coin.

Let's see how this approach to marketing analysis might look within a typical business marketing process described below. Notice how you stimulate the buyer to raise his hand and let you know he's in the market for the solution, so you can begin to sell to him.

First, the buyer identifies a problem ("We need some widgets") and identifies the need for a solution ("Let's call in the widget dealers"). You want to be in the buyer's consideration set. This means making him aware of your existence. Your campaign strategy at this point might involve advertising in trade publications read by the buyer and his analysts/consultants, who are familiar with your offerings in widgets. Since you need "buzz" and a place on the widgets radar screen, your company is likely to invest in public relations (PR) and advertising.

Once you are in the picture, you need to explain (to the buyer, or prospective customer) why your solution to his problem is superior to the next guy's. The prospect will be considering a number of vendors, so you prepare collateral material on widgets, sponsor widget-related research studies, and speak at widget industry conferences.

Perhaps most important, you stimulate the buyer to raise his hand, to let you know he's in the market for a widget, so you can begin to sell to him. At last, we have come to that key point in the marketing process — neatly mapped to the customer's buying process — the point of lead generation. Your lead-generation campaign strategy will emerge naturally from here.

Every business marketer will have some variation in his go-to-market process, perhaps involving resellers and distributors, or using a hybrid model wherein the most efficient sales resource is assigned to each stage of the selling process. But the fundamental process is the same, and marketers who analyze the process and break it down can figure out how to turn it to their advantage. They will know exactly when and how to generate leads for the sales team.

Gatekeepers and other parties

As you look into the buying process in detail, you'll notice that there are numerous individuals involved. Sometimes, it will appear that there is no real "buyer," per se. Instead, there are lots of people who can say "no" or "maybe," but no one, it seems, says "yes." The larger the customer, and the more its locations, the more complex the buying process and the more individuals involved.

What can be done to get a handle on this complexity? You will want to identify the various participants in the business buying process and understand their roles and motivations:

The influencer: The person in the organization who will benefit most directly from the purchase.

The user: The person who will be using the product to get the job done (may overlap with the influencer).

The buyer: The purchasing agent who actually places the order.

The decision-maker: Often a department head or senior manager who has final sign-off for the purchase decision.

The gatekeeper: The person who stands between the sales effort and any of the players, usually a secretary, administrative assistant, or people in the mail room.

The specifier: The IT professional, shop floor engineer, or other technical expert who reviews the need in detail and specifies what features and functionality are required.

The buying committee: A group assembled, usually ad hoc, to manage the purchase of a particular item (may comprise people listed above and others).

The motivations of each role will be different. The user, for example, is interested in how easy the product is to learn and to apply to his daily business operations. The decision-maker and senior managers will have higher-level productivity gains in mind than the user. If they are finance people, they usually control the company's purse strings, and will probably be interested in the ROI of the purchase. The purchasing agent may be motivated by ease of doing business, credit terms, and the like.

Fortunately, the buying process tends to be fairly similar among companies of similar size and industry. You will find this beneficial when drawing up consistent, comprehensive, and efficient campaign plans.

Chart 4.2 maps the selling process to the buying process. Observe how the buying process moves along (from top to bottom) in the first column. As the buyer's situation changes, the seller's situation changes as well. For example, as the buyer begins to figure out that he needs widgets, and starts researching the various solutions to that problem, the seller wants to stimulate that need, makes sure he has a way of knowing that the need is emerging, and becomes part of the consideration set, or short list. The point is that the buying-selling process follows a rather logical flow: sales and marketing efforts can be optimized if the personnel in those functions are introduced to the right prospects, at the right time, through the right communications methods.

CHART 4.2
Typical buying process and selling process

Buying process	Selling process	Seller's objective	Marketer's tools
Identify need	Arouse interest	Arouse interest	Advertising, PR
Research solutions	Identify need	Be known/recognized to research team	Advertising, PR
Develop short list of suppliers	Create preference	Be selected for inclusion on buyer's short list	Direct mail, e-mail, telephone, Web site, collateral
Request proposals/ quotes from short list	Propose specifically	Submit winning proposal	Face-to-face sales
Review proposals/quotes	Attempt to influence	Create preference	Face-to-face sales, direct mail
Negotiate	Negotiate	Preserve margins	Face-to-face sales
Select vendor	Compare to competition	Win	Face-to-face sales
Install product and use	Enhance usage	Satisfaction and usage	Support personnel
Upgrade	Identify need	Up-sell, cross-sell	Telesales, direct mail

Chapter 5

Campaign development

You have set your campaign objectives, figured out your lead flow needs, and analyzed your customers' buying processes. You may have even created a preliminary campaign budget. Now it is time to apply all that analytical work to the creative part of the lead generation process: campaign development.

But, wait. There's more analysis to be done at this stage. The first step in campaign development usually involves research.

I. Qualitative and quantitative pre-campaign research

Compared to consumer direct marketing, where most research takes the form of in-market testing, B-to-B marketing makes considerable use of primary research, such as surveys and focus groups.

There are a number of good reasons for this:

■ Business mailing universes are small and cannot support numerous test cells.

- Each business prospect can represent significant value, so it is usually worth carrying out any technique that allows the campaign to penetrate the universe more deeply. Pre-campaign research falls into this category.

- Campaign budgets usually justify the expense of pre-campaign research.

Pre-campaign research falls into two categories:

1. Qualitative research, which involves in-depth questions and answers. Types of qualitative research include: focus groups (face-to-face or online); one-on-one, in-depth interviews; and open-ended mail or phone surveys. Qualitative research is best used to:

- Validate assumptions about buyer motivation.
- Present sample message platforms and creative treatments to get directional reactions.
- Delve into the rational and emotional triggers of various buyer types.
- Develop a deeper understanding of the customer's point of view.
- Gather phrases for copywriting purposes.
- Compare the relative attractiveness of key benefits and features.

2. Quantitative research, which uses statistically valid samples to represent the entire universe. Quantitative research is usually performed through surveys, using telephone, e-mail, or postal mail to projectible numbers of respondents. Quantitative research can be used to validate hypotheses about any critical campaign variable. For lead generation campaigns, quantitative research is often used to test:

- Best potential offers
- List segments or list quality
- Purchase intent
- Product awareness
- Message preferences
- Creative concept rankings
- Improvements in your control package
- Willingness to participate in further research

Two leading research firms that assist B-to-B direct marketers are BAIGlobal and Harris Interactive.

Some B-to-B marketers value research so much that they find it productive to set up ongoing panels of customers and prospects who have agreed to answer questions on a regular basis. Panels can be large enough to provide statistical reliability, or smaller, such as focus groups. They can be managed by postal mail, e-mail, or at a Web site. Panels have the advantage of providing a steady, consistent source of feedback and input. Some companies create panels from their universe of "best customers," which combine the research panel concept with the special treatment of a loyalty program.

> **Print and banner advertising are best for generating leads among new prospects, and direct mail is useful for ongoing campaign work.**

II. Campaign media selection

The characteristics of B-to-B communications media were described at some length in Part One, Chapter 3, Chart 3.1. Suffice it to say that each medium has its strengths, weaknesses, and best applications. So your campaign must carefully harness the right medium for each job.

Print and banner advertising are best for generating leads among new prospects, and direct mail is useful for ongoing campaign work. Trade shows and referral marketing programs can be effective as well. Among inquirers and current customers, you may find telephone and e-mail most productive — telephone is more intrusive, and e-mail is less expensive than direct mail or print.

CHART 5.1

Media selection by prospect type

Prospect type	Key media
New prospects	Direct mail, print ads, banner ads, trade shows, referral marketing
Inquirers, current customers	Telephone, e-mail

CHART 5.2
How intrusive is the communications medium?

| TV Radio Print Web site | Mail | Fax | E-mail | Telephone | Face-to-face |

Least intrusive   **Most intrusive**

Selecting the right mix of communications media to meet the lead flow requirements of sales will be an iterative process. You will try some things, refine them, and try again. First, establish, with the sales team, the monthly (or weekly, or quarterly) requirements for the number of qualified leads per rep (or by product, territory, or whatever is needed). Then, carefully plan the media mix that will support their needs.

The media mix is a function of several variables, which you need to research:

- ROI each medium can deliver.

- Availability of the medium. For example, develop a calendar that lists industry trade shows scheduled throughout the year. Profitable Internet banner ad media may exist, but can you get enough media space to support your need for leads?

- Time horizon of the campaign. For example, print is faster to create and place than direct mail.

- Lead flow requirements. For example, sales may need more leads in the first and fourth quarters.

A spreadsheet makes an excellent iterative planning tool. Lay out the media options on a spreadsheet and start "tweaking." (See Chart 5.3. The numbers shown are hypothetical and not intended to represent current average costs or response rates. Note: Small universes typically cause B-to-B costs per thousand to be greater than consumer direct marketing.)

CHART 5.3

Calculating cost per lead by medium

Medium	Volume (in millions)	CPM	Response rate (%)	Gross inquiries	Qualification rate (%)	Qualified leads	Cost/lead
Direct mail	30	$ 1,500	2	600	25	150	$300
Print	40	$ 100	0.5	200	20	40	$100
Trade show	--	$15,000/show	--	400	10	40	$375
Banner	5	$ 50	0.5	25	40	10	$ 25
Web registration	--	--	--	100	60	60	$ 0

You can expand this spreadsheet to include other key variables, like timing and geographic territory requirements. Note: This spreadsheet breaks out the expected qualification rate by inquiry source, a refinement that will assist you in making the best media mix decisions. You are likely to end up with some very inexpensive leads in your mix. The unfortunate thing is that, typically, these leads will not be enough to meet your growth needs or support the sales force quota. So, you'll need to select several options and rank them by ROI, availability, and your lead flow criteria, to come up with the optimal mix.

III. How multiple media can work together

Keep in mind the power of combining various media channels that work together. For example, it is proven time and again that telephone follow-up to direct mail is very productive. This approach combines the deep penetration of the telephone with the persuasive power of the mail; together, they can build on each other to deliver a lower cost per action than each element on its own.

Just make sure the follow-up call is a substantive part of moving the prospect along the buying process, and not only an empty confirmation that the mail piece arrived. Some telemarketing experts recommend that you avoid mentioning the mail piece during the phone call altogether, as it diverts the discussion from the objective at hand.

Some B-to-B marketers reverse the process, by telephoning first and following up with mail later. This approach works well when you are asking for a specific action — e.g., attendance at a seminar. Telephoning is also a good way to qualify inquirers from trade shows, where many people may express interest at the booth, but only a portion of them will ever become qualified buyers. Rather than invest further by sending them an expensive fulfillment package, make phone calls to screen out the duds.

> **Just make sure the follow-up call is a substantive part of moving the prospect along the buying process, and not only an empty confirmation that the mail piece arrived.**

Mail combined with e-mail also can be effective. Some marketers find that varying the direct mail format is helpful: begin with a series of postcards, follow up with a letter and a phone call or e-mail. Because the phone is so powerful and intrusive, you may find that a simple postcard in advance is enough to grab their attention.

Similarly, you may want to mail print ads as tear sheets to current customers and prospects, as part of an ongoing program for keeping in touch with them. When accompanied by a letter saying "In case you missed our recent ad in such-and-such magazine…" this technique can make your advertising work harder for you, and provide a good excuse to contact your house file directly.

TV and print mass media awareness campaigns provide excellent "air cover" for a lead generation program. If you can time your campaigns to coincide with, or to follow shortly after, a branding campaign, the response rates will be stronger than usual.

Another way to look at media mix selection is from the point of view of cost. Communications prices vary widely, with e-mail costing pennies, and face-to-face costing hundreds of dollars per contact. Lead generation, a multistep process, is most productive when leveraging all the tools in the media tool kit. As a rule of thumb, it makes sense to use lower-cost media at the early stages of the process and the more expensive media later, as the prospect is more qualified and the likelihood of closing increases.

IV. The message platform

Developing the right message platform should be a fairly straightforward process once the pre-campaign research has been done. The message platform encapsulates the key benefit that you believe will appeal most strongly to your prospective audience.

The message platform encapsulates the key benefit that you believe will appeal most strongly to your prospective audience.

Your job is to convert the product or service features into benefits, and then select the benefits that are most meaningful to your prospects.

The following typical message platforms appeal to business buyers. Note that the benefits are attractive for business or personal reasons, or both.

- **Save time.** Other spins from this message might be: "Get to market quicker" or "Reduce manufacturing overhead."

- **Save money.** Recast this wording into other profit-oriented formats, like "Sell more" or "Spend less."

- **Grow the business.** "Penetrate new markets." "Find new customers. Sell them more."

- **Be secure in your job.** As in the adage: "No one ever got fired for buying IBM."

- **Increase efficiency or productivity.** "Do more with less."

- **Greed.** "Make money." "Increase sales." "Increase profits."

- **Avoid stress or hardship.**

- **Fear of the unknown, fear of loss, fear of failure.**

- **Make your job easier.**

For more information on developing and presenting powerful messages effectively, see "Creative Strategies" on pages 84 – 88. And don't ignore one of the most powerful benefits you can stress in lead generation: the offer itself. A platform that does nothing more than sell the offer can work wonders at driving response.

One last tip: Take advantage of the sales force in developing messages. They know what's on the minds of customers, prospects, and others with whom they interact and communicate daily.

V. Offer development

An offer is a critical factor in moving the prospect to action.

Like any direct marketing effort, lead generation offers are designed to elicit responses. The offer should provide a reason for prospects to act, in order to overcome their natural inertia. A consumer-like incentive may have personal benefit to the recipient, or be relative to solving a business problem. An offer is a critical factor in moving the prospect to action. No sales rep is there to "ask for the order," so the offer needs to do the job of gaining a response.

Here are a number of considerations to keep in mind as you develop lead generation offers:

- **Keep the offer simple.** Because business buying can be a long process, it is tempting to try to cover all the steps in a single communication. But lead generation is simply about getting a response and moving the process forward step by step.

- **Create offers that provide value.** Industry white papers are an excellent incentive, whether the customer plans to buy or not.

- **Match the offer to the customer's stage in the buying process.** If the customer needs to see a demo of the product before he will buy, then offer one.

- **Try service-oriented offers.** Use faster service or higher service levels as an incentive to respond or buy.

- **Consider use of "soft" or "hard" offers.** Offers can be divided into two types. Soft offers are attractive and low-risk, with high perceived value and/or broad appeal. Free premiums, like a T-shirt or a calculator, are popular soft offers in B-to-B marketing. Hard offers tend to stress business value, and require more effort on the part of the respondent — such as a free seminar or an invitation for a salesperson to call. When it comes to offers, there is a clear inverse relationship between lead quality and lead quantity. If you are looking for a more qualified prospect, use a harder offer. You will receive fewer responses, but they will be more likely to buy.

- **Combine both hard and soft offers.** For example, offer a meeting between customers and a salesperson, and say that the salesperson will hand over a T-shirt when he arrives.

- **Make sure the offer is clear, understandable, and compelling.** How the offer is presented will impact its effectiveness.

- **Test offers regularly.** Your testing criteria must evaluate both the front end (initial response) and the back end (conversion to sales). There's a chance that your soft offers may convert as well as your hard ones, allowing you to increase your results and lower your marketing costs.

- **Don't be afraid to offer a personal benefit.** Remember: the business buyer is a person, with his own self-interest. While he may be buying for his company, his response motivators are as much about his own benefit as the company's.

- **Use an offer in every lead-generation communication.** The incentive offer is the surest way to get a response. However, business people sometimes are so enamored of a product's benefits that they overlook offers because they believe "the product will sell itself."

■ **Match the offer to the medium.** What is effective in print may not carry over to the mail or telesales. The only way to be sure of an offer's efficiency is to test it.

■ **Match the offer to the objective.** Soft offers will trigger many inquiries that can be nurtured along later on. These nurturing offers provide information that will move the prospect along the buying chain.

■ **Hard offers are useful at the end of the chain,** when the prospect is ready to see a salesperson and make a commitment. Retention offers—e.g., frequency discounts—make sense after the transaction is completed.

■ **Keep the offer appropriate to your industry and your company image.**

■ **Select a premium that is not only compelling, but also easy to ship.**

> Hard offers are useful at the end of the chain, when the prospect is ready to see a salesperson.

■ **Calculate the entire cost of making the offer.** Include the costs of fulfillment, packing, and shipping for a physical item. Electronic media can help cut costs; use PDF files for white papers, and Webinars for seminars.

■ **Apply the basics of consumer direct marketing.** Use guarantees, stress exclusivity, make the offer easy to understand, add urgency, and always test.

■ **Avoid very soft offers — e.g., sweepstakes.** These offers can be productive in B-to-B marketing, for building a database, or when there are other good reasons to widen the net and scoop up a large number of responses. But, they must be used with caution. If you do use a sweepstakes offer, engage a company or agency that specializes in sweepstakes to keep you in compliance with all the rules.

■ **Experiment with several offers in a single message.** The customer can then select the offer most appropriate to his stage in the buying process — whether it be a white paper, a seminar, or a sales call.

Offer checklist

Experiment with as many offers as you can. Remember: the objective of the offer is to get the recipient to stop what he is doing and respond to you. Therefore, the offer must be compelling enough to persuade him to take the action you want him to take. And, the offer serves only one purpose: to get the desired response.

Below are the types of offers frequently used for lead generation:

■ Free information (brochure, newsletter, white paper, reprint, video, demo CD)
■ Premium (gift, book)
■ Free trial
■ Free sample
■ Free self-assessment tool
■ Seminar or Webinar
■ Demonstration
■ Discount
■ Sales call
■ Free consultation or audit
■ Free estimate

Just as the buying process dictates the most productive selling process, so does it also provide valuable guidance in your selection of the most productive direct marketing offer to use at each stage. Follow the buying process in the first column of Chart 5.4. Then, consider the most appropriate media channel for influencing each particular stage of the buyer's process. Finally, consider the best possible offer that will stimulate the buyer to move in the desired direction — namely, buying from you.

CHART 5.4

Matching the offer to the buying process stage

Customer's buying process	Marketing communications tools	Marketer's offer options
Identify need	Advertising, PR	Free information
Research solutions	Advertising, PR	Free premium, free trial
Develop short list	Direct mail, e-mail, Web site	Free premium, trial, sample
Request proposals	Face-to-face sales	Seminar, demonstration, sales call
Review proposals	Face-to-face sales, direct mail	Trial, sample, demonstration
Negotiate	Face-to-face sales	Lunch, golf game
Select vendor	Face-to-face sales	Lunch, golf game
Install product and use	Support personnel	Consultation
Upgrade	Telesales, direct mail	Information, premium

VI. Creative strategies

The secret to successful lead generation creative is to understand customers' needs, attitudes, and motivations. The business buyer is spending the company's money, so he must justify his purchases with facts and persuasive arguments. While he objectively evaluates various potential solutions to his business problem, he is a human being who is responding to emotional appeals. He represents his company, yet also has his own needs, fears, and aspirations.

Here lies the challenge of developing powerful message platforms, persuasive copy, and eye-catching art in lead generation. The job requires not only that you understand the business buyer's motivation on behalf of his company, but also that you speak to the consumer within.

Here are some guidelines to think about in the lead generation creative process:

- **Do your homework before beginning your creative development.** Analyze the market situation, the competitive situation, and your product's strengths and weaknesses. Research your prospects' needs and preferences. Develop a solid value proposition and message platform.

- **Remember: business people justify their decisions with facts.** So, make sure to give your prospects the facts they need. Ask your product manager to spend as much time as necessary to give your copywriter and art director a thorough understanding of the product and its benefits.

The secret to successful lead generation creative is to understand customers' needs, attitudes, and motivations.

- **Unleash your creativity.** Breakthrough ideas cut through the clutter, grab the attention of the prospect, and communicate the benefits of a product or service. The trick is to balance the facts with the creativity, and the features with the benefits.

- **In lead generation, your objective is to get a response.** You needn't tell your prospects everything there is to know about your product in each communication. Just tell them enough to get a response and move the process along.

- **To get a response, make an offer.** Then, present the offer in the most compelling way possible. Make it clear what you want the prospect to do, and then make it extremely easy for him to respond.

- **Integrate your DR communications strategy with your brand communications.** While asking for a response, have the message reflect the look and feel of the image being conveyed throughout the communications mix. This way, your lead generation will support your brand messaging and gain leverage from whatever awareness has already been built.

- **Employ or hire a copywriter and art director with strong DR background, if possible.** They are rare in B-to-B marketing, but worth the investment.

Copy tips

- **Keep the writing simple.** No matter how complex the product or the industry, clarity sells. Make sure prospects can grasp your offer immediately.

- **Convert your product features to benefits.** People don't buy based on what the product does, but what it does for them.

- **Describe the benefits as specifically as possible.** Instead of "saves money," specify how much money is saved. Concrete information sells.

- **Use euphemisms.** Instead of "salesperson," refer to "industry specialist." Substitute "free, no-obligation consultation" for "sales call."

- **Add guarantees.** Use testimonials and success stories. Stress your company's stability and long track record in the industry. Make it easy for the customer to feel comfortable that he won't lose his job if he does business with you.

- **Keep in mind direct marketing basics.** The writing must be clear, friendly, and personal. Make it easy for the buyer to respond to you via a variety of response media. Even though he is acting on behalf of his company, he is still a person and, therefore, will respond to emotional triggers and benefits.

Design tips

- **Graphic design does not encompass only photos and illustrations.** Rather, it draws in and takes the reader through the message. It helps organize the copy and move the reader along toward the call to action.

> ### Creative checklist for headline ideas and letter leads
>
> - **News:** "Here's a way to increase your sales. . . fast."
>
> - **Emotional connection:** "Doesn't it drive you crazy when a customer service rep puts you on hold?"
>
> - **Problem/solution:** "Is your factory floor covered with dangerous greasy film? We can help."
>
> - **Testimonial:** "Just listen to what our satisfied customers say about us."
>
> - **Compelling question:** "Would you like to sell more and spend less, in the very next quarter?"
>
> - **Guarantee:** "60-day free trial, and your money back if you are not completely satisfied."
>
> - **Benefit:** "Here's an idea that you can put to use tomorrow."
>
> - **Fear:** "What would you do if you lost your job tomorrow?"
>
> - **Greed:** "I want to give you this special free gift, just for reviewing my helpful new guide to human resource management."

- **Use all the space you need to deliver your message in a compelling way.** But don't use all the space just because it's available. Let the message drive the size of your communication.

- **In direct mail, begin with the basics.** These include the proven standard: an outer envelope, letter, response device, and brochure. Then, test against the standard into other formats, such as self-mailers and postcards.

- **Include a true business letter in the communication.** No matter what direct mail format is used, keep in mind that nothing is more powerful than a letter, especially a personalized one.

- **Include a pass-along message at appropriate points in your message.** In direct mail, opportunities include the postscript, order form, or behind the window so that the pass-along message is visible when the envelope contents are removed. This will increase the likelihood that your communication will get to the right person and extend your reach to additional prospects at a very low cost.

- **Repeat the offer and the response media (phone, e-mail address, URL, fax) on the response device.**

- **Add a deferral option to every response device.** For example, "Not interested now. Please contact me again in _____ months." This will help you increase responses and gain leads to put into the pipeline for later conversion.

Convert your features into benefits

B-to-B marketers frequently fall into the trap of stressing product features in their communications. This is especially true in technical fields, where product managers tend to get very excited about all the wonderful aspects engineered into their products.

As a B-to-B marketer, however, you need to overcome this trap by converting the product features into customer benefits. The marketer must know what is on the target customer's mind, and then set about translating the wonderful features into benefits that are meaningful, relevant, and valuable to the customer.

One term for this approach is WIIFM (What's In It For Me?), which is what customers really care about. Customers care about themselves and how the product helps them, not the product per se. So this is what you have to identify, highlight, and then communicate.

However, by no means should you ignore the product features, details, and specifications, which must be taken into consideration in order to justify the purchase price. Both features and WIIFM deserve equal billing in any campaign message.

According to some marketers, the most successful products are positioned to meet one or more of the two strongest human emotions: fear and greed. Notice that benefits can be very personal, expressed in human terms.

Here's an example of how product features can be recast as business or personal benefits:

Feature	Benefit
Lightweight	Reduces stress; saves money
24-hour tech support	Eliminates downtime and data loss
Multiplatform file sharing	Saves time; increases reliability
Plug and play	No connection headaches; get started immediately
Peel-off adhesive backing	Makes workflow organization easy

> **Seasonality**
>
> B-to-B lead generation is generally impervious to the seasonality considerations apparent in the consumer direct marketing world. Business buyers, on the other hand, need what they need when they need it, and purchasing continues steadily throughout the year. There may be some spikes related to end-of-fiscal-period budget issues, but these are likely to be unique to a handful of companies, and thus smoothed out across the board. The lesson here is the same one you already know well: in B-to-B, you must match your marketing outreach to your prospect's buying cycle.
>
> Business mailing list owners do report a modest uptick in list rentals in the months of March, May, and July. Since lists are ordered somewhat in advance of mail date, this may indicate an increase in campaigning in April, June, and August. But the variances against the other months are slight. And the data reveals inconsistencies: one office supplies list owner reported increased mail activity in March/April, June/July, September/October, and December.
>
> In certain industries — such as holiday cards and corporate gifts — seasonality may be more of a factor.

VII. Response planning

Response planning is a critical, yet sometimes sorely neglected, part of preparing a lead generation campaign. You will never regret any efforts you put into being sure your prospects' responses are properly handled and tracked. In fact, some would argue that if response planning is not done right, then you are throwing your entire marketing investment out the window.

Keep in mind the following points:

- The best way to track and measure the results of each lead generation message is via a key code on the outbound communication.

- Codes can take the form of a "priority code" number in the letter or on the response device, a special "extension" after an 800 number, or a special URL or URL extension address.

■ Set up internal processes in advance to capture and record these codes for later analysis. Make sure the teams handling the responses — whether internal call centers or outsourced fulfillment companies — are well trained and motivated to capture as many codes as possible.

The best way to track and measure the results of each lead generation message is via a key code on the outbound communication.

■ Despite your best efforts, a certain amount of inbound responses will inevitably go uncaptured. The best way to handle them for analysis is to separate the uncoded responses, sometimes known as "white mail," and analyze the trackable responses on their own.

■ Offer as many response media channels as possible in your messages. Unless there is a particular reason to limit the response to certain media, make every communication channel available for your prospects' convenience — phone, Web, business reply card, fax, e-mail, etc.

■ Use prepaid business reply mail for mail-in forms, whether cards or envelopes. Also, design the mail-in forms to be faxable, and include the fax number as an option.

■ Personalize your reply forms where possible, to ensure accuracy, improve key code capture, and make it easy and convenient for the prospect to complete the form.

■ Include qualification questions on all response forms, whether printed or electronic.

■ Schedule your campaign drops to create a smooth inflow of responses, which will reduce pressure on the response handlers as well as regulate the lead flow to the sales team.

VIII. Testing strategies

One of the best features of DR marketing is that it allows marketers to test such key variables as audience, medium, product, offer, message, art, and copy. As a result of testing, marketers can do more of what works and less of what doesn't. In theory, DR marketers are continually able to refine their work, increase response, save money, improve ROI, and be considered "heroes" by the company at large.

If only this were as easy in B-to-B marketing! There are a number of reasons why lead generators may find it difficult to institute testing as a regular part of their campaign programs. You need to know these possible roadblocks to be prepared to overcome them.

- Small mailing universes may preclude a test-and-rollout strategy, since there may not be enough names left for rollout.

- Due to frequent product changes, control packages are rarely used in B-to-B. With new creative treatments for each campaign, the concept of test and roll-out becomes moot.

- B-to-B campaigns involve a series of communications touches that are designed to move the customer steadily along the buying continuum. The logistics of test and control in a multi-touch world can be daunting.

- Testing may be unpopular with some observers who are untrained in direct marketing. Salespeople, for example, may worry about problems in managing their accounts when some segments of their customer base receive different offers from other segments.

- Testing involves additional expense that some decision-makers and others in the company may not view as justifiable.

So, the campaign testing question becomes, "Do you do it, or duck it?" There are no easy answers. One obvious strategy is to include a healthy amount of pre-testing in campaign planning. Also, introduce qualitative and quantitative research at a number of stages along the campaign trail, including post-testing, to dig into the audience's attitudes about the campaign, as well as surveys to understand whether and how they took some sort of action.

Testing pays off, however, in finding the best lists, offers, and creative platforms, and in supporting continuous improvement for your programs. Here are some points to keep in mind when you include test panels in your campaign:

- Test only what's important. The problem with testing is that it satisfies curiosity. Marketers are often curious about many things, but you must resist the urge to answer every random interesting question you have about your customers and prospects. Limit your testing to variables that can make an economic difference when they are rolled out.

- Consider all the testing options, not just the usual A/B splits and direct mail panels. For example, if you are working with a compiled list of prospects and have no other list to test it against, telephone a few of the names to get a very good early sense of the list's quality.

- If possible, include an offer test in every one of your campaigns. Offer testing can have sizable leverage, and it's helpful to build up a stable of usable offers for various purposes, such as inquiry generation or lead nurturing.

- Test new ways to reach the same audience. If you are advertising successfully in a trade publication, try renting the mailing list. If you are mailing, also try telemarketing or e-mail communications. If you are mailing a list by name, test it by title slug.

Introduce qualitative and quantitative research at a number of stages along the campaign trail, including post-testing.

- Test into areas of strength. If you have a good list, test additional selects on it. If you have a strong offer, test variations against it.

- Testing can be done cheaply and with minimal risk to the field if you limit it to certain media. Split testing of headlines, copy, and offers, for example, is cheap and fast to execute in e-mail, out-bound telemarketing, and print advertising.

■ Test the qualification process. If you add more qualification questions to your reply form, response will suffer — but your inquiry qualification rate will rise. Test to find the optimal balance in this equation.

IX. Campaign results analysis

Results analysis is an oft-neglected area of lead generation campaigning. After a campaign is over and "out the door," marketers find themselves moving on to the next project, the next quarter, or the next crisis. It may be difficult for you to look backward, no matter how much you recognize the importance of follow-through.

It helps to schedule post-mortem sessions as a regular part of the ongoing campaign process. Involve parties from all parts of the company — business partners, sales, call centers, service providers, finance, and anyone whose role has impacted the campaign or who stands to benefit from it. Let marketing report on campaign results, and have everyone offer suggestions for improvement the next time.

Campaign results need to be measured against campaign objectives. In the campaign planning stage, you established such objectives as the number of qualified leads, cost per qualified lead, lead-to-sales conversion ratio, and campaign ROI. So, let these be the benchmarks against which you measure the success of any given campaign.

This is not to suggest that results analysis is easy, though, as a number of obstacles conspire against you:

■ Campaign leads are developed and nurtured by a number of touches. Assigning a value to each element in the process can be an extremely complex task.

■ Long sales cycle times mean that final ROI results will not be available until several interim campaigns are already planned and executed.

- Salespeople may claim that they were already handling the account before the campaign started; therefore, they — not the campaign — should receive full credit for sales.

- When leads are handled by distributors or other third parties, it can be impossible to motivate them to report at all. Distributors are independent business people, and you may have little leverage over them.

- Campaign ROI may be meaningless in high-value sales situations, where the result might be in the thousands of a percent. The expense-to-revenue ratio is a better measure in such cases.

In the face of such odds, some companies divide their results analysis into two parts: activity-based metrics and results-based metrics. During the long stretch, until sales results come in, marketers can get some interim benefit by analyzing the inquiry and qualification campaign activities themselves.

Activity-based metrics include such indicators as:	**Results-based metrics include such indicators as:**
Cost per thousand (CPM)	Conversion-to-sales rate
Response rate	Sales revenue per lead
Cost per inquiry	Campaign ROI
Campaign turnaround time	Campaign expense-to-revenue ratio
Qualification rate	
Cost per qualified lead	

Campaign results analysis will be covered in "Closing the Lead Generation Marketing Loop" in Part Three, Chapter 7, beginning on page 105.

Roles and responsibilities by function

Since lead generation involves so many people and such a cross-section of functions within the company, there will always be some confusion about who should do what for whom. Therefore, clarify roles early on during the planning process — it will save much pain later. Each organization should make its own decisions, but here are some suggested guidelines for assigning roles and responsibilities. There will be much overlap, of course.

Function	Role/responsibility
Marketing	Strategic planning, budgeting, sales, and marketing objectives
Marketing	Advertising, PR for building brand awareness communications
Direct marketing	Lead generation, lead management, lead tracking
Database marketing	Marketing database management, data analysis, list selection
Sales force	Lead conversion, reporting on lead status; lead generation within territory
Resellers/distributors	Lead conversion, reporting on lead status; lead generation within territory
e-commerce	Web site management
IT	Install software tools, tech support

Do not allow the lead management (qualification, nurturing, and tracking) function to rest with the sales team, even if they make a strong case for controlling this function. Ultimately, lead management belongs in marketing. Salespeople, who are highly skilled and well-paid, need to be focused on selling.

Chapter 6

Budgeting

Budgeting can be extremely complicated in lead generation, because there are so many moving parts. You need to pull together the costs of creating and executing the campaign. You also need to account for fulfillment expense, qualification expense, and lead management expense. Finally, you need to gather costs from your call centers, your support staffs, and your vendors. With all this complexity, it is a good idea to have your finance department help you develop the right cost accounting for your campaign.

> It is a good idea to have your finance department help you develop the right cost accounting for your campaign.

As you begin thinking about the budgeting process, you might consider the following point: in B-to-B marketing, salespeople usually are responsible for sales quotas in the millions or hundreds of thousands of dollars per year. Their salaries and benefits packages may begin in the low six figures. So, give a thought to the expense — and the opportunity cost — of a salesperson who is working on cold prospecting or under-developed, unqualified leads. You might argue that marketing cannot possibly spend enough money to offset the expense of unproductive sales efforts. If you take this argument to its logical conclusion, any money invested in lead generation and qualification appears to be money worth spending.

Of course, even if you subscribe to the notion that lead generation is always going to be a good investment when compared to unproductive sales activity, you have to develop a budget of some sort. Not only do you want each lead to be productive; you also want to prove that each lead pays for itself. So, let us now look at some calculations.

I. Calculating an allowable cost per lead

One of the most important budgeting factors in lead generation is to be certain that leads are delivered to sales at an affordable price. One way to approach this is by calculating an allowable cost per lead.

Begin with the total direct campaign costs, including all fixed and variable costs that can be directly attributed to the campaign. This would include creative and pre-production costs, plus the costs of developing and producing fulfillment materials, as well as the normal variable costs of campaign development and execution. Divide this amount by the number of expected campaign responses to get a cost per inquiry figure.

Next, you need to estimate the costs associated with qualifying a lead. If you try to calculate this number on a per campaign basis, you will quickly be forced to run screaming from the room. The most logical alternative is to calculate an average qualification cost for inquiries over a set period — e.g., a year. Therefore, gather up all the back-end inquiry handling costs — i.e., the costs of the direct head count involved in inquiry capture, and the costs of fulfillment, of qualification, and of nurturing. If the back-end processes are outsourced, the data gathering is as simple as adding up the bills. Once you have a number for the year, divide it by the number of inquiries handled in the year. This number will serve as your average cost to qualify an inquiry.

The next step is to gather data from finance and sales. You also need the average order size — namely, the total revenue divided by the total number of orders. You need the margin (or its opposite, the cost of goods sold) and the direct sales expense per order, which is calculated by the total sales expense divided by the total number of orders.

Chart 6.1 uses some hypothetical numbers to arrive at the cost of a lead that has converted to a sale, and compare it to an allowable cost per lead.

CHART 6.1
Calculating an allowable cost per lead

Cost per inquiry (campaign cost ÷ no. of responses)	$100
Average cost to qualify an inquiry (back-end handling costs ÷ inquiries per year)	$50
Total cost per inquiry qualified (cost per inquiry + cost to qualify)	$150
Lead qualification rate	25%
Cost of qualified lead (cost per lead ÷ qualification rate)	$600
Lead conversion rate	30%
Cost of a closed lead (cost of qualified lead ÷ conversion rate)	**$2,000**
Average order size (annual revenue ÷ number of orders)	$10,000
Net margin per order (revenue per order × margin, 60%)	$6,000
Allowable cost per lead (net margin per order − direct sales expense, $3,500)	**$2,500**

To arrive at the allowable cost per lead, it's not actually necessary to know how many inquiries will be generated, qualified, and converted. Instead, you need to know the cost per inquiry, the cost to qualify an inquiry, the qualification and conversion rates, the net margin per order, and the direct sales expense per order.

In this example, the cost of a campaign, say, was $15,000 and generated 150 inquiries. Whatever the cost and the responses, though, the important number is the cost per inquiry. Total cost per inquiry is $100. Separately, the average cost to qualify an inquiry for the year was calculated at $50. Now, divide the qualification rate (25%) into the total cost per inquiry qualified ($150) to calculate the cost of a qualified lead. Then, divide that number by the conversion rate (30%) to get the cost of a closed lead ($2,000). Compare this number with the allowable cost per closed lead ($2,500), which is a simple calculation of the net margin per order minus the cost of sales (set here as $3,500). In this example, the campaign looks promising, since the expected cost per converted lead is $500 less than the allowable cost per lead.

By putting this information on a spreadsheet and "tweaking" it, you will see how much leverage there is on the back end. A few efficiencies on qualification rate and conversion rate can work wonders on campaign ROI.

II. Establishing break-even campaign response rates

Another useful approach to campaign budgeting is figuring out what kind of response rate is needed to break even on an outbound campaign. With the break-even number in hand, it is possible to "eyeball" the numbers and decide whether you are comfortable with the likelihood of making that response rate once the campaign is executed. If you decide you need more wiggle room, then adjust your numbers to suit — whether by lowering variable costs or improving the power of the offer, or doing whatever will get you the pro forma numbers you think the campaign can deliver.

Calculating the break-even begins with the same calculation performed above, to identify the allowable cost per lead closed. Then, work back from the allowable cost per closed lead, to the allowable cost per lead qualified, to the allowable cost per inquiry, and ultimately to the response rate required to break even.

Working with the same hypothetical numbers as in Chart 6.1, Chart 6.2 provides an example of what this might look like:

Chart 6.2
Calculating break-even response rate

Average order size (annual revenue ÷ no. of orders)	$10,000
Net margin per order (revenue per order × margin, 60%)	$6,000
Allowable cost per closed lead (net margin per order − direct sales expense, $3,500)	**$2,500**
Lead conversion rate	30%
Allowable cost per qualified lead (allowable cost per lead × conversion rate)	$750
Inquiry qualification rate	25%
Allowable cost per inquiry (allowable cost per qualified lead × qualification rate)	$187.50
Campaign cost per piece (at $1,500 per thousand)	$1.50
Break-even campaign response rate (cost per piece ÷ allowable cost per inquiry)	**0.8%**

So in this case, you would ask yourself whether you can be fairly sure you'll get at least 0.8%, or eight responses per thousand. If that doesn't feel realistic, then you need to lower your cost per thousand (CPM), strengthen your offers and lists, or improve your qualification or conversion rates.

3

Part Three
Response Management
and Lead Conversion

Chapter 7

Response management

Now that we have covered the tools and strategies used for generating responses, it's time to turn to response management, also known as inquiry handling. What do you do when the inquiry comes in? This question is important for the company, since a mere inquiry represents only a modest step along the road to generating qualified leads, and there is still much to do before the company sees any sales results.

But the question is also important when you consider that an inquiry represents a need in the market. An inquiry is, in fact, a miraculous thing. A prospective customer has indicated an interest in your product or service. You have encouraged that interest. So, it is your responsibility and your opportunity to satisfy it effectively.

Response management must follow close on the heels of campaign planning and execution. If campaign planning is sometimes called the front end of the lead generation process, then response management may be called the back end. It is on the back end where the most business leverage really lies. Small improvements in the back end can have immediate and significant results on the ROI of lead generation.

Some marketers tend to focus on the front end, the creative part, where campaign strategies are developed, messages are crafted, and copy is written. They view this arena as more fun and engaging, and resist having a disciplined focus on what they feel are the mundane details of the back end. This is a very unfortunate thing, resulting in great waste. It also increases the likelihood that inferior leads will make their way to the sales team.

Response management is also where the competitive advantage kicks in. Managing, qualifying, and converting inquiries to sales is not easy. Many companies do it poorly. So, a company that develops and executes a solid back-end process is going to pull ahead in the marketplace. Test your own processes by pretending to be an inquirer, and see how you are treated (sometimes called "mystery shopping"). Also test the processes of your competitors, and make sure your back-end processes are stronger in every way.

You must allow enough time and money to manage the back end properly. Be sure that response management is an integral part of your campaign planning process. And allow at least 10% of your campaign budget to support the back end.

Response management involves the following general steps:

- Response capture

- Inquiry fulfillment

- Inquiry qualification

- Lead nuturing

- Tracking to closure

But, of course, nothing is quite as easy as it first appears. Many responses will not qualify immediately, so they need to be put into a process called lead "nurturing," or "incubation." (Nurturing will be discussed later in the "Lead Nurturing" section in this chapter.) Marketing may deem that responses are qualified, so it hands them over to sales as leads; sales, however, may

Leads are gold

Take the time to instill within company employees an appreciation of the value of the inquiries and the qualified leads that they later become. Each lead may cost hundreds, perhaps thousands, of dollars to generate; but each may represent thousands, perhaps millions, of dollars in sales potential. Therefore, you need to consider inquiries and leads as gold. Here are some ways to spread the word:

- Encourage your senior managers to refer to leads as "valuable."

- Post messages in the call centers and elsewhere around the company that state how much an average sales lead is worth.

- Compensate salespeople on lead follow-up rates.

reject those leads for a variety of reasons. For example, a salesperson may be unsuccessful at closing the lead, and marketing will need to take the lead back for further nurturing, or hand it off to another salesperson.

In short, the response management process has many steps. Each company must decide for itself which elements belong where, and how to tailor the process to fit the company's industry and culture. Let us now review each of these steps in detail.

I. Response capture

Inquiries will come in from outbound campaigns, from current customers, or unsolicited over the transom. You need to have a well-planned process in place to capture the inquiries so they can be fulfilled, qualified, and managed properly.

Inquiries come through a variety of media, among them:

- **Mail.** Include business reply mail and bingo cards.

- **Telephone.** Arrange for an 800 number, or use your company office number. Have scripts in place to capture qualifying information and source codes. Make sure the call center is open during business hours that serve all time zones where customers do business.

- **Fax.** If possible, set up a dedicated line just for responses, so they don't become confused with regular business communications.

- **E-mail.** Like phone and fax, responders expect fast turnaround.

- **Web response form.**

- **Notes.** Scribbled from sales contacts.

The inquiry handling process should be capable of handling inquiries from all sources. Designing a process that captures inquiries from all media channels is not a trivial task, especially when the inbound channels are under separate management. Therefore, assign personnel from each channel to a task force to set this process up and then serve as point people on its smooth operation.

Inquiry handling must include the following:

- Log the inquiry in a database, whether it be a dedicated lead management database or the general marketing database. Match the inquiry against prior sales and marketing contacts to make sure it is not a duplicate. Capture the qualification criteria from the response.

- Fulfill the inquiry with the appropriate materials. A well-run campaign will have prepared collateral materials specific to the campaign. You also need to plan for non-campaign inquiries, so have a set of materials relevant to those prospects as well. Develop informational materials on products or services that receive the most inquiries, as well as a generic product or company "catch-all" brochure.

- Conduct a first screening of the inquiry. The qualification questions on the response form may already provide enough information to identify that the lead is ready to be given to a sales rep. If so, move the lead immediately to the hand-off process. The rest of the inquiries will need to flow to qualification. Some inquiries, such as those that came from publicity or over the transom, will have no additional information, and need to be qualified from scratch.

- Begin the qualification process.

II. Inquiry fulfillment

The first step in the back-end process is fulfillment. In the excitement of campaign development, some campaign planners neglect to think beyond the frenzy of getting the inquiry-generating message out the door. But, it is critically important to your success in lead generation that you think through each stage of what will happen from the moment the prospect responds.

Furthermore, it is particularly important to consider this process from the customer's point of view. How quickly will he receive the materials he requested? What kind of impression will they make? What is the next step? What do we want him to do?

In the art and science of response handling, keep in mind a number of principles:

- Speed is of the essence. Studies show that the faster fulfillment materials are received, the more likely the lead is to be qualified. The need is still fresh, and competitors are less apt to be in the way. As a rule of thumb, inquiries should be fulfilled no later than 24 hours after receipt.

- Plan carefully. To deliver on the 24-hour fulfillment mission requires that processes are well designed and working smoothly. Test, "mystery-shop," and refine the process regularly.

Inquiries should be fulfilled no later than 24 hours after receipt.

  - In the interest of speed, use the Internet for fulfillment where possible. Web-based collateral material is not only fast, it is also infinitely flexible for continuous updating and customization to the individual inquirer's need.

  - Create incentives for speed. If an inquiry sits on an employee's desk until he "gets to it," your system will fail. Every single person involved in the process needs a motivator to put the response-handling task at the top of the daily to-do list.

- Make the fulfillment package look and feel reminiscent of the original campaign message. This will provide a consistent experience for the respondent, reinforce the brand's image, and increase the fulfillment material's perceived relevance and value.

- Remember that the purpose of the package is to move the prospect closer to a sale. Make sure the contents provide the information that the customer needs at this particular stage of his buying process.

■ Keep the contents relevant to the original inquiry. You may be tempted to consider adding product or company brochures, or whatever spare collateral material you have lying around — but then the package will end up appearing disorganized and unprofessional.

■ De-duplicate inquiries against your inquiry database. Respondents may forget they have already expressed an interest, so duplicate inquiries are common. In such a case, you may decide to send the prospect another, less expensive, fulfillment package to satisfy the inquiry. However, if the original inquiry has been qualified and is in the hands of a salesperson, notify the rep of the new inquiry's arrival.

■ Initial screening of the inquiry is a good idea. Look out for competitors, students, librarians, and other information seekers who are unlikely to be true sales prospects. They, too, may be candidates for a less expensive fulfillment package.

■ "Here is the information you requested." To get your fulfillment package opened, include a reminder message on the outer envelop. This indicates to the mail sorter that materials are expected, and will serve as a memory trigger to the recipient.

■ Personalize the fulfillment message. The fulfillment package represents "the beginning of a beautiful friendship," to quote Rick of *Casablanca* fame. So treat the inquirer right, from the start.

■ Consider further qualifying the prospect by telephoning in advance of sending the fulfillment package. This lets you find out more about the specific information he needs, and helps in the personalization of your cover letter.

> ### Components of a traditional printed fulfillment package
>
> Include the following components in a traditional printed fulfillment package:
>
> - An outer envelope proclaiming the arrival of the materials requested.
>
> - A short, personalized cover letter acknowledging the prospect's expression of interest, describing the package contents and their purpose, and telling the prospect what to do next.
>
> - Sales materials filled with eye-catching devices like sticky notes, or handwritten margin notes. Include information on where to buy, such as a list of local dealers, or contact information for the sales rep in the territory.
>
> - An involvement device, like a survey or a checklist of product features and benefits.
>
> - Packaging that encourages the customer to hold on to the materials, like a file folder.
>
> - A response device and instructions for what to do next. This can be a BRE, a business card with your contact information, or a Rolodex card — whatever will allow the customer to take some action to keep in touch with you.

III. Inquiry qualification

You must correctly qualify responses before delivering them as leads to the salespeople. Marketers often misunderstand their mission to be that of generating lead volume alone. In fact, it is quality that counts. The objective is to generate enough qualified leads so that each sales territory is optimally busy, productive, and fulfilling its quota. Delivering too many leads can be as wasteful as delivering too few. And delivering qualified leads is what provides real leverage to an expensive and constrained resource: the sales force.

Your goal, as a B-to-B marketer, is to identify those inquirers whose pocketbooks are open, who have a budget, who have a business problem to solve, and who can influence or make a purchase decision. You need to separate out these inquirers from those who are merely doing some research. The latter group of folks needs to be handled differently.

CHART 7.1
The inquiry mix

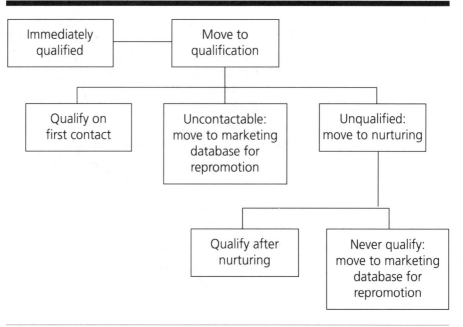

Setting qualification criteria

The best approach to setting qualification criteria is to follow the needs of your sales force. After all, it is they who will be handling the leads and taking them to closure. They know better than anyone the nature of the sales process and the kinds of buying characteristics that are most likely to be workable for them.

Qualification criteria will vary by company and by industry. However, as a general rule, most criteria involve the following categories. Taken together, these key variables are abbreviated as BANT (budget, authority, need, and time frame):

- **Budget.** Is the purchase budgeted? What size budget does the prospect have available? You will want to set up categories or ranges for easier scoring. Some companies request information about the prospect's credit history.

- **Authority.** Is the respondent authorized to make the purchase decision? If not, try to capture additional relevant contact information.

- **Need.** How important is the product or solution, and how deep is the company's pain? Approach such situations by roundabout questions such as: "What problem is your company experiencing?" "What alternative solutions are you considering?" "How many do you need?" "What product do you currently use?"

- **Time frame.** When will the customer be ready to make the purchase? Depending on industry and sales cycle length, this can be broken down into days, months, or even years. Also be sure to ask whether they would like to see a salesperson.

Qualification criteria will vary from company to company.

Other than BANT, you may consider such additional criteria as:

- **Potential sales volume.** How many departments in the company might use this product? How much of the product might they need? How often are they likely to buy?

- **Predisposition to buy from you.** Are they past customers of yours? Are they similar to your current customers? Would they recommend you to their colleagues? Will they call you back?

- **Account characteristics.** What is the company size? Make the distinction of whether this is measured by number of employees or revenue volume. Note the industry of the company. Establish if this is the parent company, or a subsidiary of a larger organization.

Qualification form example
Two qualification form examples, courtesy of The Hacker Group

Qualification form example I
Thank you for your participation.

In appreciation for your assistance, ABC Company will send you a free trial-version of ABC Plus to use for 30 days with no obligation.

To complete this survey online, go to **http://www.(company).com/survey**

Priority Code: C025904LH

Jane Doe
Software Developer
JR Investments
MS1
1 Main St
Anywhere, NY 10036

When you have completed this questionnaire, please return to A Research Group, P.O. Box 1, Somewhere, NY 10035 by **March 1, 2002**. A return envelope is enclosed for your convenience.

For more information about ABC Company and ABC Plus, please go to http://www.(company).com.

Q1. How many employees does your organization have?
- ☐ 1-500
- ☐ 501-750
- ☐ 751-1,000
- ☐ 1,000+

Q2. Which of the following areas are you responsible for? (Please mark all that apply.)
- ☐ Help Desk
- ☐ Network Maintenance
- ☐ System Compatibility
- ☐ User Workstations
- ☐ Software Applications
- ☐ File Sharing Capability
- ☐ Other_____

Q3. Does your organization receive e-mails with attachments from the following sources? (Please mark all that apply.)
- ☐ Clients/customers
- ☐ Vendors
- ☐ Business partners
- ☐ Off-site personnel
- ☐ Professional services
- ☐ We do not receive outside e-mail attachments
- ☐ Other _____

Q4. How does your organization currently view incoming files? (Please mark all that apply.)
- ☐ We use the application that created the file to open it
- ☐ If we do not have the appropriate application, we ask the sender to resend the file in a compatible format
- ☐ If we do not have the appropriate application, we buy a version to enable our users to open future incoming files
- ☐ We have the following file viewing application:
  _____

Q5. Are you satisfied with the way you currently view incoming files? (Please mark all that apply.)
- ☐ Not satisfied
- ☐ Somewhat satisfied, but would like improvements
- ☐ Very satisfied
- ☐ Do not currently have a file viewer

Q6. Are you currently considering upgrading your ability to view incoming files?
- ☐ Yes
- ☐ No

Q7. What are your biggest concerns in considering file viewing options? (Please mark all that apply.)
- ☐ Budget limitations
- ☐ Timing, I'm swamped right now
- ☐ Don't know enough about my options
- ☐ Other_____

Q8. The perfect time for me to get control of file viewing in my organization would be:
- ☐ Tomorrow
- ☐ Within the next 1-3 months
- ☐ Within the next 4-6 months
- ☐ Within the next 7-12 months

- ☐ More than 12 months from now

Q9. Would you like to receive additional information of file viewing software?
- ☐ Yes
- ☐ No

Q10. May ABC Company contact you by e-mail?
- ☐ Yes

My e-mail address is:

_____

ABC Company will not sell, lease, or lend any personal information you give without your written permission.

Qualification form example II

A GPS Legend Handheld Global Positioning System

is reserved for:

Jane Doe

Reservation number: ZZZ-99999999999

Expiration Date: March 30, 2002

To accept this gift from ABC Company, simply **call toll-free 1.800.555.5555.** You can also return this form by fax to 1.800.555.1234, or mail it in the postage-paid envelope we've included. (Certain restrictions may apply.)

Shipping Address: *(please make any corrections needed)*

Jane Doe
Software Developer
JR Investments
MS1
1 Main St
Anywhere, NY 10036

☐ I accept your offer of a FREE GPS Legend unit. Please contact me to arrange delivery as soon as it is convenient.

My phone number is: (_____) _____. The best time to reach me is:_____a.m._____p.m.

☐ You may reach me by e-mail at: _____

Company will not sell, lease, or lend any personal information provided here.)

To help us serve you better, please answer these 3 quick questions:

1. On a scale of 1 to 5, how important is knowing the exact physical location of your telecom prospects (with 1 being not important at all and 5 being extremely important)?
   - ☐ 1
   - ☐ 2
   - ☐ 3
   - ☐ 4
   - ☐ 5

2. How many people does your company employ?:
   - ☐ 1-49
   - ☐ 501-1,000
   - ☐ 50-100
   - ☐ 101-500
   - ☐ 1,001-10,000
   - ☐ 10,000+

3. Which of the following best describes your telecom marketing needs?
   - ☐ Strategic planning
   - ☐ Capital deployment
   - ☐ Market execution
   - ☐ Locating geographic concentrations of prospects
   - ☐ All of the above

Call toll-free 1.800.555.5555

Here are the guiding principles on qualification criteria:

- Set these criteria in consultation with the sales force.

- Ask the questions on your response forms, whether they are paper-based, by voice, or electronic. Asking questions on the front end introduces the risk of reducing response, but you will make it up many times over by increasing qualification rates and reducing the expense of outbound qualification efforts.

- Don't be shy. Be sure you are collecting all the information needed by the sales team. If you ask, business buyers will answer. Your question is a service to them as well as to you. If you don't ask, your conversion rates will fall dramatically.

- Don't hesitate to ask for the order. Be sure to include a hard option like "Have a sales specialist contact me" as one of the possible check-off boxes on every form. You might even ask what is the best time for the rep to make contact.

- Set criteria that will be used consistently across campaigns, if possible. They will allow you to analyze results over time and across campaign variables like list, offer, and creative. They will also reduce confusion and extra work during campaign planning.

The inquiry qualification process

Traditionally, qualification has been the province of the call center, and the key medium for qualification was a series of outbound telephone calls. Now, however, e-mail is proving to be a potent medium for qualification. In some cases — when the prospect has provided no other contact information, for example — direct mail is also effective.

What's important is that inquiries, once they are fulfilled, must move into the qualification pipeline quickly. The processes need to be designed for speed and efficient handling. The functions may be staffed by full-time dedicated resources, outsourced, or operated by employees who have other duties as well. The staff needs to be motivated and compensated to encourage 100% handling of inquiries within a very short, pre-determined time frame. However the process is set up, it must be funded to support the expected inquiry flow.

Here are the types of inquiries that will need to be qualified:

- Inquiries that have no information other than contact name and address — e.g., those from bingo cards and over the transom.

- Inquiries where the qualification questions were filled out incompletely — this occurs 40% of the time with qualification forms.

Some points to keep in mind as you plan your qualification process:

- Business people are often away from their desks, so tele-qualification will require three to five attempts.

- These days, e-mail is the most powerful medium for qualification communications. Your e-mails can be designed to link to a Web-based qualification form. Like other communications, the e-mail should offer several response media options, including phone, fax, and postal mail.

- Wherever possible, direct your inquiries to the Web for preliminary qualification, especially in a high-volume environment. Self-reporting on the Web saves money for you, and it saves time for your prospects.

- Set up an alternating qualification message series. If e-mail doesn't work, try the phone, and vice versa.

- When using the telephone for qualification, script the call to focus more on the prospect and his needs, and less about your company and your products.

- Set your tolerance limit for touches in advance, based on a reasonable number of contacts. Call it quits if the prospect is unreachable after five phone attempts and five e-mails.

- If you cannot contact a prospect, there is little alternative than to put the name back into the marketing database for re-promotion. Be sure to flag the record, however, to indicate this history. If the prospect raises his hand again and you cannot contact him the second time around, you may want to place a stop on further investments.

- Consider a step-wise qualification process. Depending on the industry and the product complexity, you may find that someone who simply requests company information is not yet ready to be qualified. So, design a series of interim contacts that will move him to the point where a qualification contact makes sense.

- Adjust the process to the customer's needs. You can't force him to be ready. However, it is your job to be there when he becomes ready.

- Manage the inquiries on a first-in, first-out basis, so that no lead gets too old and cold while waiting to go to sales.

- Motivate your qualifiers to qualify, not to sell. Their job is to gather information only.

- Handle orders based on the incoming medium. Respondents by e-mail, Web, and fax have higher expectations of quick action than postal mail users.

Lead scoring strategies

There are many ways to sort and score leads, so select the process that best suits your sales team and your industry. Remember: get input from the sales team about their preferences.

1. A, B, C, D

One common strategy is a simple alphabetical ranking. Here's an example:

- "A" means the prospect is ready to see a sales rep. Either the prospect has agreed to this (e.g., "Have a sales specialist call me.") or the predefined qualification criteria for a sales call have been met.

- "B" means the prospect still needs nurturing, but the sales team is to make the contact. This might involve a telephone call to establish the relationship, in anticipation of an imminent readiness to buy.

- "C" means the inquiry still needs nurturing — by marketing.

- Include a "D" to indicate an inquiry that is not worth nurturing. In this case, there needs to be a decision on whether to put the inquiry into the marketing database for ongoing communications, or to throw it away.

Lead ranking systems vary widely. Some companies classify leads as "hot," "warm," or "future;" others label them as "hard" or "soft." However they are organized, be sure to set up the criteria in consultation with the sales Unqualified leads should *never* be passed along to sales.

2. Weighted scoring

The Chart 7.2 shows how assigning a simple numerical score to each answer to the qualification questions can be a great help. Numerical scores allow a quick evaluation by both marketing and sales about the readiness of a lead. This approach provides flexibility, as

CHART 7.2

Design of a sample weighting scheme

Criterion	Score
Budget:	
$250k+	5
$100–250k	4
$50–100k	3
$0–50k	2
Authority to:	
approve	5
recommend	4
specify	3
use	2
purchase	1
Time frame:	
1–3 months	5
3–6 months	3
6–12 months	1
Have sales rep call:	
yes	10
no	0
Budgeted:	
yes	5
no	0

the weightings can be changed by the campaign, by the product, or even by the current level of pressure to deliver fast revenues.

In this example, assume that sales asks you to hand off immediately any lead with a score of 15. Here is the kind of prospect they would see: an inquirer with an approved budget (5 points) of $80,000 (3 points), who is planning to buy this quarter (5 points), who is the end user of the solution (2 points), and who is likely to be a strong influencer on the purchase decision. They would also see an inquiry from a purchasing agent (1 point) who has an urgent need (5 points), and wants to see a salesperson (10 points), but does not yet have a budget approved. For the industry and product line depicted here, the sales team deems it wants to work on these leads right away. Note: in this example, we assume that a purchasing agent simply performs an administrative function — the person types up purchase orders, but has no decision-making authority.

IV. Lead nurturing

When an inquiry is only partially qualified and does not make the grade of readiness for the sales team, it needs to be nurtured, in a process sometimes called "incubation" or lead "development." Nurturing involves a series of marketing communications intended to build trust and awareness, and maintain a relationship until the prospect is ready to buy.

The objective of the nurturing program is to be in touch with the prospect when a prospect is ready to buy.

Things change rapidly in businesses. The only way you can know when a prospect is ready to buy is by regular communication.

The nurturing process can be fast or slow — or endless. Some prospects never get the budget needed to make the purchase, their needs change, or they buy from a competitor. This can be discouraging. But, take heart. The fact is, half of all business inquiries eventually result in a sale — for someone. Nurturing increases the chances that the seller will be you.

Sources of leads that require nurturing include:

- **Partially qualified inquiries.** Not ready to buy, according to the predefined qualification criteria.

- **Leads returned by the sales team.** A presumably qualified lead requires further nurturing. The contact may have changed his job, or the business need may have changed. So, sales returns the lead to marketing for further follow-up.

The series of communications used in the nurturing process varies widely. You will need to choose among communications media (telephone, direct mail, and e-mail) and also decide the best sequencing and timing strategies. To keep things simple, however, devise a standard process, and refine it as experience indicates what works best.

The objective of the nurturing program is to be in touch with the prospect when he is ready to buy.

As the nurturing process helps you gather new information about the inquirer, enter those data points into the lead management database.

There may be some internal controversy over whether nurturing is a function of sales or of marketing. Some companies split the difference and create nurturing teams that report to sales. However you decide to manage nurturing, be sure to recognize it as a separate function that can be staffed by lower-cost resources than your salespeople. That said, however, those resources will be in regular contact with prospects, so make sure they are professional and well-trained. You want them to be able to act as appropriate representatives of your company to the outside world.

Here are some typical nurturing tactics:

- Catalog mailing

- Seminar invitation

- Trade show invitation

- New product announcement

- Newsletter (e-mail or print)

- Press release

- Survey

- Testimonials

- Video or CD mailing

- White paper (downloadable or mailed)

- Article or chapter reprints

- Case study

- Personal communication — e.g., birthday or holiday card

- Letter from the CFO, customer service department, engineering, senior executives, and so on

V. Closing the lead generation marketing loop

B-to-B marketers operating in a multichannel world are continually challenged to measure the results of their lead generation campaigns. Without solid measurements, it is difficult to demonstrate the value of marketing — not to mention justifying the budget. But, when multiple people and functions are involved at various stages of the lead generation and conversion processes, evaluating the contribution of each element can be well-nigh impossible.

Here are seven techniques that allow B-to-B marketers to measure sales results in lead generation campaigns. Experiment with what may apply to your company's situation.

1. Closed-loop system. Many companies have put in place elaborate "closed-loop" processes to accomplish tracking. A closed-loop system tries to follow each qualified lead to its end result, whether it be closure, rejection, or loss to the competition. In B-to-B marketers' complex, multichannel lives, this involves expensive hand work: contacting individual salespeople and directly requesting reports on the results. Since salespeople need to focus on selling, it may be inappropriate to "hound" them. Closed loop works best on high-value products and services, such as industrial equipment or technology. However, because closed loop usually under-reports results, you may need to supplement it with other techniques.

Why responses are often mishandled

When companies invest time and money in lead generation activities, they find it frustrating to learn that inquiries sometimes go unanswered by marketers, and that leads may be ignored by the sales team. There are a number of reasons why this happens:

- Response management processes may be flawed.

- Marketers get caught up in the glamour of outbound campaigning and do not devote sufficient energy and resources to the back end of inquiry management.

- Salespeople have a natural inclination to focus on current customers, instead of on pursuing new business.

- Salespeople are unable to make contact with prospects after several attempts, and then condemn the lead as poor quality.

- Prior experience with poor-quality leads from marketing has left salespeople uncomfortable with investing more time in new leads.

- Salespeople receive more leads than they can handle, so they cherry-pick the ones they like, and toss the rest.

There are several methods for combating this problem:

- Report regularly on conversion rates. Remember, if it's not measured, it won't be managed.

- Spot-check the system. Once a month, or more often, track a sample response as it wends its way through the company, to observe the process, identify any weaknesses, and make improvements. Do the same with your competitors to find out what your customers are experiencing elsewhere.

- Involve the sales team in lead generation planning and execution, communicate with them regularly, and tailor the program to meet their requirements.

2. End-user sampling. Surveying end users who were contacted in a particular campaign can provide excellent results. It is inexpensive and reliable, and captures actual sales from multiple channels. Select a statistically projectible sample of prospects who received the campaign message. Survey them via phone, e-mail, or postal mail. Do not ask whether they received or recall receiving the campaign message — nor let anyone in marketing communications persuade you to ask this irrelevant question. Instead, ask whether they bought the product that was promoted in the campaign, and where they bought it. Also, be sure to ask whether, if they didn't buy the product, they solved the problem through some other means, such as buying from the competition. What you'll find, without fail, is that a sizable number of prospects did, in fact, buy from you, but their purchases fell through the cracks of your closed-loop tracking system. By using this kind of "Did-you-buy?" survey, you'll be able to claim, legitimately, much more campaign revenue to apply to your lead generation ROI calculations. One caveat: do not over-survey your prospects. There's a fine balance between finding out what you need to know and annoying your customers into dissatisfaction.

3. Data matchback. Analyzing the sales in accounts that have been promoted is an approach that has been used for years, and particularly suits high-volume campaigns like catalog sales or office supplies. Wait a suitable period — say, the average length of the sales cycle — and then review the revenue levels in the accounts that were selected for the campaign. This technique is not suited to marketers who rely on distribution channels, unless they can persuade their channels to share revenue data from their end-user accounts. Another problem is that data matchback captures all sales into the account and is thus likely to overstate the sales that result from any particular campaign. Politically, it can be truly dangerous for marketers to make large claims for campaign sales results. All this does is alienate the salespeople, who are convinced that it was entirely their skill and persistence that got the business.

4. Control groups. This is an ideal solution in a single channel mail order environment, but just about impossible to implement in the broader world of business marketing. A control group isolates a set of customers who won't see the campaign, and compares sales in those accounts to a set of similar accounts that do see it. This can work pretty well for long-term, multitactic campaigns, like loyalty programs. But for most campaigns using multiple media, it is unreliable because of the difficulty in "fencing off" any customer. It can also be hard to justify leaving money on the table by eliminating high-potential prospects. No management team, not to mention shareholders, will cotton to suppressing certain accounts from promotions that are likely to generate revenue.

Exclusive offers are suited to single tactic campaigns for products with short sales cycles.

5. Exclusive offers. When it is possible to create an offer that is promoted only in a particular campaign, all the sales can be credibly attributed to the campaign itself. Similarly, coupons redeemable through distribution channels, but funded by the marketer, allow reliable tracking of campaign results. Exclusive offers are best suited to single tactic campaigns for products with short sales cycles.

6. Product registration. This is the ultimate end-user sampling technique. Most registration systems ask customers to indicate where or when they bought; some systems ask customers what influenced their purchase decisions. However, it is difficult to link registration questions back to specific campaigns without an elaborate string of questions. Too many questions will reduce registration rates.

7. Activity-based measurements. Some B-to-B marketers decide that tracking leads to closure is too difficult, and they measure only their lead generation activities — i.e., response rate; conversion rate to qualified lead; cost per lead; campaign executed on time, on budget, and so forth. When the other techniques are too expensive to justify, settling for activity-based measurements can make sense.

VI. Outsourcing versus in-house handling

Businesses of all types constantly face the decision to outsource versus handle a function internally. Outsourcing can increase speed to market, reduce technology risk, improve cash flow, and conserve management resources. But, outsourcing can also cost more on a variable basis. It reduces control, and in the case of mission-critical functions, introduces a potentially risky dependence on outsiders.

Many elements in inquiry handling lend themselves well to outsourcing because they can be isolated fairly easily and are performed by relatively unskilled resources. Response handling, literature fulfillment, and lead qualification are most likely to be outsourced piecemeal. Some companies declare the entire back-end process of response management to be non-strategic, and outsource everything within it. Still other companies outsource the entire process of lead generation campaigning, response management, and lead conversion to service providers.

The decision may depend simply on volume. Fewer than, say, 500 inquiries a month should be handled easily in-house. For more than 1,000 inquiries a month, it is often economical to shift the technology and work flow risk to an outside service bureau.

A number of service firms specialize in providing pieces of the lead process, or the entire function, on a contract basis — e.g., Harte-Hanks, AdTrack, TECHMAR, and Performark. It makes good sense to compare the costs and service levels of such companies, if only as a competitive benchmark for your in-house operation.

Chapter 8

Lead conversion

Once qualified, leads are ready to be handed off to sales. There are then five questions that need to be addressed. The first is: "Who will get the leads?"

I. Deciding who gets the leads

Companies use several criteria to determine who will be selected:

- **By territory.** If the account is in the rep's territory, this is an easy decision. The only problem arises when there may be an internal resource (a field salesperson or an inside sales rep) and a third-party resource (a distributor or a business partner) in the same territory. In such cases, make a decision rule, based on relevant criteria such as dollar size or complexity of the opportunity.

- **By skill or qualification.** Salespeople may be divided into specialty categories — e.g., product or industry specialists. In this case, again, make the determination by decision rule.

- **By rotation.** When reps are equally qualified to sell, and territory is not a factor, you may decide to hand off the leads in a rotating fashion, one at a time.

- **By cooperation level.** Leads should go to the salespeople who have proven their skill and willingness to work the lead and report results. You may decide to turn off the lead flow to salespeople who don't cooperate.

Lead transfer methods

The second question to be addressed decided is: "How should we transfer the leads?" There are a number of options available:

- **Warm transfer.** If the lead is qualified over the phone, have the call center transfer the prospect to the right salesperson on the spot.

- **E-mail.** This medium — ubiquitous, inexpensive, and immediate — is history's greatest boon to lead transfer.

- **Postal mail.** While some companies still deliver leads to the field via this medium, it is no longer advisable in our electronic age.

- **Web-based systems.** Corporate intranets can serve as a timely medium for lead transfer.

- **Lead management software.** Usually Web-based, the new tools for lead tracking and management (mentioned previously) allow for quick sorting, transfer, and follow-up tracking.

II. Ensuring sales follow-up

The third question is: "How can we ensure that the leads are really being worked?" Here lies the rub between the two separate functions of sales and marketing. It is the natural order of things that salespeople do not appreciate the leads they receive from marketing. "The leads they send me are never any good," they'll say. There is certainly some basis for that attitude, given the record. Marketers have, in fact, been guilty of confusing quantity with quality, and they have in the past handed off unqualified leads to sales.

But there are two sides to this story. It's also the nature of salespeople to claim all control — and credit — for every piece of their business. And they resent the implication that marketing has actually given them any help. "I was already working that account," they'll say.

It is true that salespeople are under a great deal of pressure, in that they have to make quotas — often unrealistic ones at that. They are awash in unproductive paperwork. In addition, they never have enough good leads — i.e., leads that close immediately, or leads that produce the phantom "one-call close" that is every salesperson's dream. It is no surprise that salespeople view marketing as irrelevant and unresponsive. In their view, marketing simply doesn't "get it."

From marketing's perspective, salespeople are an inconsistent lot in terms of their lack of enthusiasm for the leads provided, their unwillingness to follow up, and their carelessness in reporting back on results. Some reps may be a joy to work with, and others more difficult.

So, it's back and forth. Neither side understands the other. Each has his own job to do, and feels at cross-purposes. These natural forces put great pressure on the system and on the relationship between the eternal enemy camps of sales and marketing. Alas, the only way to ensure that the sales team follows up on every qualified lead is to make it worth their while — by carrot and by stick.

Here are some tips for increasing the likelihood that your leads will be well-received and eagerly followed up by the sales team:

- Disburse the leads to the salespeople immediately. When the lead is hot, it's hot. Use electronic channels where possible. Don't let a long sales cycle — i.e., long buying cycle — reduce your sense of urgency. The customer is waiting for an answer, and if he doesn't get it from you, he'll go to the competition.

- Give salespeople copies of the campaign materials, plus detailed plans about intended lead flow by territory. If salespeople are brought in early, they will expect the leads and be prepared for their arrival. Perhaps more importantly, the salespeople will be more committed psychologically to the upcoming leads.

- Provide full qualification information with each lead — name, address, company name, telephone number, e-mail address (if possible), and a complete set of answers to the qualification questions. Do not let any lead go to sales without the proper levels of detail. Imagine what a sales rep will do with a lead that comes through without a phone number. Will he take the trouble to look the number up? No, more likely, he'll put the lead at the bottom of his to-do pile.

> **Insist that sales compensation plans include a clear provision about lead follow-up.**

- Send a message to the prospect at the same time you hand off the lead to sales. Give the prospect the name, title, and contact information of the sales rep who will be handling the account, and give a copy to the rep — and perhaps his manager.

- Insist that sales compensation plans include a clear provision about lead follow-up. The goal of sales and sales management must be 100% follow-up of qualified leads received, within 24 to 48 hours of receipt. Salespeople need to be rewarded for following this practice and penalized when they don't.

- Sales management will need to institute a management system that tracks follow-up practices. As the saying goes, "You can't expect what you don't inspect."

- Put in place an agreement with sales that a lead not handled in 24 hours will be withdrawn and assigned to another salesperson. Similarly, agree that if a salesperson works a lead for one week without success, he may return the lead to marketing for further nurturing.

■ Analyze which inquiries qualify as leads, but don't convert. Consider their source. Use this experience as a screener for prospect selection in campaign planning.

■ Encourage the development of a culture that thinks of a qualified lead as a valuable corporate asset. Qualified leads certainly cost a lot to generate, and represent plenty in sales potential. Leads should be treated like gold.

III. Tracking leads to closure

The fourth question is: "How will sales report back to us on the results of their lead follow-up?" Frankly, it is futile to expect a sales team to be totally conscientious on reporting. It's simply not their nature. Logically, you want salespeople to concentrate on selling.

However, you do need feedback to analyze your results and fine-tune your lead generation programs. So, what is the solution? If lead tracking software is available to the sales team, your chances of receiving timely information increase dramatically. If not, the best approach is to make the reporting system as easy and convenient for the sales rep as possible. And, have your marketers "hound" sales when reports are delayed.

The kinds of data elements you need reported from sales include:

■ Leads that have been followed up.

■ Leads that have been converted to sales.

■ Leads that are lost to the competition.

■ Leads that have been returned to marketing for further nurturing.

Non-closed leads

The fifth question that needs your attention is: "Should non-closed leads be returned to marketing for nurturing?" If, after a reasonable amount of time, a lead has not closed, see that it is returned to marketing. At this point, here are several options for handling the situation:

- **Give the lead to another sales rep.** It may be that a fresh approach will do the trick.

- **Give it a rest.** The situation in the account may have changed and the prospect may no longer be ready to buy.

- **Requalify it.** Consider the lead an inquiry, and put it back through the qualification process.

- **Start over.** Put it back into the marketing database and consider it a prospect.

Whatever you decide, be sure to keep track of how each situation performs, so that you can continue to refine your approach. For example, you may find that "second-effort" marketing pays off well — or is a waste of time.

Who gets the credit?

No one is ever happy in B-to-B. Who gets credit for the sale if a lead is generated from a Web site and closed by a field rep? Of course, the salesperson deserves his commission, no matter where the business originated. The field team deserves to credit the sale against its channel quota. But, what about the Web marketing team, as well as the fulfillers, the qualifiers, and the nurturers?

Crediting the sale to the right parties involved is, in effect, the flip side of the problem of assigning marketing costs to the various parties. It isn't easy, but it's worth coming up with some kind of agreement that will reduce squabbling and allow a modicum of peace in the environment. Many companies solve the problem by double counting, for internal purposes, which allows each group that touched the process to make some claim on the revenue — and take some hit for the expense. It is also important to put in place clear decision rules on who gets the lead from any given source.

Chapter 9

Lead generation: A case narrative

Note: This case is intended to illustrate the application in a realistic business situation of some of the principles introduced in *The DMA Lead Generation Handbook*. The characters and the situation described herein are fictional. This narrative relates a month in the lives of a B-to-B marketing director named Robert and his sales management counterpart, Cindy.

▶ *August 5*

Robert decided in early August to get a head start on planning for the next fiscal year. As marketing director for General Gasket (GG), he knew his plans and budgets didn't really require corporate sign-off until late October, but he also knew from experience that plenty of advance planning would make his life easier in the long run.

In planning for the next year, Robert expected that he would be facing two issues. First, he knew that direct mail, one of GG's key inquiry generation media, was showing signs of fatigue, and response rates had declined steadily over the previous 12 months. Second, Robert had learned from his boss that the company was developing a new product line for an entirely new market segment, and that he would be required to create a marketing plan to support the launch.

GG makes pumps, seals, and gaskets for industrial and marine use. A company with a proud history of operations from its Annapolis headquarters since 1923, GG sells worldwide through a network of distributors, plus a team of field salespeople who call on large house accounts.

Cindy, the company's sales manager, is responsible for both the field sales group and the distributor relationships. She and Robert make a solid team, having driven a satisfactory level of revenue increases every year, even through cyclical downturns.

It hadn't always been that way. Cindy and Robert each joined the company three years earlier. When they arrived, sales were flat, and the sales and marketing teams were at war, with plenty of finger-pointing and ill will hampering their ability to work together. Both Cindy and Robert dedicated themselves to rebuilding the GG business, as well as restoring good relations between their departments.

Robert's first step in planning for the following year involved taking Cindy to lunch. His objective was to celebrate their success in meeting revenue and profit targets in the first half, and find out her sales objectives for the following year. Over lunch, Cindy explained that management would be expecting a 9% increase from her, but one third of that could probably come from additional sales to current accounts, especially if she devised her team quotas properly and instituted a couple of sales contests in each half of the fiscal year.

She expressed some concern about developing a sales plan for the new line of pneumatic seals that engineering had been developing over the previous 12 months. The new product line, known internally by the code name Robinson, was going to be ready to launch in the first quarter. It was targeted to the plastics industry, a completely new market for GG. Cindy proposed that she and Robert work together over the next couple of months to develop a comprehensive sales and marketing plan for Robinson's launch.

Cindy also shared with Robert her plans to add two new field sales reps and one new distributor during the second half, expecting them to be ready for full quota participation the following year. The distributor and one new rep — both with plastics industry experience — would be assigned to the Robinson project. Cindy had already identified the distributor she would use: Plastics Distributors Inc, or PDI, located in northern Virginia. The other new field sales rep, she said, would focus on current products. Cindy intended to redraw some sales territories so the new rep could focus on a couple of areas with growth potential. She expected the Robinson line would begin generating serious revenue by the second half, but decided not to count on it when planning for her 9% sales increase target.

Hearing that, Robert had a pretty good idea of what level of lead flow he would need to provide Cindy with next year. Given that three percentage points of the sales increase would come from current accounts in the normal course of business, Robert figured he could target a 6% increase in the revenue value of his lead output year on year and be in fine shape. But he knew he would have to do some careful adjusting of leads by territory to support Cindy's new rep. And he would need to set up a special team to help plan for the new plastics industry product line.

Over dessert, Robert took the opportunity to ask Cindy what the salespeople were saying about the leads coming from marketing in the first half of this year, and whether Cindy thought they needed to fine-tune the qualification criteria a bit for the inquiries currently going into the qualification pipeline. Cindy offered to set up a meeting for Robert with some key members of the sales team to discuss their views.

▶ August 5, afternoon

Robert directed his team to pull together their preliminary media plans for next year. Specifically, he wanted them to identify the key trade shows where GG would exhibit, and recommend the timing and cadence of the direct mail campaigns they wanted to do. He also asked the team to estimate the number of inquiries they figured they could generate from each media channel, for each quarter. "Don't worry about the expense numbers at the moment," he said. "I want to begin the process from the leads we think we can generate, and then match them to the lead levels that sales says they need.

Later in October or so, we can get specific about the marketing budgets we'll need to ask for."

▶ August 6

Robert called together two of his most skilled team members, Audrey and Phil, and asked them to begin researching the plastics market — its size, its needs, and its buying processes. Audrey agreed to take the lead on the Robinson project with the goal of delivering a marketing plan by October 1, when the new rep was expected to be on board. Phil offered to visit the new distributor, PDI, to begin a relationship and pick up some early insights into the plastics market.

▶ August 6, afternoon

There was one more preliminary phone call Robert wanted to make. He dialed up Al, one of his pals on the field sales team, to ask a couple of questions. Al was someone Robert could trust to give him a straight story, but at the same time be sympathetic and appreciative of the efforts made by the marketing group. Robert wanted an early warning on any problems with the quality and flow of the current leads in the pipeline. "Just keep 'em coming, Robert," said Al. "Our problem is not with your leads. Our problem now is with persistence among the reps. We know from experience that 75% of all sales are closed after the fifth call, but we are finding that only 7% of the salespeople keep on calling after they've been turned down a couple of times. So our big challenge is not leads — it's sales training and incentives."

▶ August 10

For marketing communications purposes, GG segments its market by industry served. It is active in three industries, each with very different needs: paper manufacturing, shipping, and industrial cooling towers. To each segment, Robert's team crafts separate messages about the benefits of their seals and pumps. However, the buying process is quite similar across the three industries: buyers gather information, get their questions answered, ask for quotes, negotiate the deal, and then send a purchase order.

Robert has designed his marketing process to mirror this sequence. First, he makes sure GG is well known in the three industries by advertising in industry publications and arranging for senior GG executives to speak at conferences and be quoted in the press. A few years ago, Robert enhanced his advertising with an offer for a free white paper on developments in sealant technology that are cutting costs and reducing needed repairs. Now all GG ads both create awareness and generate responses, which Robert can send through his qualification process and convert to valuable sales leads.

Maintaining awareness levels is fairly straightforward in each of his three industry segments because they are all such close-knit communities, with little employee turnover. As a result, the industry trade shows are a powerful source of opportunity for GG. At these trade shows, much business gets done, and nearly everyone on the exhibit floor is both a motivated and a qualified prospect. So, Robert makes the trade show calendar the anchor of his marketing plan and counts on it to generate about 40% of his qualified sales leads annually.

The marketing team presented to Robert their findings and recommendations for lead flow for next year. They were confident that the trade-show productivity would hold up solidly. But, they were quite concerned about the steady response-rate decline they were seeing in their lead generation direct mail campaigns. The GG marketing group counts on direct mail to generate at least 30% of its leads, so the concern was serious. The group devoted the rest of the meeting to brainstorming ideas about solutions to this problem. Robert asked them to sift through all the ideas and come back with a detailed set of recommended steps the following week.

▶ August 15

Solving problems always gives Robert a rush of energy, so he eagerly awaited the marketing team's plans. They came to the meeting with a list of proposed steps:

- Profile the customer base. Have the characteristics of our customers changed?

- Analyze lists by response rate. Are there any categories that show signs of weakness or strength? Can we get more productivity by using narrower selects?

- Ask the list broker to research the source of current lists. Are the list owners using different offers?

- Perform a penetration analysis by six-digit SIC code, to see where there may be untapped opportunity.

- Talk to our friendly competitors. Are they experiencing similar declines?

- Test new offers.

- Test new creative, message platforms, and formats.

- Launch an e-mail newsletter, with subscription offers at the Web site.

- Redesign the Web site to make stronger offers and capture more registrations.

- Create and host dedicated Web sites for our distributors.

- Expand outbound telemarketing. Test phone follow-up to the mail.

- Research e-mail prospecting lists.

- Review the lead qualification criteria and the lead nurturing program. If direct mail is fatiguing as a medium, what can be done to get more out of less?

Robert approved the plan, and the team set to work on getting the analyses and tests in the works.

▶ *August 20*

Robert and Cindy led a planning meeting for the Robinson project. In attendance were Audrey, Phil, and a sales manager from PDI — the new distributor who was hired due to its plastics industry experience. Audrey presented her action plan for developing a marketing program to the new industry. "Since there is no one in-house who has worked in plastics, we have to start from scratch," she said. "But Phil has met with PDI and picked up some good ideas. Also, we are all aware of the opportunity for GG in plastics, and we're looking forward to the challenge of taking on an entirely new market segment."

Audrey's action plan outlined the following steps:

- Research the plastics industry buying process through interviews, focus groups, and meetings with PDI sales reps.

- Research the need within the plastics industry for GG's new pneumatic seals, and identify any meaningful industry segments based on various needs. Hypothesis: GG seals will appeal to the high end of the injection molding manufacturing business.

- Identify key media in the plastics industry: trade shows, professional associations, trade publications, mailing lists, and Web sites.

- Formulate potential message platforms and test their effectiveness with focus groups of plastics industry insiders.

- Brainstorm offer possibilities with the marketing team.

- Review lead qualification criteria with the distributor to get his input and approval.

- Create a campaign budget based on the media identified.

Robert and Cindy were both pleased with the plan, and suggested they regroup once the new sales rep was hired, to monitor the team's progress and get additional input from the new rep.

▶ *August 30*

Robert attended the meeting Cindy set up with three of her key sales reps and two distributors. Robert's objective was to get feedback on the leads his team had provided them so far in the year. He also intended to ask for some preliminary insights into where they'd be focusing their sales efforts next year.

Cindy invited the reps and distributors to comment on the lead quality. Just as Al had said when Robert called him for a heads-up, the salespeople were generally satisfied with the leads. They did raise a couple of red flags, though. Some of the lead sheets coming through were not completely filled out, they said. Robert made a note to review his internal process and fix any quality control issues that may have developed.

Also, one of the distributors commented that he was seeing more growth in the marine market than they expected, and he requested that Robert see if he could pump up the lead flow in that segment to take advantage of the growth. Robert agreed to tweak some of his campaign plans to increase the emphasis on prospects in the shipping business.

As the meeting broke up, Cindy congratulated Robert on the relative calm that had set in between their departments. "Isn't it amazing?" she said. "We haven't had to break up a fight in months. I guess our messages of cooperation and mutual respect are being heard. And, of course, it doesn't hurt that the business is growing and we're meeting our quotas!"

4

Part Four
Customer Retention

Chapter 10

Retention strategies

Philosophically, business marketers are generally very savvy about the value of retention. Having small universes in which to play, B-to-B marketers instinctively know that they need to focus on satisfying their customer base. This is how good salespeople manage their territories. B-to-B direct marketing does nothing more than replicate the time-honored approaches of the salesman — only more efficiently.

So, how should you nurture your best customers? Answer: the same way a salesperson would. Get to know your customers and their needs. Make them feel good about doing business with you. Spend time and money on them according to their worth to you — e.g., play golf with the big accounts. Sell to them the way in which they want to buy. Watch your competitors, and make sure you provide at least as much value as they do.

By now, it is a marketing maxim that it's more profitable to retain a customer than continually to acquire new ones. In recent years, many companies have jumped enthusiastically onto the retention marketing bandwagon. Their main focus seems to be in instituting loyalty programs that are designed to increase retention and reduce attrition. Some of these programs have borne fruit, but others have been abandoned.

It is becoming clear that the core concept in retention marketing is not frequent buyer points or other artificial attempts to buy a customer's loyalty and repeat purchases. Instead, the basis of customer loyalty is customer satisfaction — both personal and professional — with the product, service, and entire experience of interacting with the company.

As products improve and as features become commoditized, companies are finding that the best way to differentiate themselves is through service levels and excellent customer experience.

I. The customer experience

The concept of customer experience marketing has important implications. B-to-B marketers must do everything possible to enhance customers' total experience with the company, the product, and the service. The marketing mix, the product, the packaging, the product quality, and the communications that customers receive are just the tip of the iceberg, however. B-to-B marketers also need to pay attention to customers' experiences with field salespeople, telemarketers, business partners and distributors, customer service personnel, and billing practices. In fact, every point of contact is an opportunity to satisfy — or annoy — customers.

The basis of customer loyalty is customer satisfaction — both personal and professional — with the product, service, and entire experience of interacting with the company.

Now, where does this leave you as a marketer? It means that your influence must be carried throughout the organization. You must analyze every point of contact a customer may have with your company. You must then do everything possible to ensure the quality of any and all contacts. And, you must define quality in terms that are meaningful to your customers.

Here is a series of steps that marketers should take to ensure customer satisfaction at all points of contact:

1. Analyze all the points of contact a customer or prospect may have with your product, service, company, employees, or representatives.

2. Establish standards of required quality for each point of contact. The metrics must be specific (e.g., number of minutes on hold in the call center, product/service defect rates, or logo design standards for color, size, and usage).

3. Survey customers regarding their experiences and expectations at each touch point.

4. Apply those expectations to the metrics and standards by which you operate the business.

5. Establish processes for ongoing updates and refinements as the customer experience and expectation levels change.

II. Customer value segmentation

Another strategic approach to retention marketing is based in customer value segmentation. It is true that all customers are not created equal. Further, any company is likely to earn the bulk of its profits from a relatively small percentage of its customers. The 80/20 rule is a rule for good reason. It is the most valuable customers that we are most desperately seeking to retain.

How do you decide who is your best customer? Most direct marketers rely on the technique of recency/frequency/monetary (RFM) value to segment customers by value. RFM is a great tool for analyzing customers by their past behavior. But RFM isn't the whole story. To evaluate "bestness," RFM analysis can be a misleading indicator for two reasons. First, a customer who has bought a lot from you — however often — is not necessarily loyal. He may drop off without giving you a chance to respond if he can get a better price, better quality, and better delivery terms elsewhere. Second, looking at his monetary value doesn't say much of anything about his total value — or about your share of his budget. He may be spending just a little money with you, but a lot more with the competition.

To supplement RFM, you must focus on wallet share. Also known as share of customer, this is, frankly, not easy to calculate. Information about budgets in some large public companies or sizable industries may be publicly available in annual reports or industry statistics. Otherwise, you have to gather the information by hand. Your best information resource is your sales force, who know very well the size of the company budgets in their accounts and what share of those budgets your company is enjoying. Sales will also know what competitors are servicing the account and what the competitive spend is.

Therefore, segment the customer base by value. Customers will fall roughly into three segments: best, medium, and worst. Next, decide on an appropriate strategy for the treatment of each segment. Ideally, you will develop plans to serve the best customers well and retain them at all costs. With the second group, the strategy will be to migrate them closer to the kind of behavior exhibited by the first group. In some cases, you may find that some customers in the third group are more trouble than they are worth, and that it no longer makes sense to invest in serving them. In fact, it may make more sense to introduce them to your competitors!

Whatever strategies you follow, open and nurture robust lines of communication with your customers. Establish an ongoing dialogue with them. E-mail, Web-based surveys, and electronic newsletters are ideal tools for this kind of communication. Encourage your customers to contact you, and make it easy for them to do so. But, be prepared to respond to them when they reach out to you.

III. Retention metrics

There is much heated debate over how to measure customer loyalty and retention. On the face of it, retention might appear to be a fairly clear concept: the number of customers, year on year, who continue to buy. Specifically, retention can be expressed in a number of ways:

- The ratio of repeat buyers to the total number of buyers

- The ratio of new buyers to the total number of buyers

- The "churn rate," or the ratio of lapsed buyers to the total number of buyers

However you decide to measure retention, compare your results against one or both of the following benchmarks:

- **Yourself, over time.** Track your results quarterly or annually, and reward your employees for improvements.

- **Your industry.** Some trade organizations and trade publications will gather and publish statistics for the respective industries they cover. If no such statistics are available, you might informally share information among your colleagues in the industry. To avoid doing anything that could be construed as anticompetitive, though, be sure to keep your legal department apprised of your activities.

Generally, there are three useful measures of customer retention:

- **"Buy more"** — The rate at which your current customers repeat buy, expressed in dollar or unit amounts.

- **"Stay longer"** — The length of time customers are actively buying.

- **"Refer"** — The level of referral business your customers give you.

Retention marketing myths

As retention marketing has grown in importance, it has spawned some interesting but dangerous myths. Here are some of them, and what they mean to you as a B-to-B marketer:

"Customers want to have a relationship with you." Marketers are heard to boast about "building customer relationships," but instead they fall into the trap of "marketing myopia." Marketers fail to think from the customer's point of view. That is, they do not say, "What do business buyers really want?" The correct answer to this question is that customers want to do their jobs well, to have fewer headaches, and to make more money. It is your job, as a marketer, to help them do that — by delivering great value, being responsive and easy to deal with, and otherwise serving customers' needs. The only reason a customer might want a relationship with a marketer is to make his own life easier.

"Customers define loyalty the way marketers do." Marketers are likely to define "loyalty" via the typical retention measures: buy more, stay longer, and provide referrals. But the customer may have a different point of view. The customer's sense of "loyalty" may be more about his attitude than his behavior. For instance, you may find that many customers feel loyal to you, yet have not bought anything in years because of changing conditions in their business needs. However, they may say that they have every intention of buying from you again when the need next arises. So, customers initially viewed as "lapsed" or "lost" must be handled with care.

"Customers are all worth retaining." No retention strategy can effectively be designed as "one size fits all." If you break down your customers into segments, you will likely find that certain sets of them are costing you more to serve than they are worth.

IV. Customer retention tactics

Once the hard work of developing the right strategic approach to customer retention is completed, then comes the relatively fun part — namely, deciding on the right tactics to apply to the retention imperative.

Here is a list of retention tactics that have proven successful in business marketing:

- **Surveys/feedback.** It's amazing how much people like to share their opinions. The simple act of being asked for feedback can be a powerful stimulator of loyal feelings in the heart of a customer.

- **Outbound communications.** One inexpensive and powerful technique is to send a follow-up message after a purchase, reaffirming the customer's decision to buy from you.

- **Newsletters.** Whether electronic or print, newsletters are welcomed by customers and prospects as a source of valuable information. It's best to keep the selling messages to a minimum, and to provide content that can truly help readers with their daily jobs.

- **Proprietary magazines.** Creating a specialized magazine for your product users involves considerable expense, but the benefits can also be great. Many trade publishing companies have custom publishing divisions that will handle editorial, production, circulation, and ad sales for you on an outsourced basis.

- **Special events.** Client conferences, outings, and seminars — ranging from the classic junket to educational sessions — provide real business value.

- **Contests and awards.** Conduct a contest for the most creative use of your product or service.

- **Special service levels.** Give top customers a dedicated sales and services team, branded with the name of the level, such as "Gold" or "Platinum." Create dedicated extranets to these customers, so that they can interact with you online in a customized environment with their particular terms and conditions in operation.

- **Automated marketing communications.** These messages are triggered by predetermined events in the relationship between you and the customer. The message can be as simple as a bounce-back thank-you note when an order is placed. Or, it can be a series of relationship-nurturing touches customized to each customer's interactions. With the arrival of e-mail-based systems from companies like MarketFirst and E2 Communications, automated marketing has become even easier to manage.

- **Welcome programs.** Special treatment is a powerful and effective way to get the relationship with a new customer on the right track for long-term satisfaction and profitability. Institute a welcoming phone call or letter from the account rep or a senior manager. Gather information about the customer's needs and preferences, and act on it.

- **Rewards programs.** As the airlines' frequent-flier programs have become quickly commoditized, serious questions have arisen about the value of rewards programs that temporarily drive purchase behavior — but not necessarily loyalty. However, business marketers have used variations of rewards programs successfully for years. Their techniques include volume discounts, premium service levels, and custom product development. There can be a big payoff in making top customers feel rewarded for their business. Relationship marketing companies like Frequency Marketing Inc., Directech/eMerge, Digitas, and Direct Results Group can help design and operate customized programs.

- **Advisory board or special club.** Invite your top customers to become part of an inner circle that gets special perks and attention from top management.

- **Occasional thank-you messages.** Customers are surprised and pleased to receive unsolicited messages of gratitude for their business. Send spontaneous thank-you notes, gifts, and even birthday greetings.

- **Sales force incentives.** These compensation plans reward account penetration and repurchase.

- **Winback, reclaiming lost customers.** When you have only a few accounts and each of them represents great value, it's important to reconvert customers wherever possible. Some B-to-B marketers create special sales and marketing teams dedicated to winback. One of the best techniques is loss prevention — i.e., identifying accounts that are likely to defect to the competition, and putting resources against the loss before it happens.

Measuring customer satisfaction

While customer satisfaction is a critical driver of retention, it needs to be managed. That is, it must be tracked, measured, and linked to employee compensation. However, the measuring of customer satisfaction raises a number of problems, since it is so subjective and so inextricably related to customers' expectations, which vary widely.

Customer satisfaction measurement has a long and glorious history, with experiments involving all kinds of qualitative and quantitative metrics.

These days, most formal programs that measure satisfaction are based on the following steps:

- Segment the customers to be measured (e.g., new customers, repeat buyers, lapsed buyers, and prospects).

- Establish links to employee compensation.

- Identify the specific areas to measure (e.g., perceived image of the company overall, product performance, the purchase experience, and competitive preferences).

- Determine the survey methodology, such as e-mail or postal mail, telephone, in person, and the timing and frequency you will use.

Other points to keep in mind:

- Measurement can cause some internal friction. Be sure from the outset that senior management supports the program and will champion it aggressively.

- Budget appropriately. Regular survey-taking consumes considerable expense. Be sure you have the budget in place for an initial baseline survey as well as several comparison runs to follow.

- If survey budgets are unavailable, consider proxy indicators of satisfaction, like customer correspondence, and reports from customer service.

- The Internet offers a low-cost vehicle for gathering satisfaction input. Post a quick survey offer on your home page. Or, set up a Web-based "consumer panel" of customers who are willing to be polled for regular feedback.

Remember: customer satisfaction is only part of the retention equation. Just because a customer is happy with you doesn't necessarily mean that he will buy or continue to buy. You must supplement your satisfaction data with harder measures, like how much, and how recently, customers have repurchased.

Appendix 1

Listing of key resources

Here is a compendium of key resources for B-to-B direct marketers:

Books

Business to Business Direct Marketing by Robert W. Bly, 2nd ed. One of the great copywriters in the direct marketing industry, Bob Bly explains why every type of business communication should be a DR communication, and then shows you how to put this into effect. Bly covers creative approaches and offer development, and then takes the reader through all the key media types in detail.

Business-to-Business Internet Marketing by Barry Silverstein, 3rd ed. After a superb chapter on the basics of B-to-B direct marketing, Barry Silverstein covers every conceivable aspect of how to harness the Internet for business marketing purposes. No surprise, he has updated this book twice to keep it current, and provides a special "members only" Web site so that readers can view the latest ideas and information.

Business to Business Marketing: Creating a Community of Customers by Victor L. Hunter. One of the thought leaders of our time, Vic Hunter puts direct marketers' daily activities of acquiring and retaining customers into a new perspective. Citing the changes in the way customers buy, he explains how business marketers need to change their strategies and focus on their customers' needs.

S.U.R.E.-Fire Direct Response Marketing by Russell Kern. The latest contributor to the B-to-B direct marketing library, Russell covers the gamut of planning and research, and campaign development and execution in all media.

Managing Sales Leads by Donath, Dixon, Crocker, and Obermayer. Everything you need to know about lead planning, generation, and qualification. This book is officially out of print, but The DMA bookstore still has some in stock.

Trade publications

BtoB: The Magazine for Marketing and E-Commerce Strategists (www.btobonline.com) is published by Crain Communications. It has regular coverage of news and developments in direct and interactive marketing, and a very good e-mail newsletter called *Hands On*, with case studies and an "Ask the Expert" column.

Conferences

Direct Marketing to Business (DMB), the annual conference and trade show sponsored by The DMA and Primedia Business Exhibitions, is the place to keep up with the latest in the industry. With two full days of sessions and a pre-conference day of workshops, this show also provides attendees with a sizable soft-cover book of slides and notes from each session. Session audiotapes are sold on site (www.dmbshow.com).

The B-to-B Marketing Conference is an annual conference and trade show produced by The DMA. It is designed to address broader B-to-B marketing issues including direct response marketing. For more details, please go to (www.dmab2b.org).

B-to-B newsletter

The DMA also publishes a newsletter following the DMB conference called *In Case You Missed It*, which contains articles culled from session content. Subscribe by contacting The DMA.

Web-based resources

www.b2bmarketingbiz.com. An excellent weekly newsletter with very detailed case studies. The editor, Anne Holland, elicits amazing quantities of real numbers from her subjects.

www.wordbiz.com. Debbie Weil's newsletter, WordBiz *Brief,* educates readers on how to strategize and write outstanding business e-mail communications, whether solo mail or newsletters.

www.b2btalk.org. A forum for business marketers, with regular live chats and plenty of good articles, operated by a marketing agency outside of Philadelphia.

www.marketing.org. When you are ready to integrate your direct marketing with the rest of your marketing communications mix, the Business Marketing Association might be a big help.

www.the-dma.org/b2b. Information on The DMA's resources and activities for business marketers.

Appendix 2

B-to-B direct marketing statistics from The DMA

Excerpts from The DMA's State of the E-Commerce Industry Report 2002

The tables that follow are excerpts of The DMA's fifth annual e-commerce survey. The objective of this study is to identify current business practices and trends regarding the use of interactive media in marketing programs for both the business-to-business and consumer marketplace.

The sample was comprised of the following sources:

• The DMA e-mail list of domestic U.S. voting members from both business-to-business and consumer marketers (total = 3,652).

• A banner ad was also placed on the DMA Web site for *I-Marketing News* and AIM (Association for Interactive Marketing) to solicit additional respondents.

• Two follow-up postcards to 9,115 individuals comprised of DMA and AIM members and the subscribers to *I-Marketing News.*

The following tables are selected business-to-business highlights of the final report. A total of 694 companies participated in the research — with more than half of the respondents being b-to-b marketers. The data is organized to show responses by whether companies market solely to other businesses or to a combination of business and consumer companies. It is also sorted by whether companies classify themselves as suppliers versus those that are sellers using direct response channels.

I. Profile of B-to-B Web Site Marketers
(By Target Market)

B-to-B marketers use their Web sites primarily to provide product and service information and to generate leads. Those marketing to both business and consumer audiences generally have more traffic than B-to-B only Web sites. B-to-B only Web sites are more likely to have a greater percentage of e-mail addresses on their house files than those targeting both B-to-B and consumer markets.

	Web Site Targeted To:	
	B-to-B	Consumer/ B-to-B
Web Site Use		
Have had Web sites for 3 years or more	62%	61%
Use Web site mostly for product and service information	96%	81%
Use Web site mostly for lead generation	68%	54%
Use Web site mostly for sales/e-commerce	25%	63%
Use Web site mostly for public relations/image	56%	56%
Use Web site mostly for customer service	22%	46%
Web Site Traffic		
Have less than 100K unique traffic daily	63%	28%
Have more than 100K unique traffic daily	37%	72%
Have less than 100K total page views per day	49%	18%
Have more than 100K total page views per day	51%	82%
Making a profit from online transactions	58%	53%
Breaking even	22%	20%
Operating online transactions at a loss	20%	27%
Drive traffic through direct mail	55%	58%
Drive traffic through e-mail marketing	52%	58%
Drive traffic through online advertising	24%	46%
Use of Banner Ads		
Have banner ads at other sites	27%	50%
Do not pay for banner ads at other sites	33%	36%
Target by section or search	82%	76%
Accept varying sizes	75%	84%
Accept banner ads at your Web site	11%	28%
Compensated for these ads	74%	85%

	Web Site Targeted To:	
	B-to-B	Consumer/ B-to-B
Measuring Effectiveness of Interactive Media		
Ability to reach new members/segments	56%	68%
Greater visibility	56%	44%
New business opportunities	62%	42%
Cost savings	39%	49%
Better customer service	35%	37%
Web Marketing Statistics		
Average # of products marketed on Web site	10	32.5
Average # of products marketed with e-online catalogs	275	700
Can conduct electronic financial transactions	20%	55%
Up-sell on primary Web site	39%	39%
Do Web business overseas	62%	44%
Cross-sell by targeting offline buyers online	65%	62%
Cross-sell by targeting online buyers offline	56%	72%
Online and Offline Tracking		
Distinguish or segment customer prospects	36%	45%
Track % of net sales generated by outside media sources	24%	35%
Use tracking information in focusing marketing campaigns	94%	89%
Use tracking information in personalization	39%	56%
Tracking Online and Offline Budgets		
E-mail marketing ranks 1st of online promo budget portion	✔	✔
E-mail marketing ranks 1st of online traffic portion	✔	✔
Catalog ranks 1st of offline budget portion		
Telemarketing ranks 1st of offline budget portion	✔	
Print ranks 1st of offline budget portion		✔
E-mail Marketing Statistics		
Median % of house file that has e-mail addresses	72.5%	40%
Mean % net interactive sales from e-mail based promotions	9.3%	20.1%
E-mail marketing sales have increased	59%	68%
Future Investments in Interactive Media		
Anticipate increase in investment over next 3 years	74%	75%
Expect interactive media to increase revenue over 3 years	76%	87%

Source: The DMA's State of the E-Commerce Industry Report 2002. Direct Marketing Association, Inc., 2002.

II. Profile of B-to-B Web Site Marketers
(Supplier vs. Seller)

Web site usage is very similar between b-to-b suppliers and sellers. Sellers generally offer more products on their Web sites and are more likely to up-sell and conduct business overseas.

	Type of Business:	
	Supplier	User Bus.
Web Site Use		
Have had Web sites for 3 years or more	64%	67%
Use Web site mostly for product and service information	93%	91%
Use Web site mostly for lead generation	62%	60%
Use Web site mostly for sales/e-commerce	36%	37%
Use Web site mostly for public relations/image	60%	58%
Use Web site mostly for customer service	36%	40%
Web Site Traffic		
Have less than 100K unique traffic daily	60%	47%
Have more than 100K unique traffic daily	40%	53%
Have less than 100K total page views per day	49%	35%
Have more than 100K total page views per day	51%	65%
Making a profit from online transactions	49%	52%
Breaking even	19%	24%
Operating online transactions at a loss	33%	24%
Drive traffic through direct mail	60%	56%
Drive traffic through e-mail marketing	52%	59%
Drive traffic through online advertising	32%	32%
Use of Banner Ads		
Have banner ads at other sites	33%	32%
Do not pay for banner ads at other sites	33%	46%
Target by section or search	77%	76%
Accept varying sizes	77%	83%
Accept banner ads at your Web site	15%	21%
Compensated for these ads	84%	88%

	Type of Business:	
	Supplier	**User Bus.**
Measuring Effectiveness of Interactive Media		
Ability to reach new members/segments	57%	59%
Greater visibility	49%	43%
New business opportunities	47%	45%
Cost savings	41%	37%
Better customer service	37%	45%
Web Marketing Statistics		
Average # of products marketed on Web site	10	14.5
Average # of products marketed with e-online catalogs	100	200
Can conduct electronic financial transactions	34%	41%
Up-sell on primary Web site	37%	50%
Do Web business overseas	33%	50%
Cross-sell by targeting offline buyers online	65%	71%
Cross-sell by targeting online buyers offline	70%	50%
Online and Offline Tracking		
Distinguish or segment customer prospects	40%	38%
Track % of net sales generated by outside media sources	31%	35%
Use tracking information in focusing marketing campaigns	89%	98%
Use tracking information in personalization	43%	33%
Tracking Online and Offline Budgets		
E-mail marketing ranks 1st of online promo budget portion	✔	✔
E-mail marketing ranks 1st of online traffic portion	✔	✔
Catalog ranks 1st of offline budget portion		
Telemarketing ranks 1st of offline budget portion		✔
Print ranks 1st of offline budget portion	✔	
E-mail Marketing Statistics		
Median % of house file that has e-mail addresses	70%	50%
Mean % net interactive sales from e-mail based promotions	13.4%	12.6%
E-mail marketing sales have increased	58%	57%
Future Investments in Interactive Media		
Anticipate increase in investment over next 3 years	75%	75%
Expect interactive media to increase revenue over 3 years	79%	80%

Source: The DMA's State of the E-Commerce Industry Report 2002. Direct Marketing Association, Inc., 2002.

163

III. The Primary Purpose(s) of B-to-B Web Sites
(By Target Market)

Those targeting their Web sites towards both consumers and the B-to-B segment more often identified their sites purpose to be sales/e-commerce (63%) than B-to-B only (25%). The same pattern emerged for customer service where 46% of the consumer/B-to-B segment used the Web site for this purpose, compared to only 22% of the B-to-B segment. Those targeting their Web sites to the B-to-B segment were more likely to find the Web site's primary purpose in lead generation (68%).

	Web Site Targeted To:	
	B-to-B	**Consumer/ B-to-B**
Information about products and services	96%	81%
Advertising	40%	44%
Sales/E-commerce	25%	63%
Lead generation	68%	54%
Human resources management	12%	13%
Collect e-mail addresses other than for lead generation	22%	37%
Public relations/general image enhancement	56%	56%
Customer service	22%	46%
Technical support	11%	16%
Conduct survey/market research	10%	17%
Build online community	10%	26%
Fund raising	2%	7%
Program development and management	4%	10%
Fulfillment	8%	18%
Real-time inventory management	2%	4%
Other	4%	6%

Source: The DMA's State of the E-Commerce Industry Report 2002. Direct Marketing Association, Inc., 2002.

IV. The Primary Purpose(s) of B-to-B Web Sites
(Supplier vs. Seller)

Suppliers and business-users more often noted the Web site's primary purposes as providing information about products and services, (93% of suppliers and 91% of business users), lead generation (62% of suppliers and 60% of business-users), and public relations (60% of suppliers and 58% of business users).

| | Type of Business: | |
	Supplier	User Bus.
Information about products and services	93%	91%
Advertising	43%	39%
Sales/E-commerce	36%	37%
Lead generation	62%	60%
Human resources management	12%	8%
Collect e-mail addresses other than for lead generation	31%	32%
Public relations/general image enhancement	60%	58%
Customer service	36%	40%
Technical support	11%	17%
Conduct survey/market research	14%	18%
Build online community	20%	23%
Fund raising	5%	8%
Program development and management	7%	9%
Fulfillment	13%	12%
Real-time inventory management	3%	3%
Other	2%	3%

Source: The DMA's State of the E-Commerce Industry Report 2002. Direct Marketing Association, Inc., 2002.

V. Methods to Drive Web Site Traffic
(By Target Market)

Direct mail, including catalogs, and e-mail are the top drivers of Web traffic. Online advertising and print ads drive traffic more so among those targeting their sites to B-to-B and consumers than B-to-B only.

Ways of Driving Web Site Traffic	Web site Targeted To:	
	B-to-B	Consumer/ B-to-B
Direct mail	55%	58%
E-mail marketing	52%	58%
Print ads	36%	55%
Search engine optimization	37%	44%
Online advertising	24%	46%
Offline promotions	22%	38%
Paid search engine placement	17%	25%
Online promotions	11%	29%
Sponsorship of e-newsletters	17%	18%
Incentive programs	7%	17%
TV ads	2%	18%
Other	23%	15%

Source: The DMA's State of the E-Commerce Industry Report 2002. Direct Marketing Association, Inc., 2002.

VI. Methods to Drive Web Site Traffic
(Supplier vs. Seller)

Suppliers and sellers use basically the same methods to drive Web traffic — sellers are somewhat more inclined to use e-mail.

Ways of Driving Web Site Traffic	Type of Business: Supplier	User Bus.
Direct mail	60%	56%
E-mail marketing	52%	59%
Print ads	41%	42%
Search engine optimization	36%	33%
Online advertising	32%	32%
Offline promotions	34%	37%
Paid search engine placement	22%	23%
Online promotions	20%	22%
Sponsorship of e-newsletters	20%	26%
Incentive programs	8%	8%
TV ads	8%	8%
Other	19%	23%

Source: The DMA's State of the E-Commerce Industry Report 2002. Direct Marketing Association, Inc., 2002.

VII. Status of Financial Transactions and e-Commerce Profitability (By Target Market)

Only 20% of "pure" b-to-b Web marketers conduct transactions online, while a little over the majority of those targeting both b-to-b and consumer audiences are conducting e-commerce. Of those not yet profitable, dual Web site marketers more frequently project being profitable in 2002 than B-to-B marketers.

	Web Site Targeted To:	
	B-to-B	Consumer/ B-to-B
Can conduct financial transactions		
Yes	20%	55%
No	80%	45%
Financial status of primary Web site		
Making a profit	58%	53%
Breaking even	22%	20%
Operating at a loss	20%	27%
Expect Web site to be profitable in:		
2001	27%	14%
2002	47%	59%
2003	13%	14%
More than 4 years	13%	14%

Source: The DMA's State of the E-Commerce Industry Report 2002. Direct Marketing Association, Inc., 2002.

VIII. Status of Financial Transactions and e-Commerce Profitability
(Supplier vs. Seller)

Of those b-to-b marketers who are conducting online financial transactions, approximately half are making a profit. Among those who aren't yet in the black, suppliers (60%) expect Web site profitability in 2002, compared to 36% of business-users.

	Type of Business:	
	Supplier	**User Bus.**
Can conduct financial transactions		
Yes	36%	41%
No	66%	59%
Financial status of primary Web site		
Making a profit	49%	52%
Breaking even	19%	24%
Operating at a loss	33%	24%
Expect Web site to be profitable in:		
2001	20%	36%
2002	60%	36%
2003	10%	9%
More than 4 years	10%	18%

Source: The DMA's State of the E-Commerce Industry Report 2002. Direct Marketing Association, Inc., 2002.

Economic Impact: U.S. Direct Marketing Today 2002

The following tables were derived from the DMA's econometric database, which provides historical and forecast information on direct marketing advertising expenditures, revenue, and employment in both the business-to-business and consumer markets. Working with the economic forecasting firm, DRI-WEFA, The DMA annually updated the following statistics in the seven direct response media and for 52 major industry categories.

The tables that follow highlight business-to-business direct response activity in terms of ad spending, revenue, and employment across all media and industries.

Business-to-Business Direct Marketing Advertising Expenditures by Medium
(Millions of Dollars)
Advertising expenditures for business-to-business direct marketing are forecast to grow by 6.99% annually from 2001-2006.

	1996	2000	2001	2002	2006	Compound Annual Growth '96-'01	'01-'06
Magazine	$3,793	$5,204	$5,287	$5,474	$7,028	6.87%	5.86%
Direct Mail	$12,894	$17,444	$18,405	$19,608	$26,148	7.38%	7.28%
Newspaper	$5,380	$7,450	$7,670	$8,051	$10,547	7.35%	6.58%
Other	$4,993	$7,030	$7,222	$7,505	$10,449	7.66%	7.67%
Radio	$2,551	$3,913	$4,051	$4,250	$5,736	9.69%	7.20%
Telephone	$33,663	$46,474	$48,934	$51,899	$68,486	7.77%	6.95%
Television	$7,595	$10,752	$10,921	$11,345	$15,256	7.53%	6.91%
All	$70,869	$98,267	$102,489	$108,132	$143,649	7.66%	6.99%

Source: The DMA Report: Economic Impact- U.S.Direct & Interactive Marketing Today, 2002.

Business-to-Business Direct Marketing Driven Sales By Medium
(Millions of Dollars)

Business-to-Business sales growth is expected to increase 8.79% per year in the five year period from 2001-2006.

	1996	2000	2001	2002	2006	Compound Annual Growth '96-'01	'01-'06
Magazine	$28,117	$43,430	$46,956	$50,574	$68,543	10.80%	7.86%
Direct Mail	$132,782	$202,088	$223,412	$246,005	$347,445	10.97%	9.23%
Newspaper	$55,840	$85,875	$93,068	$101,085	$138,988	10.76%	8.35%
Other	$18,507	$29,355	$32,092	$34,740	$50,451	11.64%	9.47%
Radio	$12,264	$20,896	$22,896	$24,947	$35,433	13.30%	9.13%
Telephone	$223,019	$350,972	$387,631	$424,254	$587,789	11.69%	8.68%
Television	$30,464	$48,384	$52,057	$56,118	$79,134	11.31%	8.74%
Total	**$500,992**	**$780,999**	**$858,113**	**$937,723**	**$1,307,783**	**11.36%**	**8.79%**

Source: The DMA Report: Economic Impact- U.S. Direct Marketing Today, 2002.

Business-to-Business Direct Marketing Employment by Medium
(Number of Employees).

Business-to-Business Direct Marketing Employment growth is projected to grow by 4.73 % annually from 2001-2006.

	1996	2000	2001	2002	2006	CAGR '96-'01	CAGR '01-'06
Magazine	256,992	336,944	355,536	373,422	430,511	6.71%	3.90%
Direct Mail	1,174,084	1,526,440	1,649,214	1,767,470	2,123,806	7.03%	5.19%
Newspaper	456,934	593,281	625,156	660,052	772,175	6.47%	4.31%
Other	237,140	309,031	326,340	341,726	423,274	6.59%	5.34%
Radio	122,939	174,342	185,243	195,995	235,934	8.55%	4.96%
Telemarketing	2,464,119	3,249,906	3,484,941	3,707,079	4,367,988	7.18%	4.62%
Television	318,106	425,548	443,707	464,225	554,337	6.88%	4.55%
All Media	5,030,315	6,615,492	7,070,138	7,509,969	8,908,027	7.05%	4.73%

Source: The DMA Report: Economic Impact- U.S. Direct & Interactive Marketing Today, 2002

Business-to-Business Direct Marketing Advertising Expenditures Ranked by Industry
(Millions of Dollars)

Business Services, Communications and the Wholesale Trade Lead in
Business-to-Business Direct Marketing Advertising Expenditures Ranked by Industry*

Rank	SIC	Industry	1996	2000	2001	2006	Compound Annual Growth '96-'01	'01-'06
Total	Total	Total	$70,869	$98,267	$102,489	$143,649	7.66%	6.99%
1	73	Business Services	$7,367	$11,175	$11,833	$17,055	9.94%	7.58%
2	48	Communications	$5,976	$8,844	$9,494	$13,356	9.70%	7.06%
3	WST	Wholesale Trade	$5,253	$8,061	$8,892	$13,808	11.10%	9.20%
4	TRNX45	Transportation, excluding Airlines	$4,481	$5,957	$6,252	$8,412	6.89%	6.11%
5	27	Printing & Publishing	$4,699	$5,894	$6,065	$8,255	5.24%	6.36%
6	63&4	Insurance Carriers & Agents	$3,286	$4,808	$5,292	$8,625	10.00%	10.26%
7	81&7&9	Other Services	$2,632	$4,322	$4,836	$7,765	12.94%	9.93%
8	36	Electrical Machinery & Equipment	$3,257	$4,669	$4,266	$4,836	5.55%	2.54%
9	28	Chemicals & Allied Products	$3,476	$3,879	$3,911	$5,777	2.39%	8.11%
10	35	Industrial Machinery & Equipment	$2,377	$3,718	$3,520	$3,888	8.17%	2.01%
11	65	Real Estate	$1,925	$3,004	$3,356	$4,957	11.76%	8.11%
12	62&7	Security & Commodity Brokers	$1,688	$2,836	$2,966	$4,268	11.93%	7.55%
13	70	Hotels	$1,403	$2,197	$2,366	$3,344	11.02%	7.16%
14	72&5&6	Personal & Repair Services	$1,339	$2,020	$2,238	$3,320	10.82%	8.21%
15	61	Nondepository Institutions	$1,425	$2,039	$2,085	$2,371	7.91%	2.60%
16	20	Food & Kindred Products	$1,767	$1,996	$2,048	$2,865	3.00%	6.94%
17	60	Depository Institutions	$1,660	$1,983	$2,034	$2,503	4.15%	4.24%
18	78&9	Entertainment	$1,112	$1,783	$1,950	$3,218	11.89%	10.54%
19	37	Transportation Equipment	$1,178	$1,624	$1,616	$2,474	6.53%	8.89%
20	53	General Merchandise Stores	$1,195	$1,564	$1,571	$1,969	5.62%	4.62%
21	38	Instruments & Related Products	$1,098	$1,404	$1,497	$2,091	6.40%	6.91%
22	45	Airlines	$1,104	$1,359	$1,402	$1,969	4.90%	7.03%
23	59	Non-Store Retailers	$858	$1,119	$1,137	$1,378	5.79%	3.92%
24	32	Stone, Clay & Glass	$854	$1,010	$905	$1,042	1.17%	2.86%
25	34	Fabricated Metals	$853	$966	$904	$1,180	1.17%	5.47%
26	30	Rubber & Plastic Products	$709	$799	$752	$936	1.18%	4.47%
27	86	Membership Organizations	$412	$660	$742	$1,183	12.49%	9.78%
28	26	Paper & Allied Products	$735	$757	$732	$941	-0.08%	5.15%

Business-to-Business Direct Marketing Advertising Expenditures Ranked by Industry
(Millions of Dollars)

Business Services, Communications and the Wholesale Trade Lead in
Business-to-Business Direct Marketing Advertising Expenditures Ranked by Industry*

Rank	SIC	Industry	1996	2000	2001	2006	Compound Annual Growth '96-'01	01-'06
29	GGE	Government & Government Enterprises	$515	$630	$700	$1,136	6.33%	10.17%
30	25	Furniture & Fixtures	$572	$699	$677	$840	3.43%	4.41%
31	33	Primary Metals	$709	$757	$666	$837	-1.24%	4.68%
32	22	Textile Mill Products	$646	$689	$647	$766	0.03%	3.43%
33	49	Electric & Gas Utilities	$469	$502	$532	$682	2.55%	5.09%
34	39	Miscellaneous Manufacturing	$451	$528	$524	$640	3.05%	4.08%
35	24	Lumber & Wood Products	$500	$520	$434	$505	-2.79%	3.08%
36	MIN	Mining	$314	$344	$424	$406	6.19%	-0.86%
37	CON	Construction	$307	$387	$398	$503	5.33%	4.79%
38	AGR	Agriculture	$252	$315	$330	$406	5.54%	4.23%
39	52	Building Materials & Garden Supplies	$243	$300	$292	$333	3.74%	2.66%
40	29	Petroleum & Coal	$281	$256	$290	$328	0.63%	2.49%
41	82	Educational Services	$134	$241	$275	$467	15.46%	11.17%
42	23	Apparel & Other Textiles	$294	$307	$274	$265	-1.40%	-0.67%
43	55	Auto Dealers & Service Stations	$205	$263	$273	$357	5.90%	5.51%
44	57	Household Appliance Stores	$236	$289	$268	$284	2.58%	1.17%
45	58	Restaurants	$188	$222	$219	$241	3.10%	1.93%
46	54	Food Stores	$161	$203	$206	$246	5.05%	3.61%
47	56	Apparel Stores	$88	$107	$106	$112	3.79%	1.11%
48	80	Health Services	$66	$92	$102	$189	9.10%	13.13%
49	83	Social Services	$45	$85	$102	$201	17.78%	14.53%
50	21	Tobacco Products	$32	$42	$43	$50	6.09%	3.06%
51	31	Leather & Leather Products	$35	$28	$25	$26	-6.51%	0.79%
52	84	Museums & Galleries	$8	$18	$21	$44	21.29%	15.94%

* Based on 2001 projections

Source: The DMA Report: Economic Impact- U.S. Direct & Interactive Marketing Today, 2002

Business-to-Business Direct Marketing Revenue Ranked by Industry
(Millions of Dollars)

Business Services, Insurance Carriers, and Real Estate Lead in
Business-to-Business Direct Marketing Revenue Ranked by Industry*

Rank	SIC	Industry	1996	2000	2001	Compound Annual Growth 2006	'96-'01	'01-'06
		Total	$500,992	$780,999	$858,113	$1,307,783	11.36%	8.79%
1	73	Business Services	$73,915	$154,888	$176,879	$286,882	19.07%	10.16%
2	63&64	Insurance Carriers & Agents	$36,349	$55,339	$61,437	$104,233	11.07%	11.15%
3	65	Real Estate	$31,549	$51,449	$58,936	$92,953	13.31%	9.54%
4	50&51	Wholesale Trade	$25,971	$35,806	$38,842	$56,292	8.38%	7.70%
5	81&87&89	Other Services	$18,468	$30,729	$34,649	$55,126	13.41%	9.73%
6	28	Chemicals & Allied Products	$24,142	$30,086	$31,705	$51,220	5.60%	10.07%
7	35	Industrial Machinery & Equipment	$19,712	$30,247	$31,154	$36,115	9.59%	3.00%
8	27	Printing & Publishing	$23,339	$29,837	$31,058	$39,195	5.88%	4.76%
9	62&67	Security & Commodity Brokers	$11,222	$26,013	$30,741	$55,087	22.33%	12.37%
10	36	Electrical Machinery & Equipment	$15,186	$27,093	$30,087	$54,530	14.65%	12.63%
11	48	Communications	$16,435	$26,603	$29,852	$44,235	12.68%	8.18%
12	45	Airlines	$16,855	$24,163	$26,110	$41,994	9.15%	9.97%
13	20	Food & Kindred Products	$19,874	$23,697	$25,360	$35,068	5.00%	6.70%
14	72&75&76	Personal & Repair Services	$14,525	$21,616	$24,067	$35,701	10.63%	8.21%
15	78&79	Entertainment	$11,343	$17,402	$19,306	$31,963	11.22%	10.61%
16	59	Non-Store Retailers	$9,533	$16,193	$17,873	$26,586	13.39%	8.27%
17	TRNX45	Transportation, excluding Airlines	$9,625	$13,493	$14,551	$21,099	8.62%	7.71%
18	60	Depository Institutions	$10,443	$12,805	$13,491	$16,407	5.26%	3.99%
19	38	Instruments & Related Products	$9,499	$12,303	$13,439	$19,669	7.19%	7.92%
20	86	Membership Organizations	$7,561	$11,833	$13,335	$20,989	12.02%	9.50%
21	53	General Merchandise Stores	$7,855	$11,549	$12,759	$18,713	10.19%	7.96%
22	70	Hotels	$6,844	$10,126	$11,233	$17,751	10.42%	9.58%
23	55	Auto Dealers & Service Stations	$6,925	$10,573	$11,190	$17,408	10.07%	9.24%
24	GGE	Government & Government Enterprises	$7,351	$8,984	$9,767	$13,131	5.85%	6.10%
25	61	Nondepository Institutions	$4,605	$7,769	$8,311	$10,335	12.53%	4.46%
26	37	Transportation Equipment	$6,420	$8,625	$8,285	$9,901	5.23%	3.63%
27	CON	Construction	$4,715	$7,108	$7,659	$10,553	10.19%	6.62%

Business-to-Business Direct Marketing Revenue Ranked by Industry
(Millions of Dollars)

Business Services, Insurance Carriers, and Real Estate Lead in
Business-to-Business Direct Marketing Revenue Ranked by Industry*

Rank	SIC	Industry	1996	2000	2001	2006	Compound Annual Growth '96-'01	Compound Annual Growth '01-'06
28	35	Fabricated Metals	$4,575	$5,837	$5,630	$6,814	4.24%	3.89%
29	52	Building Materials & Garden Supplies	$3,279	$5,133	$5,528	$7,932	11.01%	7.49%
30	26	Paper & Allied Products	$4,255	$4,723	$4,741	$5,955	2.19%	4.67%
31	25	Furniture & Fixtures	$3,092	$4,357	$4,492	$5,647	7.76%	4.68%
32	20	Rubber & Plastic Products	$3,249	$4,033	$3,978	$4,833	4.13%	3.97%
33	33	Primary Metals	$3,809	$4,265	$3,915	$4,713	0.55%	3.78%
34	23	Apparel & Other Textiles	$3,589	$3,936	$3,779	$3,497	1.04%	-1.54%
35	22	Textile Mill Products	$3,758	$3,694	$3,451	$3,319	-1.69%	-0.78%
36	58	Restaurants	$2,235	$3,029	$3,307	$4,622	8.15%	6.92%
37	39	Miscellaneous Manufacturing	$2,110	$3,070	$3,261	$4,444	9.10%	6.39%
38	57	Household Appliance Stores	$1,872	$2,858	$3,038	$4,308	10.17%	7.24%
39	54	Food Stores	$2,169	$2,676	$2,843	$3,441	5.56%	3.89%
40	32	Stone, Clay & Glass	$1,719	$2,519	$2,418	$2,675	7.06%	2.04%
41	49	Electric & Gas Utilities	$2,034	$2,154	$2,275	$2,815	2.26%	4.35%
42	24	Lumber & Wood Products	$2,238	$2,465	$2,166	$2,373	-0.65%	1.84%
43	AGR	Agriculture	$1,635	$1,779	$1,851	$2,165	2.51%	3.18%
44	80	Health Services	$733	$1,253	$1,509	$3,790	15.54%	20.22%
45	MIN	Mining	$1,043	$1,262	$1,506	$1,567	7.62%	0.80%
46	82	Educational Services	$722	$1,256	$1,470	$2,662	15.28%	12.61%
47	29	Petroleum & Coal	$919	$1,389	$1,452	$1,611	9.58%	2.10%
48	21	Tobacco Products	$565	$1,052	$1,184	$1,505	15.95%	4.91%
49	83	Social Services	$487	$925	$1,117	$2,251	18.06%	15.04%
50	56	Apparel Stores	$465	$681	$735	$909	9.59%	4.34%
51	84	Museums & Galleries	$142	$298	$367	$774	20.91%	16.10%
52	31	Leather & Leather Products	$41	$28	$25	$22	-9.42%	-2.52%

* Based on 2001 projections

Source: The DMA Report: Economic Impact- U.S. Direct & Interactive Marketing Today, 2002

Appendix 3

Glossary of terms

Address Standardization:

The U.S. Postal Service (USPS) worked with B-to-B mailers to develop guidelines/standards for address formatting, abbreviations, and address compression. These guidelines are designed to help alleviate the following problems that can result in processing B-to-B lists: inefficiencies in the merge/purge process, poor address hygiene, missed opportunities for bar-coding discounts, and ultimately non-deliverability. Most B-to-B list maintenance companies have adopted the USPS standards as part of their processing procedures. For a quick and easy reference, visit the USPS Web site *(www.usps.com)* and search for Publication 28, *Postal Addressing Standards.* Chapter three in Publication 28, focuses on B-to-B addressing.

Affiliate Programs:

Many Web marketers find success in placing an offer on someone else's Web site, and then compensating the other site owner for any traffic it generates. Business marketers can benefit by setting up such deals with all kinds of relevant sites: business partners, trade associations — anywhere prospects are likely to visit.

Allowable Cost Per Lead:

Being certain that leads are delivered to a sales force at an affordable price is one of the most important budgeting factors in lead generation. The allowable cost per closed lead is the average order size minus the cost of sales per order. The cost per closed lead is calculated by dividing the conversion rate into the cost per qualified lead. In campaign planning, you want to be sure your cost per closed lead will be lower than your allowable.

Appended Information:

Large business file owners make their information available for appending to clients' house files. Files can be over-laid with such important data fields as SIC code, title, phone number, credit rating, executive contacts, and company size, at a very low cost — ranging from $0.15 to $6.00 per piece matched, depending on the data element required.

Banners:

Internet advertising that appears as bars running horizontally across the screen. When users click on these ads, they are linked to the company's Web site.

BANT:

This is the acronym for typical lead qualification criteria — budget, authority, need, and time frame.

Bingo Cards:

A prepaid card bound into a magazine listing multiple free offers by advertisers. Most business marketers find that the inquiries coming in from bingo cards need a high degree of qualification before they are of any value.

Brand Advertising:

The marketing of a company's specific brand name. A brand name is defined as the identifying mark, symbol, word(s), or a combination of all three, that separate one company's product or services from another firm's.

Business Reply Card (BRC):

Promotion reply postcard preaddressed to the mailer and usually requiring no postage payment by responder.

Buyer:

The purchasing agent who actually places the order.

Buying Committee:

A group assembled, usually ad hoc, to manage the purchase of a particular item.

Call Center/Contact Center:

Traditionally, business marketers have operated in-house call centers, where customer service handled inbound calls, while sales and marketing made outbound calls. In recent years, with the arrival of the Internet, these call centers are rapidly being converted to "contact centers" that handle inbound and outbound communications through a variety of media channels, among them telephone, fax, and e-mail. Contact centers play a key role in the lead generation process. They handle inbound inquiries, qualify and nurture leads, and maintain ongoing contact with customers.

Campaign Objectives:

The first step in campaign planning should be to set campaign objectives. Campaign objectives will typically cover the number of leads expected, their degree of qualification, the time frame during which they will arrive, the cost per lead, lead-to-sales conversion ratio, revenue per lead, campaign ROI, and expense-to-revenue ratio.

Campaign Results Analysis:

Results analysis is an often-neglected area of lead generation campaigning. Parties from all parts of the company should be involved: business partners, sales, call centers, service providers, finance, and anyone whose role has impacted the campaign or who stands to benefit from it. Campaign results need to be measured against campaign objectives.

Card Decks:

Some trade publications offer additional access to their subscribers by publishing card decks, which are mailed separately to the subscriber base. While this approach can be a productive source of inquiries, a card often doesn't have enough space to describe the value proposition in depth. As a result, many responders are unqualified. It is important to have a solid qualification process in place to deal with card deck inquiries.

Catalogs:

Catalogs are an important and versatile B-to-B tool, bridging both the sales and marketing functions. They can be used to sell, or as a mail order channel. They can also serve as collateral material, providing an easily referenced and long-lasting source of detailed product or service information for customers.

Closed Lead:

A lead that has been converted to a sale.

Compiled Files:

Compiled lists are those created from directories or other public and private sources for the purpose of resale or rental to mailers. The names on compiled files have some characteristics in common, whether they be geographic or demographic, or related to industry, job function, or product type.

Controlled Circulation:

Copies of publications distributed free of charge to qualified readers of interest to the advertisers. Most industry trade magazines and newspapers operate on a controlled circulation basis.

Conversion:

When a lead becomes a sale.

Conversion Rate:

The rate at which qualified leads convert to sales. It is calculated by dividing the number of closed leads by the number of qualified leads delivered to the sales force.

Creative Checklist:

The secret to successful lead generation creative is to understand customers' needs, attitudes, and motivations. The following message platforms are frequently used to appeal to potential buyers: news statements; emotional connections; problems/solutions; testimonials; compelling questions; guarantees; benefit offers; appealing to buyers' greed; and inspring a need.

Credit Score:

An indicator of credit-worthiness, either internally generated or commercially available from a provider.

Customer:
An individual or company that has made a purchase from you.

Customer Relationship Management (CRM):
CRM is a philosophy that attempts to put the customer in the center of all business activity. CRM can be enabled by new software tools that automate the sales, marketing, and customer service functions, and connect those functions to real-time marketing databases. CRM is clearly central to the job of acquiring and retaining customers profitably — the core of any business.

Customer Service:
This function is now being seen as critically important to a company's success in a number of areas, including lead generation. Customer service manages the contact center, which includes many aspects of inquiry management and lead qualification. The key contribution to lead generation by customer service is up-selling and cross-selling. Customer service reps can enhance their usual function of solving problems and providing support by becoming alert to and identifying sales opportunities.

Data Hygiene:
Business data tends to degrade quickly, so it is important to invest in data hygiene. Hygiene tactics include the development of processes to capture all non-delivered mail and update the database accordingly.

Data Mining:
A technique for accessing data and analyzing it. It is used by companies to learn more about their customers, improve response rates, increase sales to current customers, decrease attrition, or optimize the efficiency of their next campaign.

Database Modeling:
Database modeling refers to both predictive and segmentation models that use the data in a customer or prospect database as the basis for predicting behavior or for segmenting customers, prospects, or areas. Database modeling should not be confused

with data modeling, which has to do with the organization of a company's data from a data processing or database management perspective.

Decision-Maker:

Often a department head or senior manager who has final sign-off for the purchase decision.

Direct Mail:

Marketing communications via the postal system usually intended to elicit a direct response. The standard elements of a direct mail package — outer envelope, letter, brochure, reply form, and business reply envelope (BRE) — work solidly for lead generation.

Dimensional Mail:

These are oversized, cleverly designed, and typically very expensive pieces that are intended to cut through the clutter of an administrative person's in-box, and actually get past the gatekeeper and onto the desk of a decision-maker. They often contain a physical premium: a video, gift, or other item that someone in the office thinks the boss will want to see. These packages can be quite effective in business marketing because they prove to be affordable.

Electronic Newsletters:

Ongoing communications via e-mail, often distributed on a subscription basis. Electronic newsletters are an excellent tool for keeping in touch with customers and prospects at little cost. While primarily seen as a relationship management tool, they can also serve as a way to generate new leads with the addition of a "viral," or pass-along, component.

Extranets:

Dedicated Web sites built behind the firewalls of key customers. Extranets allow for purchasing and inquiries to be conducted at any time of day, from sites all over the corporation, using the special terms and conditions pre-negotiated between the supplier and customer. Like the corporate Web site, dedicated extranets can include registrations, subscription sign-up, links to the sales team covering the account, and other lead generation techniques.

Gatekeeper:

The person who stands between the sales effort and any of the players in the buying process, usually a secretary, administrative assistant, or person in the mail room.

Incentive Programs:

A motivation technique that offers cash, gifts, special recognition, or other awards to stimulate an action.

Influencer:

The person in the organization who will benefit most directly from the purchase.

Inquiry:

An inquiry is the first inbound contact from a prospective customer. It may also be from a current customer seeking a refill, replacement, upgrade, or new product or service.

Integrated Marketing Communications:

Marketers find value in synchronizing their outbound communications across media channels, in a process known as integrated marketing communications. Print advertising, e-mail, telephone, direct mail, and collateral materials are all communications media channels that can be put to good use in lead generation. They work best when they reinforce one another and provide the prospect with a consistent series of messages.

Key Codes:

Usually in an alpha-numeric format, key codes are the best way to track and measure the results of each lead generation message. Key codes can take the form of a "priority code" number in the letter or on the response device, a special "extension" after an 800 number, or a special URL or URL extension address.

Lead (also called qualified lead):

An inquiry that has met the agreed-upon qualification criteria, such as having the right budget, decision-making authority, need for the product or service, and readiness to make the purchase in a suitable amount of time. Once an inquiry has become a qualified lead, it is ready to be worked by the sales force.

Lead Generation:

The process of identifying prospective customers and qualifying their likelihood to buy, in advance of making a sales call. First, establish a series of outbound and inbound contacts to generate the inquiry and qualify it as a lead; next, hand the lead over to sales; then, track the lead through conversion to sales revenue.

Lead Nurturing:

The process of moving an unqualified inquiry to the point where it becomes qualified. Nurturing involves a series of marketing communications intended to build trust and awareness, and maintain a relationship until the prospect is ready to buy. The objective of the nurturing program is to be in touch with the prospect when he is ready to buy.

Marketing Database:

The marketing database is the essential element of the lead generation tool kit. It allows customer and prospect data to be gathered, maintained, and analyzed, for the purpose of having a deep understanding of customer value, customer needs, and business opportunity, as well as selecting the right targets for marketing communications and sales activities.

Merge/Purge:

Merge/purge is a computerized process of matching records to eliminate duplicate records or correct records with incorrect or insufficient data. It is critically important to B-to-B data management. It allows a new record or new data elements to be introduced to the marketing database correctly. It enables marketers to keep track of the various contacts within a site that they want to influence, and it allows records to be efficiently selected for campaigns.

Mini-sites:

A mini-site is something like a combined Web response form and Web site. Frequently used as a landing page for an outbound campaign, mini-sites are often created to support new product introductions, limited-time deals, or some other offering that deserves special highlighting. Mini-sites can be populated with contests, demos, downloads, cross-sell offers, or whatever makes sense. They should always contain a form to collect contact information for follow-up.

Online Fulfillment:

Fulfilling prospects' requests for information by offering Web-based downloads, instead of sending out printed collateral material or white papers. This lets marketers update the material regularly, and avoid the carrying costs of warehousing printed brochures. Materials can also be made customizable before download so the prospect only receives what matters most to him.

Postcards:

Postcards are widely used in lead generation — typically over-sized ones that announce a new product feature, service, or an upcoming seminar. This type of communication serves the need to stay in touch with a prospect but does not require much detailed explanation or content. Postcards appeal to marketers because of their low cost, and to recipients because they can be skimmed and absorbed quickly.

Print Advertising:

Direct response advertising in trade, industry vertical, and business publications can provide a steady, reliable stream of new prospective sales leads. Print advertising can be very powerful in generating awareness and building brand recognition and positive attitudes. If the objective is to get leads, print ads must be created for response.

Product History:

Information about products purchased by a particular customer and maintained in the marketing database. This includes the price, category, stock-keeping unit (SKU) numbers, and product names of item(s) purchased by the customer. Records should be kept if the purchased product was later discontinued and removed or uninstalled.

Profiling:

Characterizing the best and worst customers in a process known as profiling will offer some solid direction on new customers to pursue or avoid. It involves identifying the key characteristics of a group and using those characteristics to identify look-alikes in a prospect universe. Predictive characteristics are likely to include industry, company size (using number of employees as a proxy), company revenues, and geographic territory.

Promotion History:

The frequency, medium, offer code, cost, and type of outbound contacts with the account, maintained in the marketing database. This data can be helpful in two ways: as a predictor of purchase propensity, and as part of a customer value analysis.

Prospect:

An individual or company that is likely to need your product or service, but has not bought from you yet.

Prospecting Databases:

A database of prospects for use in lead-generation campaigns. Typically, a prospecting database will be built and maintained by a list broker or manager, using the rental lists that are most productive. The benefit is fast and convenient access to pre-de-duplicated names that have appropriate appended information in place, and with approvals already secured.

Purchase History:

Database elements that capture what the account has purchased in the past, the date, the dollar amount, the order placement method, the payment method, and the frequency. Purchase history can be highly predictive of future purchase propensity.

Purchase Preference:

Database element that records details about how accounts like to buy, their preferred channels, their terms, and other information that may be predictive.

Qualification:

The process by which you establish whether the inquiry is qualified to become a lead.

Qualification Rate:

The rate at which inquiries migrate to qualified leads. Qualification rates are calculated by dividing the number of qualified leads during a time period, or from a particular campaign, by the number of inquiries in the period, or from the campaign.

Recency/Frequency/Monetary (RFM) Value:

These three measures are considered jointly to determine the value of a customer in terms of: the time since the last purchase was made, the number of purchases made during a period of time, and the dollar value of the purchases made.

Referral Marketing:

Name of a prospective customer acquired from a current customer or other third party. From a marketer's point of view, referrals are an outstanding source of new business. Recommendations from a colleague have great credibility, so, not only is the referred prospect likely to be qualified, he is also likely to be motivated. Because of its speed and informality, the Internet lends itself well to referral practices.

Response Rate:

The rate at which prospects or customers respond to an outbound campaign. It is calculated by dividing the number of responses by the number of prospects promoted. Once received, responses are called inquiries.

Research — Qualitative:

Qualitative research involves in-depth questions and answers. Types of qualitative research include focus groups (face-to-face or online), one-on-one, in-depth interviews, and open-ended mail or phone surveys. Qualitative research is best used to: validate assumptions about buyer motivation; present sample message platforms and creative treatments to get directional reactions; delve into the rational and emotional triggers of various buyer types; develop a deeper understanding of the customer's point of view; gather phrases for copywriting purposes; or compare the relative attractiveness of key benefits and features.

Research — Quantitative:

Quantitative research uses statistically valid samples to represent the entire universe. Quantitative research is usually performed through surveys using telephone, e-mail, or postal mail to reach projectional numbers of respondents. Quantitative research can be used to validate hypotheses around any critical campaign variable. For lead generation campaigns, quantitative research is often used to test: the best potential offers; list segments or list quality; purchase intent; product awareness; message preferences; creative concept rankings; improvements in your control package; or willingness to participate in further research.

Response Management:

The process of handling responses from a lead-generation campaign. Response management must follow close on the heels of campaign planning and execution. If campaign planning is sometimes called the front end of the lead generation process, then response management may be called the back end. Response management involves the following general steps: response capture, inquiry fulfillment, inquiry qualification, hand-off to sales, and tracking to closure.

Retention:

The process of developing a customer, continuing to satisfy him, stimulating him to buy again and more frequently, and preventing him from defecting to the competition.

Retention Metrics:

Retention equals the number of customers, year on year, who continue to buy. Retention metrics can be expressed in a number of ways: the ratio of repeat buyers to the total number of buyers; the ratio of new buyers to the total number of buyers; or the "churn rate" (the ratio of lapsed buyers to the total number of buyers).

Retention Tactics:

The following is a list of retention tactics that have proven successful in business marketing for stimulating repeat purchase: surveys/feedback; outbound communications; newsletters; proprietary magazines; special events; contests and awards; special service levels; automated marketing communications; welcome programs; rewards programs; advisory boards or special clubs; occasional thank-you messages; sales force incentives; and winback programs to reclaim lost customers.

Search Engine Optimization:

Internet search engines can direct interested inquirers to a marketer's site. To achieve high-ranking results, companies must submit their sites to the top search engines and apply optimizing techniques. Another approach is to pay for certain keywords relevant to the company's product/service or company to pop up at the top of the search engine list whenever prospects undertake a search on the Internet.

Segmentation:

The first step in targeting is to divide the prospective universe into groups, based on a number of defining characteristics. This process is known as segmentation. Segmentation offers a way to group campaign targets in order to create the right messages, use the right communications channels, and increase the likelihood of response. Segmentation also allows each segment to operate as a small universe on its own for testing and roll-out. Marketers can test their messages to a part of the segment and later expand the communication to the rest of the segment with confidence that it will respond similarly.

Segmentation Criteria:

Segmentation criteria include the relationship existing today between the company and the buyer, geographics, demographics — sometimes known as "firmographics," — and purchase history.

Self-mailers:

Self-mailers are widely used to promote seminars and trade shows. The main advantages of self-mailers are their low cost, and the fact that they are more likely than enveloped pieces to be passed along from one in-box to another within an office.

Service History:

Service history documents the contacts the customer has had with your service center, such as inquiries, returns, and problems, plus their resolution.

SIC or NAICS:

The U.S. government is currently in the process of migrating the four-digit Standard Industrial Classification (SIC) system to a new six-digit system called NAICS, or North American Industry Classification System. NAICS was developed in cooperation with Canada and Mexico. Read all about it at *http://www.census.gov/epcd/www/naics.html*. NAICS is a more modern classification system, reflecting the new realities of how our information economy operates. Check into *http://www.osha.gov/oshstats/sicser.html*, where you can search for SIC codes by keyword, and vice versa.

Source Code:

This indicates where the first contact with this person originated. Some companies also record the most recent source of the contact, which serves as an indicator of campaign results.

Specifier:

The IT professional, shop floor engineer, or other technical expert who reviews the need in detail and specifies what features and functionality are required.

Telephone — Inbound:

Inbound, the phone is frequently used as a response device — one of several options for prospects to express their interest, if they prefer the phone to the Web or to a business reply card (BRC).

Telephone — Outbound:

Outbound phone calls are usually used in lead generation as a substitute for — or a supplement to — direct mail. This function is typically known as telemarketing, and its power lies in its ability to effectively penetrate small universes.

User:

The person who will be using the product to get the job done (may overlap with the influencer).

Webinars:

Web-based seminars, sometimes called "webinars," are quickly growing in popularity, because they combine the rich content of a traditional face-to-face seminar with the wide reach, flexibility, and low cost of the Internet. Webinars play the same role in lead generation as the traditional seminar — namely, they provide qualified prospects with detailed product or service information, case studies, and demonstrations.

Web Response Forms:

As a substitute for, or supplement to, a BRC, Web response forms invite targets to visit a particular URL to respond to your campaign. Sometimes called "splash pages," "jump pages," or "landing pages," these forms offer numerous advantages. Instantaneous and highly convenient, their response mechanism appeals to business buyers. They also permit campaign tracking and measurement via the assigned URL.

Winback:

The process of persuading a lapsed customer to buy again. Winback involves understanding the reason for the defection, solving any outstanding problems, and motivating the customer to consider repurchase. Business marketers often create dedicated teams who specialize in winback sales.

5

Part Five
Directory of Suppliers

Advertising & Direct Response Agencies

AdSouth, Inc.
1220 Compass Pointe Crossing
Alpharetta, GA 30005
Phone: (770) 346-8600
Fax: (770) 346-8601
www.adsouth.com

A. Eicoff & Company
401 N Michigan Ave
Chicago, IL 60611
Phone: (312) 527-7100
Fax: (312) 527-7179
www.drtvadvertising.com

Alcott Routon, Inc.
830 Crescent Ctr
Franklin, TN 37067
Phone: (615) 261-7111
Fax: (615) 261-7211
www.alcottrouton.com

Allen & Gerritsen
85 School St
Watertown, MA 02472
Phone: (617) 926-4005
Fax: (617) 926-0133
www.a-g.com

Alternative Marketing Solutions
P.O. Box 942
Valley Forge, PA 19482
Phone: (610) 783-1320
Fax: (610) 783-1324
www.amsolutions.com

Archer/Malmo Direct
65 Union Ave
Memphis, TN 38103
Phone: (901) 523-2000
Fax: (901) 524-5578
www.archermalmo.com

Baker-Blais Marketing, Inc.
295 Hymus Blvd
Pointe Claire, QC H9R 6A5
CANADA
Phone: (514) 693-9900
Fax: (514) 693-9960
www.bakerblais.com

Banner Direct Inc.
630 5th Ave
Ste 2109
New York, NY 10111
Phone: (212) 218-7520
Fax: (212) 218-7527
www.bannerdirect.com

BBDO New York
1285 Avenue of the Americas
New York, NY 10019
Phone: (212) 459-5000
Fax: (212) 459-6645
www.bbdo.com

Beacon Group, Inc.
8320 Bellona Ave
Windsor Ct
Ste 250
Baltimore, MD 21204
Phone: (410) 583-1203
Fax: (410) 583-1506
www.beacon.com

Beyond DDB
200 E Randolph St
Chicago, IL 60601
Phone: (312) 552-6000
Fax: (312) 552-2370
www.ddb.com

Bienestar LCG Communications
230 W 41st St
New York, NY 10036
Phone: (212) 730-7230
Fax: (212) 730-7450

Biggs-Gilmore Communications
100 W Michigan Ave
Ste 300
Kalamazoo, MI 49007
Phone: (616) 349-7711
Fax: (616) 349-3051
www.biggs-gilmore.com

Billington Advertising
594 Caudill Way
Branson, MO 65616
Phone: (417) 334-1545
Fax: (417) 334-1545

Blattner Brunner, Inc.
11 Stanwix St
5th Fl
Pittsburgh, PA 15222
Phone: (412) 995-9500
Fax: (412) 995-9501
www.blattnerbrunner.com

B/M/C Advertising
2419 E Skelly Dr
Tulsa, OK 74105
Phone: (918) 743-4600
Fax: (918) 743-9188
www.bmcadv.com

BMD
901 N Washington St
Ste 300
Alexandria, VA 22314
Phone: (703) 549-3500
Fax: (703) 549-2358
www.b-m-d.com

Brody Smythe Direct
8665 Wilshire Blvd
Ste 301
Beverly Hills, CA 90211
Phone: (310) 360-0887
Fax: (310) 360-1078
www.brodysmythe.com

Campbell Ewald/C-E Communications
30400 Van Dyke Ave
Warren, MI 48093
Phone: (810) 558-7089
Fax: (810) 558-5896
www.cecom.com

Carey Color Inc.
P.O. Box 609
6835 Ridge Rd
Sharon Center, OH 44274
Phone: (800) 555-3142
Fax: (330) 239-6016
www.careyweb.com

Carl Bloom Associates, Inc.
232 Madison Ave
Ste 1107
New York, NY 10016
Phone: (212) 679-6900
Fax: (212) 679-6913
www.carlbloom.com

Carlson Marketing Group
205 Lexington Ave
6th Fl
New York, NY 10016
Phone: (212) 252-5815
Fax: (212) 252-5816
www.carlsonmarketing.com

Carlson Marketing Group
3055 Kettering Blvd
Ste 220
Kettering, OH 45439
Phone: (937) 299-0700
Fax: (937) 299-9175
www.carlsonmarketing.com

Carlson Marketing Group
735 Battery St
Ste 500
San Francisco, CA 94111
Phone: (415) 398-5165
Fax: (415) 398-5397
www.carlsonmarketing.com

Carlson Marketing Group
2800 Livernois
Ste 600
Troy, MI 48083
Phone: (248) 824-7600
Fax: (248) 824-7606
www.carlsonmarketing.com

Carmichael Lynch
800 Hennepin Ave
Minneapolis, MN 55403
Phone: (612) 334-6219
Fax: (612) 334-6171
www.carmichaellynch.com

Catalyst Direct Inc.
110 Marina Dr
Rochester, NY 14626
Phone: (716) 453-8331
Fax: (716) 453-8361
www.catalystdirect.com

CCMR Advertising & Marketing Communications
260 Fair St
Kingston, NY 12401
Phone: (845) 331-4620
Fax: (845) 331-3026
www.gotoccmr.com

Chadwick Communications
49 W 27th St
New York, NY 10001
Phone: (212) 251-0555
Fax: (212) 251-0533
www.chadwickcomm.com

Chinnici Direct LLC
411 Lafayette St
3rd Fl
New York, NY 10003
Phone: (212) 561-6000
Fax: (212) 260-3710
www.pavlikachinnici.com

Clarion Marketing & Communications
Greenwich Office Park 5
Greenwich, CT 06831
Phone: (203) 862-6000
Fax: (203) 862-6009
www.clarionmarketing.com

Connect Direct
61 Renato Ct
Redwood City, CA 44061
Phone: (650) 306-9060
www.connectthe.com

Cosgrove Associates
747 Third Ave
16th Fl
New York, NY 10017
Phone: (212) 888-7202
Fax: (212) 888-7201
www.cosgrovejuro.com

CPC Loyalty Communications
2001 Sheppard Ave E
Toronto, ON M2J 428
CANADA
Phone: (416) 494-9995
Fax: (416) 494-2328
www.cpchealthcare.com

Creative Strategy, Inc.
5454 Wisconsin Ave
Ste 1655
Chevy Chase, MD 20815
Phone: (301) 718-4550
Fax: (301) 718-8828
www.creativestrategy.com

Customer Growth, Blau Moritz Partnership, Inc.
37 Franklin St
Ste 201
Westport, CT 06880
Phone: (203) 226-8795
Fax: (203) 227-8601
www.customer-growth.com

Devon Direct Euro RSCG
200 Berwyn Park
Berwyn, PA 19312
Phone: (610) 651-2651
Fax: (610) 651-2671
www.devondirect.com

DiMassimo Brand Advertising
20 Cooper Sq
6th Fl
New York, NY 10003
Phone: (212) 253-7500
Fax: (212) 228-8810
www.dimassimo.com

Direct Impact, Inc.
8420 Delmar Blvd
Ste LL6
Saint Louis, MO 63124
Phone: (314) 567-0024
Fax: (314) 567-1497
www.directimpactinc.com

eMerging Marketing
2931 Donnylane Blvd
Columbus, OH 43235
Phone: (614) 923-6000
Fax: (614) 923-6006
www.emergingmarketing.com

More than just great response.
Great *quality* leads.

It's not a thing of the future. It's a necessity now. Your direct marketing program needs to produce more than a killer response rate, although, we'll be happy to do that for you. You also need a steady stream of qualified sales leads.

And that's when you need The Hacker Group. With over 4.5 million leads generated in 2001 alone, we are one of the most successful lead generation specialists in the country. Give us a call and find out how you can get . . .

A strong winner on the first try

Ask about The Hacker Group's Power*Test*™ proprietary methodology for getting you a winning package when you need it most. With it, you can simultaneously test hundreds of package, offer, list and price combinations.

Call (425) 454-8556 for a FREE 1-year subscription!

A system to electronically qualify and distribute leads

Our WebTrapper™ system puts together a comprehensive sales machine, from prospecting to CRM. As your program generates responses, WebTrapper qualifies them based on your sales force's definition of a qualified lead.

Razor-sharp strategic insight

If the strategy is wrong, the greatest creative execution in the world won't save the program. Direct is the one piece of the marketing communications puzzle that truly is measurable, and *The Hacker Group knows exactly how and what to count.*

For a **FREE consultation** with The Hacker Group and a **FREE 1-year subscription to** *High Performance Direct,* give Spyro Kourtis a call at (425) 454-8556.

The Hacker Group
high performance direct

1110 112th Avenue NE, Suite 200, Bellevue, WA 98004-4504 • Phone: 425.454.8556 • Fax: 425.455.5694 • www.hackergroup.com

ESG Consulting, Inc.
1440 N Lake Shore Dr 8E
Chicago, IL 60610
Phone: (312) 664-3727

e2 Communications
6404 International Pkwy
Ste 1200
Plano, TX 75093
Phone: (972) 931-7000
Fax: (972) 931-8883
www.e2software.com

Euromarketing AG
VORLAUFSTRASSE 3
A -1010 Vienna, AUSTRIA
Phone: 43-1 53759
Fax: +43-1 5327678
www.euromarketing.ag

Fishbowl.com
1127 King St #3
Alexandria, VA 22314
Phone: (703) 836-3421
Fax: (703) 836-3422
www.fishbowl.com

Gianfagna Marketing & Communications, Inc.
1991 Crocker Rd
Ste 400
Cleveland, OH 44145
Phone: (440) 808-4700
Fax: (440) 808-4707
www.gianfagnamarketing.com

Global DM Solutions
416 Main St
Boonton, NJ 07005
Phone: (973) 402-2205
Fax: (973) 402-2305
www.globaldmsolutions.com

Grizzard
229 Peachtree St
Ste 900
Atlanta, GA 30303
Phone: (404) 935-7133
www.grizzard.com

The Hacker Group
1110 112th Avenue NE
Ste 200
Bellevue, WA 98004
Phone: (425) 454-8556
Fax: (425) 455-5694
www.hackergroup.com

Harte-Hanks Direct & Interactive
2050 Cabot Blvd W
Langhorne, PA 19047
Phone: (800) 543-2212
Fax: (215) 750-7418
www.harte-hanks.com

Hawkeye Communications
551 Fifth Ave
Ste 1501
New York, NY 10176
Phone: (212) 763-0200
Fax: (212) 763-0090
www.hawkeyeww.com

HBM Associates, Inc.
20 Stuyvesant Oval
New York, NY 10009
Phone: (212) 529-1891
Fax: (212) 505-8720

Hemmings IV Direct
2500 E Foothill Blvd
Ste 204
Pasadena, CA 91107
Phone: (626) 796-7188
Fax: (626) 796-9436

Hill Holliday
200 Clarendon St
Boston, MA 02116
Phone: (617) 437-1600
Fax: (617) 572-3534
www.hhcc.com

HispanAmérica
437 Madison Ave
7th Fl
New York, NY 10022
Phone: (212) 415-3054
Fax: (212) 415-3591

Hispanic Direct, Inc.
5940 Touhy Ave
Ste 250
Niles, IL 60714
Phone: (847) 588-0088
Fax: (847) 588-2488
www.hispanicdirect.com

Horah Direct
49 W 37th St
New York, NY 10018
Phone: (212) 921-4521

Howard, Merrell & Partners, Inc.
8521 Six Forks Rd
Raleigh, NC 27615
Phone: (919) 848-2400
Fax: (919) 848-2420
www.merrellgroup.com

Husk Jennings Advertising and Public Relations, Inc.
6 E Bay St
Jacksonville, FL 32202
Phone: (904) 354-2600
Fax: (904) 354-2018
www.huskjennings.com

Ibis Communications, Inc.
1024 17th Ave S
Ste C
Nashville, TN 37212
Phone: (615) 777-1900
Fax: (615) 777-1906
www.ibisflys.com

Imagine Direct
552 Main St
Williamstown, MA 01267
Phone: (413) 458-1803
Fax: (413) 458-1804
www.imaginedirect.com

Independent Marketing
85 N Raymond Ave
Ste 270
Pasadena, CA 91103
Phone: (626) 432-4594
Fax: (626) 821-1889
www.independentmarketing.com

Indico Bellum
53 W Jackson St
Ste 1352
Chicago, IL 60604
Phone: (312) 934-5444
www.indicobellum.com

Initiative Media
5700 Wilshire Blvd
Ste 400
Los Angeles, CA 90036
Phone: (323) 370-8000
Fax: (323) 370-8957
www.im-na.com

Interactive Marketing Group
50 Commerce Dr
Allendale, NJ 07401
Phone: (201) 327-0974
Fax: (201) 327-3596
www.imgusa.com

Integrated Marketing Partners
389 Clementina St
Ste 707
San Francisco, CA 94103
Phone: (415) 369-9100
Fax: (415) 369-9200
www.imarketingpartners.com

International Business Systems
431 Yerkes Rd
King of Prussia, PA 19406
Phone: (610) 265-8210
Fax: (610) 265-7997
www.ibs4cmyk.com

InterOne Marketing Group
880 W Long Lake
Troy, MI 48098
Phone: (248) 433-6955
Fax: (248) 813-0082
www.interonemarketing.com

Interval International
P.O. Box 431920
6262 Sunset Dr
Miami, FL 33243
Phone: (305) 666-1861
Fax: (305) 663-2286
www.intervalworld.com

J. Moritz and Co.
37 Franklin St
Ste 201
Westport, CT 06880
Phone: (203) 226-8795
Fax: (203) 227-8601

Jacobs & Clevenger, Inc.
401 N Wabash Ave
Ste 620
Chicago, IL 60611
Phone: (312) 894-3094
Fax: (312) 645-0499
www.jacobsclevenger.com

JAM Communications, Inc.
1638 R St, NW
Ste 400
Washington, DC 20009
Phone: (202) 986-4750
Fax: (202) 232-9146
www.jamagency.com

JWT Specialized Communications
1239 E Newport Center Dr
Ste 110
Deerfield Beach, FL 33442
Phone: (954) 425-8525
Fax: (954) 425-8357
www.jwtworks.com

Kang & Lee Advertising
315 Fifth Ave
New York, NY 10016
Phone: (212) 889-4509
Fax: (212) 889-2924
www.kanglee.com

KMA the Agency
12001 N Central Exp
900 Coit Ctrl Twr
Dallas, TX 75243
Phone: (972) 560-1900
Fax: (972) 560-1985
www.kma.com

Kroha Direct
573 Newfield St
Middletown, CT 06457
Phone: (860) 346-4650
Fax: (860) 347-4828
www.krohadirect.com

Lawrence Butner Advertising
228 E 45th St
New York, NY 10017
Phone: (212) 338-5000
Fax: (212) 682-4866
www.LBAI.com

List Media, Inc.
251 W Garfield Rd
Ste 262
Aurora, OH 44202
Phone: (330) 995-0864
Fax: (330) 995-0873
www.dm1.com

Malcolm Decker Associates, Inc.
36 Rockwood Ln
Box 4839
Greenwich, CT 06830
Phone: (203) 422-0518
Fax: (203) 422-0519

MWA Direct Inc.
6465 Wayzata Blvd
Minneapolis, MN 55426
Phone: (952) 591-1007

Novus Print Media, Inc.
13605 First Ave N
Plymouth, MN 55441
Phone: (888) 668-8723
Fax: (763) 476-7701
www.novusprintmedia.com

OgilvyOne Worldwide
33 Yonge Street
Toronto, ON M5E 1X6
CANADA
Phone: (416) 363-9514
Fax: (416) 363-7736
www.ogilvyone.com

Ovation Marketing, Inc.
201 Main St
6th Fl
La Crosse, WI 54601
Phone: (608) 785-2460
Fax: (608) 785-2496
www.ovationmarketing.com

Passaic Parc
148 Linden St
Ste 205
Wellesley, MA 02482
Phone: (718) 431-0150
Fax: (718) 431-0170
www.passaicparc.com

Pedone/1.to.1
100 5th Ave
4th Fl
New York, NY 10011
Phone: (212) 627-3300
Fax: (212) 627-3966
www.pedonepartners.com

Peter A. Mayer Advertising, Inc.
324 Camp St
New Orleans, LA 70130
Phone: (504) 581-7191
Fax: (504) 581-3009
www.petermayer.com

Porter Direct Marketing
4181 Farquhar Ave
Los Alamitos, CA 90720
Phone: (562) 493-4676

PreVision Marketing, Inc.
55 Old Bedford Rd
Lincoln, MA 01773
Phone: (781) 259-5100
Fax: (781) 259-1548
www.previsionmarketing.com

Prime Access Inc.
345 Seventh Ave
New York, NY 10001
Phone: (212) 594-6300
Fax: (212) 594-6336
www.primeaccess.net

Publicis Dialog
111 Queens St E
Ste 200
Toronto, ON M5C 1S2
CANADA
Phone: (416) 925-5260
Fax: (416) 925-7341
www.publicis.ca

Rapp Collins Worldwide
1660 N Westridge Circle
Irving, TX 75038
Phone: (972) 582-2000
Fax: (972) 582-2519
www.rappcollins.com

Rawhide Internet Services, Inc.
521 Illinois Ave
Saint Charles, IL 60174
Phone: (630) 762-0857
Fax: (630) 443-0008
www.rawhideinc.com

Reinke & Associates, Inc.
733 N Van Buren St
Milwaukee, WI 53203
Phone: (414) 224-8833
Fax: (414) 224-8818
www.reinkeassoc.com

Response Advertising
22 Harrison Ave
Ste 301
Highland Park, NJ 08904
Phone: (732) 246-4186
Fax: (732) 846-9856

Response Associates
680 8th St
Ste 260
San Francisco, CA 94103
Phone: (415) 750-3870
Fax: (415) 621-4126
www.rareresponse.com

Response JPS
Calle Nicaragua 14-1
Madrid, SPAIN, 28106
Phone: 34-913504766
Fax: 34-913459868
www.response.es

Roberts Communications
64 Commercial St
Rochester, NY 14614
Phone: (716) 325-6000
Fax: (716) 246-0318
robertscomm.com

Roska Direct
211B Progress Dr
Montgomeryville, PA 18936
Phone: (215) 699-9200
Fax: (215) 699-9240
www.roska.com

Target + Response, Inc.
420 N Wabash Ave
Ste 201
Chicago, IL 60611
Phone: (312) 321-0500
Fax: (312) 321-0051
www.target-response.com

VentureDirect Worldwide
60 Madison Ave
New York, NY 10010
Phone: (212) 684-4800
Fax: (212) 576-1129
www.venturedirect.com

WOL DIRECT/THOMSON
925 Oak St
Scranton, PA 18515
Phone: (570) 961-4628
Fax: (570) 343-8172

Wunderman
675 Avenue of the Americas
4th Fl
New York, NY 10010
Phone: (212) 941-3000
Fax: (212) 627-8521
www.wunderman.com

Affiliate Marketing

Be Free, Inc.
154 Crane Meadow Rd
Marlborough, MA 01752
Phone: (508) 480-4000
Fax: (508) 357-8899
www.befree.com

Performics
180 N Lasalle St
Ste 1100
Chicago, IL 60601
Phone: (312) 739-0222
Fax: (312) 739-0223
www.performics.com

Alternative Media

Adchek, Inc.
2225 Sperry Ave
Ste 1050
Ventura, CA 93003
Phone: (805) 639-0006
Fax: (805) 639-0051
www.adchek.com

Advertising.com
1020 Hull St
Ste 200
Baltimore, MD 21230
Phone: (914) 747-3947
Fax: (914) 747-3971
www.advertising.com

Everyday Media
461 Park Ave S
3rd Fl
New York, NY 10016
Phone: (212) 481-7300
Fax: (212) 481-7800
www.everydaymedia.com

4anything.com
487 Devon Park Dr
Ste 204
Wayne, PA 19087
Phone: (610) 768-1444
Fax: (610) 592-1094
www.4anything.com

Independent Media Services, Inc.
2050 Center Ave
Ste 610
Fort Lee, NJ 07024
Phone: (201) 592-8282
Fax: (201) 592-6066
www.independentmediaser-
vices.com

Leon Henry, Inc.
455 Central Ave
Scarsdale, NY 10583
Phone: (914) 723-3176
Fax: (914) 723-0205
www.leonhenryinc.com

MTD Marketing, Inc.
420 Alcott Ct
Colorado Spgs, CO 80921
Phone: (719) 320-7507
Fax: (719) 481-1990
www.mtdmarketing.com

My Virtual Model
1001 Sherbrooke E
7th Fl
Montreal, QC, H2L 1L3
CANADA
Phone: (514) 523-9966
Fax: (514) 523-0100
www.myvirtualmodel.com

PlusMedia, LLC
100 Mill Plain Rd
4th Fl
P.O. Box 3949
Danbury, CT 06813
Phone: (203) 748-6500
Fax: (203) 748-6600

VentureDirect Worldwide
60 Madison Ave
New York, NY 10010
Phone: (212) 684-4800
Fax: (212) 576-1129
www.venturedirect.com

WVH Marketing & Advertising
225 Bush St
Ste 1600
San Francisco, CA 94104
Phone: (415) 281-7300
www.wvh.com

Broadcast Media Buyers

Concept Media
2255 Glades Rd
Ste 324-A
Boca Raton, FL 33431
Phone: (561) 852-1818
Fax: (561) 852-5502
www.concept-media.com

Lighthouse Strategic Projects Group
2080 Cabot Blvd W
Ste 203
Langhorne, PA 19047
Phone: (215) 750-4544
Fax: (215) 750-9795
www.lighthousespg.com

Cable TV Systems

Comcast Cable Communications
1500 Market St
34th Fl
Philadelphia, PA 19102
Phone: (215) 320-7474
Fax: (215) 655-8125
www.comcast.com

Catalog Agency

J. Schmid & Associates, Inc.
9000 W 64th Terrace
Shawnee Mission, KS 66202
Phone: (913) 236-8988
Fax: (913) 236-8987
www.jschmid.com

Pluzynski and Associates, Inc.
26 W 17th St
10th Fl
New York, NY 10011
Phone: (212) 645-1414
Fax: (212) 645-2013
www.pluzynski.com

Shasho Jones Direct, Inc.
226 W 26th St
New York, NY 10001
Phone: (212) 929-2300
Fax: (212) 929-5630
www.sjdirect.com

Catalog Consultants

Alan Glazer Associates LLC
2 Lauder Way
Greenwich, CT 06830
Phone: (203) 869-3970
Fax: (203) 869-3969

Alexander & Company, LLC
178 Water St
Stonington, CT 06378
Phone: (860) 535-9160
Fax: (860) 535-9161

Cynthia Fields & Company
230 W 22nd St
New York, NY 10011
Phone: (212) 242-6063
Fax: (212) 242-6063

iCatalogInquiry.com, Inc.
777 E Atlantic Ave
Ste Z373
Delray Beach, FL 33483
Phone: (561) 330-6207
Fax: (561) 330-6208
www.iCataloginquiry.com

J. Schmid & Associates, Inc.
9000 W 64th Terrace
Shawnee Mission, KS 66202
Phone: (913) 236-8988
Fax: (913) 236-8987
www.jschmid.com

Kris Snyder & Associates
35 Atherton Ln
Amherst, NH 03031
Phone: (603) 672-5255
Fax: (603) 672-5403

Lisa Glass
2 Whitebridge Ct
Baltimore, MD 21208
Phone: (410) 580-0355
Fax: (410) 580-0366

Maxwell Sroge Company, Inc.
522 Forest Ave
Evanston, IL 60202
Phone: (847) 866-1890
Fax: (847) 866-1899
www.catalog-news.com

Newgistics Inc.
2700 Via Fortuna
Ste 450
Austin, TX 78746
Phone: (512) 225-6000
Fax: (512) 225-6001
www.newgistics.com

Computer Service Bureaus

Acxiom Corporation
1 Information Way
Little Rock, AR 72003
Phone: (501) 342-1000
Fax: (501) 342-5610
www.acxiom.com

Affinity Processing Services, Inc.
580 Capital Dr
Unit 314
Lake Zurich, IL 60047
Phone: (847) 438-2800
Fax: (847) 438-0855
www.affinityprocessing.com

Anchor Computer, Inc.
1900 New Hwy
Farmingdale, NY 11735
Phone: (631) 293-6100
Fax: (631) 293-0891
www.anchorcomputer.com

Automated Resources Group, Inc.
135 Chestnut Ridge Rd
Montvale, NJ 07645
Phone: (201) 391-1500
Fax: (201) 391-5338
www.callargi.com

CMS, Inc.
300 2nd St, NW
St. Paul, MN 55112
Phone: (651) 636-6265
Fax: (651) 636-0879
www.netcms.com

Communication Logistics
P.O. Box 27
19270 N State Rd 1
Ferdinand, IN 47532
Phone: (812) 357-2545
Fax: (812) 357-5005
www.comloginc.com

Cornwell Data Services, Inc.
352 Evelyn St
Paramus, NJ 07652
Phone: (201) 261-1050
Fax: (201) 261-7569
www.cornwelldata.com

Cross Country Computer Corp.
75 Corporate Dr
Hauppauge , NY 11788
Phone: (631) 231-4200
Fax: (631) 231-9248
www.crosscountrycomputer.com

Data For Development, Inc.
880 Lee St
Ste 301
Des Plaines, IL 60016
Phone: (847) 768-9700
Fax: (847) 768-9707
www.dfdi.com

Direct Access Marketing Services, Inc.
33 Queens St
Syosset, NY 11791
Phone: (516) 364-2777
Fax: (516) 364-0644
www.daxcess.com

Direct Data Capture

755 New York Ave
Ste 307
Huntington, NY 11743
Phone: (631) 547-5500
Fax: (631) 547-6800
www.datacapture.com

Global-Z International

Historic Rte 7a
Box 930
Manchester Center, VT 05255
Phone: (802) 362-5000
Fax: (802) 362-9030

Hyaid Group

6 Commercial St
Hicksville, NY 11801
Phone: (516) 433-3800
Fax: (516) 822-8028
www.thehyaidgroup.com

IntraSource

619 Palisade Ave
Englewood Cliffs, NJ 07632
Phone: (201) 837-1300
Fax: (201) 837-1515
www.intra-source.net

Merkle Direct Marketing, Inc.

8400 Corporate Dr
Lanham, MD 20785
Phone: (301) 459-9700
Fax: (301) 489-8431
www.merklenet.com

Midland Marketing

11457 Olde Cabin Rd
Ste 300
St. Louis, MO 63141
Phone: (314) 993-1888
Fax: (314) 993-2349
www.midlandmarketing.com

Peachtree Data, Inc.

1854 Shackleford Ct
Ste 450
Norcross, GA 30093
Phone: (678) 987-4600
Fax: (770) 985-5663
www.peachtreedata.com

Phoenix Data Processing, Inc.

645 Blackhawk Dr
Westmont, IL 60559
Phone: (630) 654-4400
Fax: (630) 654-4470
www.phoenixdataprocessing.com

Professional Advertising Systems, Inc.

70 Memorial Plz
Pleasantville, NY 10570
Phone: (914) 741-1100
Fax: (914) 741-2788

Pro/Phase Marketing, Inc.

6550 Edenvale Blvd
Eden Prairie, MN 55346
Phone: (952) 974-1100
Fax: (952) 974-7874
www.repeatrewards.com

Creative Consultants

Bruce W. Eberle & Associates, Inc.
1420 Spring Hill Rd
Ste 490
McLean, VA 22102
Phone: (703) 821-1550
Fax: (703) 821-0920
www.bruceeberle.com

Creative Marketing Strategies
15 E Centre St
Woodbury, NJ 08096
Phone: (856) 686-2404
Fax: (856) 853-6859
www.cmsgrp.com

Daniel Gonzalez & Associates
370 Lexington Ave
Ste 1607
New York, NY 10017
Phone: (212) 682-0333
Fax: (212) 682-9833

Harvey Associates - Direct Marketing Solutions
63 Hoover Dr
Cresskill, NJ 07626
Phone: (201) 816-1780
Fax: (201) 816-1781

Lee Marc Stein Ltd.
41 Executive Dr
Hauppauge, NY 11788
Phone: (631) 724-3765
Fax: (631) 724-6202
www.leemarcstein.com

Our Tribe Marketing
70A Greenwich Ave
Ste 380
New York, NY 10011
Phone: (212) 462-0036
Fax: (212) 462-0039
www.ourtribe.com

Pat Friesen & Company
9636 Meadow Ln
Leawood, KS 66206
Phone: (913) 341-1211
Fax: (913) 341-4343

Perlman and Perlman
220 Fifth Ave
7th Fl
New York, NY 10001
Phone: (212) 889-0575
Fax: (212) 889-5228
www.perlmanandperlman.com

Credit & Collections

Credit Index
100 Stierli Ct
Mt. Arlington, NJ 07886
Phone: (973) 770-4007
Fax: (973) 770-4006
www.tcindex.com

Innovis Data Solutions
950 Threadneedle
Ste 200
Houston, TX 77079
Phone: (281) 504 2600
Fax: (281) 504-2599
www.innovis-cbc.com

CRM Software

Business Development Solutions, Inc.
133 Gaither Dr
Ste H
Mount Laurel, NJ 08054
Phone: (856) 787-1500
Fax: (856) 787-1510
www.bdsdatabase.com

E.piphany
1900 S Norfolk St
Ste 310
San Mateo, CA 94403
Phone: (650) 356-3800
Fax: (650) 356-3908
www.epiphany.com

GSP Group, Data-Driven Marketing Resources
1343 Boswall Dr
Ste 200
Worthington, OH 43085
Phone: (614) 888-7502
Fax: (614) 885-1165

Harte-Hanks CRM Software
25 Linnell Circle
Billerica, MA 01821
Phone: (800) 456-9748
www.harte-hankscrm.com

PreVision Marketing, Inc.
55 Old Bedford Rd
Lincoln, MA 01773
Phone: (781) 259-5100
Fax: (781) 259-1548
www.previsionmarketing.com

SourceLink Software Solutions Group
10866 Wilshire Blvd
Ste 650
Los Angeles, CA 90024
Phone: (310) 234-9265
Fax: (310) 208-5681
www.sourcelinkssg.com

Database Marketing Consultants

Addressing Your Needs, Inc.
8317 Cross Park Dr
Ste 400
Austin, TX 78754
Phone: (512) 349-3100
Fax: (512) 349-3101
www.ayn.com

B2B Data Corp
12707 High Bluff Dr
San Diego, CA 92130
Phone: (858) 794-1424
Fax: (760) 754-0349

Bullseye Database Marketing, Inc.
601 S Boulder Ave
Tulsa, OK 74119
Phone: (918) 587-1731
Fax: (918) 587-0450

Business Development Solutions, Inc
133 Gaither Dr
Ste H
Mount Laurel, NJ 08054
Phone: (856) 787-1500
Fax: (856) 787-1510
www.bdsdatabase.com

Computer Strategy Coordinators, Inc.
1100 Woodfield Rd
Ste 320
Schaumburg, IL 60173
Phone: (847) 330-1313
Fax: (847) 330-9155
www.computerstrategy.com

Corry Direct Marketing, LLC
109 Limekiln Rd
Ridgefield, CT 06877
Phone: (203) 438-1478
Fax: (203) 431-0217

DataMentors, Inc.
13153 N Dale Mabry Hwy
Ste 100
Tampa, FL 33618
Phone: (813) 960-7800
Fax: (813) 960-7811
www.datamentors.com

David Shepard Associates, Inc.
2 Captain Lawrence Dr
South Salem, NY 10590
Phone: (914) 763-8125
Fax: (914) 763-8299

Decide with Confidence

Dun & Bradstreet Corporation
3 Sylvan Way
Parsippany, NJ 07054
Phone: (973) 605-6000
www.dnb.com

ESG Consulting, Inc.
1440 N Lake Shore Dr 8E
Chicago, IL 60610
Phone: (312) 664-3727

GSP Group, Data-Driven Marketing Reources
1343 Boswall Dr
Ste 200
Worthington, OH 43085
Phone: (614) 888-7502
Fax: (614) 885-1165

Harte-Hanks CRM Analytics
55 5th Ave
14th Fl
New York, NY 10003
Phone: (800) 456-9748
Fax: (212) 481-6232
www.harte-hanks.com

Insight Out of Chaos
220 E 23rd St
Ste 600
New York, NY 10010
Phone: (212) 935-0044
Fax: (212) 742-1245
www.iooc.com

Integrated Marketing Technology, Inc.
50 Osgood Pl
Ste 330
San Francisco, CA 94133
Phone: (415) 352-2370
Fax: (415) 352-2373
www.imtnetwork.com

Interactive Marketing Group
50 Commerce Dr
Allendale, NJ 07401
Phone: (201) 327-0974
Fax: (201) 327-3596
www.imgusa.com

International Data Management
490 White Pond Dr
Akron, OH 44320
Phone: (330) 869-8500
Fax: (330) 869-4027
www.idmi.com

iVOX LLC
3541 Investment Blvd
Ste 3
Hayward, CA 94545
Phone: (800) 747-8271
Fax: (510) 732-5070
www.ivoxllc.com

Kestnbaum Consulting
55 W Wacker Dr
Ste 1210
Chicago, IL 60601
Phone: (312) 782-1360
Fax: (312) 782-1362
www.kestnbaum.com

KnowledgeBase Marketing
701 N Plano Rd
Richardson, TX 75081
Phone: (866) 275-4563
www.kbm1.com

msdbm
10866 Wilshire Blvd
Ste 650
Los Angeles, CA 90024
Phone: (310) 234-9265
Fax: (310) 208-5681
www.sourcelinkssg.com

PledgeMaker
2350 N Forrest Rd
Getzville, NY 14068
Phone: (716) 636-5400
Fax: (716) 636-5401
www.pledgemaker.com

Premier Data Group
616 Corte Regalo
Camarillo, CA 93010
Phone: (805) 445-7522
Fax: (805) 445-8876
www.premierdatagroup.com

PreVision Marketing, Inc.
55 Old Bedford Rd
Lincoln, MA 01773
Phone: (781) 259-5100
Fax: (781) 259-1548
www.previsionmarketing.com

PrimeNet Marketing Services, Inc.
2250 Pilot Knob Rd
St. Paul, MN 55120
Phone: (651) 405-4057
Fax: (651) 405-4100
www.pnms.com

Research & Response International
250 W 57th St
Ste 1326
New York, NY 10107
Phone: (212) 489-8610
Fax: (212) 262-3474
www.rresp.com

Sigma Marketing
1850 Winton Rd S
Rochester, NY 14618
Phone: (716) 325-7300
Fax: (716) 473-0332
www.sigmamarketing.com

Dimensional Direct Response Packaging

Porter Direct Marketing
4181 Farquhar Ave
Los Alamitos, CA 90720
Phone: (562) 493-4676

Direct Marketing Media

Brann Worldwide
241 Danbury Rd
Wilton, CT 06897
Phone: (203) 834-6900
Fax: (203) 834-7000
www.brann.com

Budco
13700 Oakland Ave
Highland Park, MI 48203
Phone: (313) 957-5100
Fax: (313) 957-5062
www.budco.com

C.D. Direct
200 Yorkland Blvd
Ste 710
North York, ON M2J 5C1
CANADA
Phone: (416) 756-0774
Fax: (416) 756-3403
www.c-d-direct.com

Campbell Mithun
222 S 9th St
Minneapolis, MN 55402
Phone: (612) 347-1827
Fax: (612) 347-1848
www.campbellmithun.com

Carat Freeman
Two Wells Ave
Newton, MA 02459
Phone: (617) 303-3029
Fax: (617) 303-3064
www.carat-na.com

Century Direct Marketing, Inc.
7404 Hollister Ave
Goleta, CA 93117
Phone: (805) 968-2020
Fax: (805) 968-9899
www.century-direct.com

Communication Concepts, Inc.
1044 Pulinski Rd
Ivyland, PA 18974
Phone: (215) 672-6900
Fax: (215) 957-4366
www.ccgroupnet.com

Cox Direct, Inc.
8605 Largo Lakes Dr
Largo, FL 33773
Phone: (727) 393-1270
Fax: (727) 393-4968

CPS Direct, Inc.
20 Cabot Rd
Woburn, MA 01801
Phone: (781) 935-5007
Fax: (781) 933-5716
www.cpsdirect.com

CPU, Inc.
6 Penns Trail
Ste 105
Newtown, PA 18940
Phone: (800) 379-9664
Fax: (215) 497-9039
www.cou.com

Cramer

425 University Ave
Norwood, MA 02062
Phone: (781) 278-2306
Fax: (781) 255-0721
www.cramerprod.com

D-J Associates

38A Grove St
P.O. Box 2048
Ridgefield, CT 06877
Phone: (203) 431-8777
Fax: (203) 438-6422
www.djassoc.com

Havas Advertising Diversified Agencies NA

410 Park Ave
Ste 1520
New York, NY 10022
Phone: (212) 753-1410
Fax: (212) 753-1409
www.haras-advertising.com

Haynes & Partners Communication, Inc.

5745 Lee Rd
Indianapolis, IN 46216
Phone: (317) 860-3000
Fax: (317) 860-3001
www.hp-inc.com

hunt.DDBdirect

1601 2nd Ave
Seattle, WA 98101
Phone: (206) 728-6245
Fax: (206) 728-0139
www.hunt.ddbdirect.com

Iris Shokoff Associates

130 W 42nd St
Ste 801
New York, NY 10036
Phone: (212) 295-9191
Fax: (212) 293-3779
www.irisshokoff.com

iWon.com

One Bridge St
Irvington, NY 10533
Phone: (914) 591-2000
Fax: (914) 591-0205
www.iwon.com

Kern Direct Marketing

20300 Ventura Blvd
Ste 210
Woodland Hills, CA 91364
Phone: (818) 703-8775
Fax: (818) 703-8458
www.kerndirect.com

Lieber, Levett, Koenig, Farese, Babcock

299 W Houston St
New York, NY 10014
Phone: (212) 206-5800
Fax: (212) 206-5801
www.llkfb.com

LinkShare Corporation

215 Park Avenue S
New York, NY 10003
Phone: (646) 654-6000
Fax: (646) 602-0160
www.linkshare.com

Marketing Services
For An Integrated World

Online, Offline, at Home, at Work...Smart Marketers
Reach Their Audiences Where Buying Decisions Are Made.

Today's audiences move faster, demand more and have greater access to information than ever before. Because of this, marketers must work harder to find cost effective solutions to acquiring new customers.

VentureDirect offers direct response integrated marketing solutions for cost-effective customer acquisition.

Print Media - Recruitment & Direct Response print advertisements in premiere publications including Fortune, Inc., Business 2.0, PC World, Sports Illustrated's Golf Plus, Entrepreneur, etc.

Online Media Services - Consumer and business-to-business lead generation and customer acquisition programs using an array of targeted online marketing techniques.

Email List Services - Email marketing, with the exclusive opt-in email lists of the XactMail Network. Email list owners can also take advantage of our superior email list management services.

Direct Mail Services - Our postal List Management & List Brokerage services ensure unparalleled rental revenue for list owners, and efficient campaigns for direct marketers.

Cooperative Direct Mail - Low cost, high return advertising in Card Pacs stretches your marketing dollars without compromising results.

For over twenty years, VentureDirect has offered a wide variety of direct response media, consistently meeting clients' demands for profitable lead generation, subscription, registration, membership and customer acquisition. By targeting hard-to-find business and consumer audiences, and generating exceptional response rates, we deliver true return on advertising investment.

Call a VentureDirect Worldwide Integrated Media Specialist today at 212.684.4800, email sales@ven.com, or visit www.venturedirect.com for a consultation.

An industry leader with twenty years of direct marketing experience.

VentureDirect Worldwide 60 Madison Avenue New York, NY 10010   Reference Code: LG2002

List Media, Inc.
251 W Garfield Rd
Ste 262
Aurora, OH 44202
Phone: (330) 995-0864
Fax: (330) 995-0873
www.dm1.com

Orlando Sentinel Communications
633 N Orange Ave
MP 312
Orlando, FL 32801
Phone: (407) 420-5790
Fax: (407) 420-5758
www.orlandosentinel.com

Paragon Direct Marketing, LLC
140 Shady Ln
Ste 3F
Randolph, NJ 07869
Phone: (973) 895-9900
Fax: (973) 895-9088
www.paragondirect.com

Presentation Packaging
870 Louisiana Ave S
Minneapolis, MN 55426
Phone: (763) 540-9615
Fax: (763) 540-9522
www.presentationpackaging.com

Price/McNabb
100 N Tryon St
Ste 2800
Charlotte, NC 28202
Phone: (704) 375-0123
Fax: (704) 375-0222
www.pricemcnabb.com

Production Management Group
7240 Parkway Dr
Ste 170
Hanover, MD 21076
Phone: (703) 218-0738
Fax: (703) 218-0749
www.dm1stop.com

Rauxa Direct
3020 Old Ranch Pkwy
Ste 250
Seal Beach, CA 90740
Phone: (562) 493-6890
Fax: (562) 493-6591
www.rauxa.com

VentureDirect Worldwide
60 Madison Ave
New York, NY 10010
Phone: (212) 684-4800
Fax: (212) 576-1129
www.venturedirect.com

Direct Response Communications

Gift Certificates.com
470 7th Ave
New York, NY 10018
Phone: (212) 465-2112
Fax: (212) 465-1965
www.giftcertificates.com

Grantastic Designs

180 S Western Ave
Ste 274
Carpentersville, IL 60110
Phone: (847) 426-8815
Fax: (847) 426-1507
www.grantasticdesigns.com

Intrapromote

2054 Kemppel
STE 100
Stow, OH 44224
Phone: (330) 650-5370
Fax: (630) 604-7656
www.intrapromote.com

Mypoints.com Inc

100 California St
12th Fl
San Francisco, CA 94111
Phone: (415) 676-3700
Fax: (415) 676-3720
www.mypoints.com

Ripple Marketing

P.O. Box 10221
Bozeman, MT 59718
Phone: (406) 585-8168
Fax: (406) 585-0047
www.ripplemarketing.com

The Sutherland Group

1160 Pittsford/Victor Rd
Pittsford, NY 14534
Phone: (716) 586-5757
www.thesutherlandgroupinc.com

Zenhits

Phone: (631) 206-5453
www.zenhits.com

Envelope Manufacturers and Distributors

Commercial Envelope Manufacturers, Inc.

900 Grand Blvd
Deer Park, NY 11729
Phone: (631) 242-2500
Fax: (631) 242-6122

Continental Envelope Corp.

1700 Averill Rd
Geneva, IL 60134
Phone: (630) 262-8080
Fax: (630) 262-1450
www.convelope.com

Husky Envelope Products

P.O. Box 868
Walled Lake, MI 48390
Phone: (248) 624-7070
Fax: (248) 624-5990
www.huskyenvelope.com

Executive Search Firms

Andrew Yoelin & Company

5524 East Waltann Ln
Ste 1079
Scottsdale, AZ 85254
Phone: (602) 482-6214
Fax: (602) 992-0398

The Beam Group
11 Penn Center Plz
Ste 502
Philadelphia, PA 19103
Phone: (215) 288-2100
Fax: (215) 988-1558
www.beamgroup.com

Bert Davis Publishing Placement
425 Madison Ave
14th Fl
New York, NY 10017
Phone: (212) 838-4000
Fax: (212) 935-3291
www.bertdavis.com

Bristol Associates, Inc.
5757 W Century Blvd
Ste 628
Los Angeles, CA 90045
Phone: (310) 670-0525
Fax: (310) 670-4075
www.bristolassoc.com

Carpenter Associates, Inc.
322 S Green St
Ste 408
Chicago, IL 60607
Phone: (312) 243-1000
Fax: (312) 243-1875

Columbia Consulting Group
767 Third Ave
29th Fl
New York, NY 10017
Phone: (212) 832-2525
Fax: (212) 832-7722
www.ccgsearch.com

Crandall Associates, Inc.
114 E 32nd St
New York, NY 10016
Phone: (212) 213-1700
Fax: (212) 696-1287
www.crandallassociates.com

Direct Marketing Resources, Inc.
P.O. Box 15353
Charlotte, NC 28211
Phone: (704) 365-5890
Fax: (704) 365-5892
www.dmresources.com

Direction Management Group
980 N Michigan Ave
Ste 1700
Chicago, IL 60611
Phone: (312) 397-0101
Fax: (312) 397-1040
www.dmgusa.com

DM Network
342 Madison Ave
Ste 926
New York, NY 10173
Phone: (212) 490-5959
Fax: (212) 697-0962

Executive Solutions
P.O. Box 1133
Cairo, NY 12413
Phone: (518) 622-4016
Fax: (518) 622-4017
www.exsolutions.com

Gundersen Partners, LLC
30 Irving Pl
2nd Fl
New York, NY 10003
Phone: (212) 677-7660
Fax: (212) 358-0275
www.gpllc.com

J.M. Generao & Associates
88 Kinderhook St
Chatham, NY 12037
Phone: (518) 392-7227
Fax: (518) 392-7742

Karen Tripi Associates
305 Madison Ave
Ste 2140
New York, NY 10017
Phone: (212) 972-5258
Fax: (212) 599-3809
www.karentripi.com

Kenzer Corporation, Inc.
777 3rd Ave
26th Fl
New York, NY 10017
Phone: (212) 308-4300
Fax: (212) 308-1842
www.kenzer.com

Kole & Company
11973 N 114th Way
Scottsdale, AZ 85259
Phone: (480) 391-9898
Fax: (480) 391-1011

LeadersOnline
18401 Von Karman
Ste 500
Irvine, CA 92612
Phone: (949) 752-1000
Fax: (949) 752-1085
www.leadersonline.com

Madison Executive Search
54 Danbury Rd
Ste 368
Ridgefield, CT 06877
Phone: (203) 431-6565
Fax: (203) 431-6060
www.directexec.com

Ken Malek Associates, Inc.
P.O. Box 383
Yardley, PA 19067
Phone: (215) 579-2070
Fax: (215) 860-3498
www.kenmalek.com

Mangieri Solutions LLC
One Riverside Rd
Sandy Hook, CT 06482
Phone: (203) 270-4800
Fax: (203) 270-4815
www.mangierisolutions.com

Media Recruiting Group, Inc.
1 Bridge St
Ste P-2
Irvington, NY 10533
Phone: (914) 591-5511
Fax: (914) 591-8911
www.mediarecruitinggroup.com

MLB Associates
110 Main St
Ste 301
Lake Placid, NY 12946
Phone: (518) 523-2371
Fax: (518) 523-9011
www.mlbassociates.com

1 to 1 Executive Search
20 Glover Ave
Norwalk, CT 06850
Phone: (203) 642-1403
Fax: (203) 642-1401

Peter N. Carey & Associates, Inc.
1010 Jorie Blvd
Ste 400
Oak Brook, IL 60523
Phone: (630) 573-4260
Fax: (630) 573-0529

Ray & Berndtson
301 Commerce St
Ste 2300
Fort Worth, TX 76102
Phone: (817) 334-0500
Fax: (817) 334-0779
www.rayberndtson.com

The Resource Group
705 Boston Post Rd
Guilford, CT 06437
Phone: (203) 453-7070
Fax: (203) 453-7580
www.eresourcegrp.com

Ridenour & Associates
1555 N Sandburg Terrace
Ste 602
Chicago, IL 60610
Phone: (312) 787-8228
Fax: (312) 787-8528
www.ridenourassociates.com

Robin Portnoy & Company
156 Fifth Ave
Ste 800
New York, NY 10010
Phone: (212) 242-2772
Fax: (212) 691-7889
robinportnoyandcompany.com

Smith Hanley Associates
107 John St
2nd Fl
Southport, CT 06490
Phone: (203) 319-4300
Fax: (203) 319-4320
www.smithhanley.com

SpencerStuart
401 N Michigan Ave
Ste 401
Chicago, IL 60611
Phone: (312) 822-0080
Fax: (312) 822-0116
www.spencerstuart.com

Stephen-Bradford Search
1140 Avenue of the Americas
10th Fl
New York, NY 10036
Phone: (212) 221-6333
Fax: (212) 391-7826
www.stephenbradford.com

Tesar Reynes, Inc.
500 N Michigan Ave
Ste 1400
Chicago, IL 60611
Phone: (312) 661-0700
Fax: (312) 661-1598
www.tesar-reynes.com

TradeLion.com
4728 E Michigan St
Ste 6
Orlando, FL 32812
Phone: (407) 382-3163
Fax: (407) 382-3162
www.tradelion.com

Victoria James Executive Search, Inc.
1177 Summer St
Stamford, CT 06905
Phone: (540) 657-8885
Fax: (540) 657-6083
www.victoriajames.com

Wright-Nelson Enterprises
111 North Ave
Barrington, IL 60010
Phone: (847) 304-0293
Fax: (847) 304-0296

Fulfillment Services

Access Canada Direct
328 Guelph St
Georgetown, ON L7G 4B5
CANADA
Phone: (905) 877-5163
Fax: (905) 877-2862

AIM Marketing
525 N "D" St
P.O. Box 129
Fremont, NE 68025
Phone: (402) 721-2077
Fax: (402) 721-9171
www.solution-group.com

Ambrosi
1100 W Washington Blvd
Chicago, IL 60477
Phone: (312) 666-9200
Fax: (312) 666-8660
www.ambrosi.com

American Industries,Inc.
800 Granada Ave
Nashville, TN 37206
Phone: (800) 695-2153
Fax: (615) 227-9041

APL Direct Logistics
1301 River Place Blvd
Jacksonville, FL 32207
Phone: (904) 858-4405
Fax: (904) 396-3984
www.apldirectlogistics.co

Arnold Logistics
4410 Industrial Park Rd
Camp Hill, PA 17011
Phone: (717) 731-4374
Fax: (717) 761-6688
www.arnoldlogistics.com

Arrowmail Canada
1415 Janette Ave
Windsor, ON N8X 1Z1
CANADA
Phone: (313) 961-8334
Fax: (313) 961-7849
www.mailingcanada.com

Artisan Creative
1950 Sawtelle Blvd
Los Angeles, CA 90025
Phone: (818) 947-4709
Fax: (818) 947-0317
www.artisancreative.com

Berlin Industries
175 Mercedes Dr
Carol Stream, IL 60188
Phone: (630) 682-0600
Fax: (630) 682-3093
www.berlinindustries.com

Bradley Direct
7100 Jamesson Rd
Midland, GA 31820
Phone: (706) 565-2100
Fax: (706) 565-2132
www.bradleydirect.com

Buffkin Associates, LLC
424 Church St
Ste 2925
Nashville, TN 37219
Phone: (615) 742-8491
Fax: (615) 742-8470
www.buffkinassociates.com

CanadaPlus.com
2001 Huron Church Rd
Windsor, ON N9C2L
CANADA
Phone: (519) 966-3003
Fax: (519) 966-1363
www.CanadaPlus.com

Catalogs by Lorel
780 Fifth Ave
King of Prussia, PA 19406
Phone: (610) 337-9133
Fax: (610) 768-9511
www.lorel.com

Direct Marketing Research Associates
4151 Middlefield Rd
Ste 200
Palo Alto, CA 94303
Phone: (650) 856-9988
Fax: (650) 856-9192
www.dmrainc.com

Direct Marketing Resources, Inc.
P.O. Box 15353
Charlotte, NC 28211
Phone: (704) 365-5892
Fax: (704) 365-5890
www.dmresources.com

Dydacomp
11-D Commerce Way
Totowa, NJ 07512
Phone: (973) 237-9415
Fax: (973) 237-9043
www.dydacomp.com

EZ Fulfillment
333 Beicht St
Beaver Dam, WI 53916
Phone: (920) 887-0391
Fax: (920) 887-9506
www.nnexfulfillment.com

Fulfillment Concepts Inc.
2200 Ampere Dr
Louisville, KY 40269
Phone: (502) 266-5555
Fax: (502) 214-4382
www.fulfillmentconcepts.com

Fulfillment Technologies
5389 E Provident Dr
Cincinnati, OH 45246
Phone: (513) 346-3100
Fax: (513) 346-3103
www.filltek.com

Hartford Direct Marketing
129 Worthington Ridge
Berlin, CT 06037
Phone: (860) 829-2121
Fax: (860) 829-2242
www.hartforddirect.com

Holden Direct Marketing Group

4900 Augusta Dr
Ft Worth, TX 76106
Phone: (817) 429-9393
Fax: (817) 429-9472
www.holdendirect.com

The Howard-Sloan-Koller Group

300 E 42nd St
Ste 1500
New York, NY 10017
Phone: (212) 661-5250
Fax: (212) 557-9178
www.hsksearch.com

Innotrac Corporation

6655 Sugarloaf Pkwy
Duluth, GA 30097
Phone: (678) 584-4025
Fax: (678) 475-5875
www.innotrac.com

Intelligent Marketing Solutions

200 Park Ave S
Ste 518
New York, NY 10003
Phone: (212) 420-9777
Fax: (212) 420-9799
www.marketingmatchmaker.com

iVOX LLC

3541 Investment Blvd
Ste 3
Hayward, CA 94545
Phone: (800) 747-8271
Fax: (510) 732-5070
www.ivoxllc.com

J. Robert Scott

255 State St
Boston, MA 02109
Phone: (617) 563-2770
Fax: (617) 723-1282
www.j-robert-scott.com

KD Mailing & Fulfillment Service

6159 W Dickens Ave
Chicago, IL 60639
Phone: (773) 889-6245
Fax: (773) 889-6246
www.kdmailing.com

Lamay Associates

P.O. Box 517
Riverside, CT 06878
Phone: (203) 256-3593
Fax: (203) 256-3594
www.lamayassociates.com

Noble Sander Search
535 Sixteenth St
Ste 620
Denver, CO 80202
Phone: (303) 825-3646
Fax: (303) 629-6056

Palm Coast Data Inc.
11 Commerce Blvd
Palm Coast, FL 32164
Phone: (386) 445-4662
Fax: (386) 445-2728
www.palmcoastd.com

Programmers Investment Corp.
125 Armstrong Rd
Des Plaines, IL 60018
Phone: (847) 299-2300
Fax: (847) 299-8286
www.pic-online.com

Promac, Inc.
38 S Grove Ave
Elgin, IL 60120
Phone: (847) 695-8181
Fax: (847) 468-0423
www.promac.com

Publishing Fulfillment Services
85 Settlers Hill Rd
Brewster, NY 10509
Phone: (845) 278 2800

Quest Management
19834 FM 2252
Ste 103
Garden Ridge, TX 78266
Phone: (210) 946-6000
Fax: (210) 946-7000

Reliance Distribution Corp.
10 Old Bloomfield Ave
P.O. Box 392
Pine Brook, NJ 07058
Phone: (973) 808-1746
Fax: (973) 808-1988
www.reliancedc.com

Robsham and Associates
4 S Market St
4th Fl
Boston, MA 02109
Phone: (617) 742-2944
Fax: (617) 523-0464
www.robshamgroup.com

Slayton International, Inc.
181 W Madison St
Ste 4510
Chicago, IL 60602
Phone: (312) 56-0080
Fax: (312) 456-0089
www.slaytonintl.com

TotalWorks, Inc.
2222 N Elston Ave
Chicago, IL 60614
Phone: (773) 489-4313
Fax: (773) 489-0482
www.totalworks.net

Versient
10231 Plano Rd
Dallas, TX 75238
Phone: (214) 553-8791
Fax: (214) 348-1726
www.versient.com

The Waters Group LLC
135 Rowayton Ave
P.O. Box 203
Rowayton, CT 06853
Phone: (203) 855-1700
Fax: (203) 855-0900
www.thewatersgroup.com

Wheelless Bennett Group Ltd.
227 W Monroe St
19th Fl
Chicago, IL 60606
Phone: (312) 596-8388
Fax: (312) 596-8801
www.wheelless.com

Fund Raising Consultants

Amergent, Inc.
9 Centennial Dr
Peabody, MA 01960
Phone: (978) 531-1800
Fax: (978) 531-0400
www.amergent.com

Inquiry and Lead Generation

Ad-Venture Network
60 Madison Ave
New York, NY 10010
Phone: (212) 655-5280

iBusinesses.com, LLC
106 Park
Covington, LA 70433
Phone: (985) 898 0400
Fax: (504) 727-5575
www.ibusinesses.com

VentureDirect Worldwide
60 Madison Ave
New York, NY 10010
Phone: (212) 684-4800
Fax: (212) 576-1129
www.venturedirect.com

International Marketing Services

Arrowmail Canada
1415 Janette Ave
Windsor, ON N8X 1Z1
CANADA
Phone: (313) 961-8334
Fax: (313) 961-7849
www.mailingcanada.com

Internet Marketing

B2BMarketingBiz.com
Marketing Sherpa, Inc.
1791 Lanier Pl NW
Ste 5
Washinton, D.C. 20009
Phone: (202) 232-6830
www.B2Bmarketingbiz.com

B2B Web Marketing Solutions
25047 Avenida Balli
Valencia, CA 91355
Phone: (661) 799-9911
Fax: (661) 799-9922
www.b2bwebmarketingsolutions.com

B2BWorks
230 W Superior
7th Fl
Chicago, IL 60610
Phone: (312) 923-7604
Fax: (312) 923-7626
www.b2bworks.com

Commission Junction
1501 Chapala St
Santa Barbara, CA 93101
Phone: (805) 560-0777
Fax: (805) 560-6678
www.cj.com

Directech | eMerge
One Van de Graaf Dr
Burlington, MA 01803
Phone: (781) 993-9222
Fax: (781) 933-9117
www.directech.com

Interactive Marketing Group
50 Commerce Dr
Allendale, NJ 17401
Phone: (201) 327-0974
Fax: (201) 327-3596
www.imgusa.com

Lieber, Levett, Koenig, Farese, Babcock
299 W Houston St
New York, NY 10014
Phone: (212) 206-5800
Fax: (212) 206-5801
www.llkfb.com

Performics
180 N Lasalle St
Ste 1100
Chicago, IL 60601
Phone: (312) 739-0222
Fax: (312) 739-0223
www.performics.com

QuinStreet, Inc.
2750 El Camino Real
Redwood City, CA 94061
Phone: (650) 474-4004
Fax: (650) 368-3553
www.quinstreet.com

Respond.com, Inc.
3290 W Bayshore Rd
Palo Alto, CA 94303
Phone: (650) 461-1100
Fax: (650) 461-1900
www.respond.com

Wunderman
675 Avenue of the Americas
4th Fl
New York, NY 10010
Phone: (212) 941-3000
Fax: (212) 627-8521
www.wunderman.com

Internet Services

CheetahMail
29 Broadway
30th Fl
New York, NY 10006
Phone: (212) 809-0825
Fax: (212) 809-6378
www.cheetahmail.com

iMatcher
Phone: (800) 633-9729
Fax: (800) 633-3292
www.imatcher.org

iPlace.com
444 Oxford Valley Rd
Langhorne, PA 19047
Phone: (267) 580-3100
Fax: (267) 580-3200
www.iplace.com

MarketFirst
2061 Stierlin Ct
Mountain View, CA 94043
Phone: (650) 691-6200
Fax: (650) 254-1287
www.marketfirst.com

MarketsOnDemand
541 N Fairbanks Ct
Ste 2800
Chicago, IL 60610
Phone: (312) 670-8000
Fax: (312) 670-8008
www.marketsondemand.net

Overture
140 W Union St
Pasadena, CA 91104
www.overture.com

Promotions.com
450 W 33rd St
New York, NY 10016
Phone: (212) 244-7173
Fax: (212) 279-3150
www.promotions.com

yesmail.com
222 S Riverside Plz
17th Fl
Chicago, IL 60606
Phone: (312) 423-5000
Fax: (312) 423-5010
www.yesmail.com

Lead Handling Services

AdTrack
9057 Simms View Ct
Loveland, OH 45140
Phone: (800) 735-3237
www.adtrack.com

CompuSystems
2805 25th Ave
Broadview, IL 60153
Phone: (708) 344-9070
Fax: (708) 344-9487
www.compusystems.com

Data Services Direct
3 Century Dr
3rd Fl
Parsippany, NJ 07054
Phone: (973) 285-1700
Fax: (973) 285-9246

DirectSynergy
16542 Venutra Blvd
Ste 305
Los Angeles, CA 91436
Phone: (818) 728-1478
Fax: (818) 728-1582
www.directsynergy.com

iVOX LLC
3541 Investment Blvd
Ste 3
Hayward, CA 94545
Phone: (800) 747-8271
Fax: (510) 732-5070
www.ivoxllc.com

TECHMAR
250 Turnpike St
Canton, MA 02021
Phone: (617) 821-8324
Fax: (617) 821-9198
www.techmar.com

Lead Tracking & Management Software

ChannelWave
One Kendall Sq
Ste 200
Cambridge, MA 02139
Phone: (617) 621-1700
Fax: (617) 621-1010
www.channelwave.com

deuxo
1621 18th St
Ste 150
Denver, CO 80202
Phone: (303) 382-1245
Fax: (303) 292-2352
www.deuxo.xom

Epicor Software Corporation
195 Technology Dr
Irvine, CA 92618
Phone: (945) 585-4000
Fax: (945) 450-4494
www.epicor.com

Webridge
1925 NW Amberglen Pk
Beaverton, WA 97006
Phone: (503) 601-4000
Fax: (503) 601-4001
www.webridge.com

Lettershops and Mailing Services

Advanced Casino Systems Corporation
200 Decadon Dr
Ste 100
Egg Harbor Township, NJ 08234
Phone: (609) 407-7440
Fax: (609) 407-2473
www.acsc-sms.com

Advertising Distributors of America, Inc.
230 Adams Ave
Hauppauge, NY 11788
Phone: (516) 231-5700
Fax: (516) 434-1063
www.advdistofam.com

Alaniz, LLC
425 North Iris St
P.O. Box 799
Mt. Pleasant, IA 52641
Phone: (319) 385-7259
Fax: (319) 385-2825
www.alanizsons.com

American Mail Union
420 Lexington Ave
Ste 502
New York, NY 10170
Phone: (212) 388-8826
Fax: (212) 388-8890

American Mailers / aNETorder
820 Frontenac Rd
Naperville, IL 60563
Phone: (630) 579-8800
Fax: (630) 579-8888
www.anetorder.com

AmeriComm Direct Marketing, Inc.
494 St. Paul's Blvd
Norfolk, VA 23510
Phone: (804) 622-2724
Fax: (804) 624-5713
www.americomm.net

Brokers Worldwide, Inc.
701 Ashland Ave
Folcroft, PA 19032
Phone: (610) 461-3661
Fax: (610) 461-4239
www.brokersworldwide.com

Calloway House, Inc.
451 Richardson Dr
Lancaster, PA 17603
Phone: (717) 299-5703
Fax: (717) 299-6754
www.callowayhouse.com

Chicago Tribune: Tribune Direct
505 Northwest Ave
Chicago, IL 60164
Phone: (708) 836-2712
Fax: (708) 836-0605

Chin Super Enterprise
1400 N American St
Philadelphia, PA 19122
Phone: (215) 765-4610
Fax: (215) 765-4637

Colorfx Marketing Services
5085 NE 17th St
Des Moines, IA 50313
Phone: (515) 270-3838
Fax: (515) 270-3837
www.colorfxmarketing.com

Connextions.net
3601 Mercy Dr
Orlando, FL 32808
Phone: (407) 926-2411
Fax: (407) 926-2402
www.connextions.net

Corporate Communications Group
14 Henderson Dr
West Caldwell, NJ 07006
Phone: (973) 808-0009
Fax: (973) 808-2762
www.corpcomm.com

Data-Mail, Inc.
240 Hartford Ave
Newington, CT 06111
Phone: (860) 666-0399
Fax: (860) 665-1226
www.data-mail.com

DIMAC Marketing Partners
200 Day Hill Rd
Windsor, CT 06095
Phone: (480) 346-1444
Fax: (480) 346-1445
www.DIMAC.com

Direct Mail Depot, Inc.
200 Circle Dr N
Piscataway, NJ 08854
Phone: (732) 469-5900
Fax: (732) 469-8414
www.directmaildepot.com

Diversified Direct
1301 Burton St
Fullerton, CA 92831
Phone: (714) 776-4520
Fax: (714) 776-2590
www.diversified-direct.com

DM Group
8903 Presidential Pkwy
Ste 201
Upper Marlboro, MD 20772
Phone: (301) 855-9808
Fax: (301) 420-5616
www.dmgroup.com

DMM, Inc.
40 Manson Libby Rd
P.O. Box 10
Scarborough, ME 04070
Phone: (207) 883-6930
Fax: (207) 883-2160
www.direct2market.com

DMW
45 Braintree Hill Office Park
Braintree, MA 02184
Phone: (781) 356-3216
Fax: (781) 356-3299
www.dmw-w.com

EU Services
649 N Horners Ln
Rockville, MD 20850
Phone: (301) 424-3300
Fax: (301) 424-3696
www.euservices.com

Excalibur Enterprises, Inc.
P.O. Box 7372
Winston-Salem, NC 27109
Phone: (336) 744-5000
Fax: (336) 767-8257
www.excaliburmail.com

Express Messenger International
121 5th Ave, NW
New Brighton, MN 55112
Phone: (651) 634-0441
Fax: (651) 636-5559

FALA Direct Marketing
70 Marcus Dr
Melville, NY 11747
Phone: (631) 391-0602
Fax: (631) 391-0680

Federal Direct
95 Main Ave
Clifton, NJ 07014
Phone: (973) 667-9800
Fax: (973) 667-0228
www.feddirect.com

Fulfillment Xcellence
5235 Thatcher Rd
Downers Grove, IL 60515
Phone: (630) 852-7600
Fax: (630) 852-6060
www.fx-inc.com

FYI Direct
1211 E Artesia Blvd
Carson, CA 90746
Phone: (310) 637-7100
Fax: (310) 637-7747
www.fyidirectla.com

Gage Lettershop/ Personalization Services
401 13th Ave N
Howard Lake, MN 55349
Phone: (320) 543-3737
Fax: (320) 543-3228

Genesis Direct
391 Roberts Rd
Oldsmar, FL 34677
Phone: (813) 855-4274
Fax: (813) 855-0969
www.gendirect.net

Graphic Innovations
101 Wordsworth Ln
North Wales, PA 19454
Phone: (215) 361-6001
Fax: (215) 361-5725
www.graphin.com

Grizzard
229 Peachtree St
Ste 900
Atlanta, GA 30303
Phone: (404) 935-7133
www.grizzard.com

Hartford Direct Marketing
129 Worthington Ridge
Berlin, CT 06037
Phone: (860) 829-2121
Fax: (860) 829-2242
www.hartforddirect.com

Holden Direct Marketing Group
4900 Augusta Dr
Ft Worth, TX 76106
Phone: (817) 429-9393
Fax: (817) 429-9472
www.holdendirect.com

Huntsinger & Jeffer, Inc.
809 Brook Hill Circle
Richmond, VA 23227
Phone: (804) 266-2499
Fax: (804) 266-8563
www.huntsinger-jeffer.com

Impact Mailing & Fulfillment
4600 Lyndale Ave N
Minneapolis, MN 55412
Phone: (612) 521-6245
Fax: (612) 521-1349
www.impactmail.com

Integrated Mail Industries
3450 W Hopkins St
Milwaukee, WI 53216
Phone: (414) 908-3533
Fax: (414) 449-2906
www.abdata.com

InteliMail
14601 W 99th St
Lenexa, KS 66215
Phone: (913) 310-4354
Fax: (913) 599-3912

International Business Systems
431 Yerkes Rd
King of Prussia, PA 19406
Phone: (610) 265-8210
Fax: (610) 265-7997
www.ibs4cmyk.com

International Direct Response Services
10159 Nordel Ct
Ste 4
Delta, BC V4G 1J8
CANADA
Phone: (604) 951-6855
Fax: (604) 951-6756

International Mailing Solutions, LLC
9 Arrow Dr
Woburn, MA 01801
Phone: (781) 376-5000
Fax: (781) 376-5001
www.mailims.com

JDM - Jetson Direct Mail Services, Inc.
100 Industrial Dr
Hamburg, PA 19526
Phone: (610) 562-1000
Fax: (610) 562-9701
www.jetson.com

Johnson & Hayward, Inc.
500 Rte 46 E at Trenton Ave
Clifton, NJ 07011
Phone: (973) 253-2323
Fax: (973) 253-2313
www.jhinc.com

Johnson & Quin, Inc.
7460 N Lehigh Ave
Niles, IL 60714
Phone: (847) 588-4800
Fax: (847) 647-6949
www.j-quin.com

Key Mail Canada Inc.
2756 Slough St
Mississauga, ON L4T 2G3
CANADA
Phone: (905) 677-1692
Fax: (905) 677-8086
www.key-mail.com

Lason
88 Long Hill St
East Hartford, CT 06108
Phone: (860) 290-6655
Fax: (860) 290-6661
www.lason.com

Lazarus Marketing
3530 Oceanside Rd
Oceanside, NY 11572
Phone: (516) 678-5107
Fax: (516) 766-3160

LCS Direct Mail Advertising & Printing
3590 NW 54th St #9
Ft Lauderdale, FL 33309
Phone: (954) 733-8105
Fax: (954) 733-8108
www.lcsdirect.com

Letter Shop S.A. de C.V.
Destajistas No 3
Col. Industrial Xhal
Cuautitlan Izcalli, MEXICO
54714
Phone: (525) 872-6512
Fax: (525) 872-3849

Mail Communications, Inc.
721 Olive St
Ste 1200
Saint Louis, MO 63101
Phone: (314) 241-5408
Fax: (314) 241-6125

Mailing Services of Pittsburgh
155 Commerce Dr
Freedom, PA 15042
Phone: (724) 774-3244
Fax: (724) 774-6996
www.msp-pgh.com

MailMarketing Corporation
4075 Gordon Baker Rd
Scarborough, ON M1W 2P4
CANADA
Phone: (416) 490-8030
Fax: (416) 490-8455
www.mailmarketing.com

Mid-America Mailers, Inc.
430 Russell St
P.O. Box 646
Hammond, IN 46325
Phone: (219) 933-0137
Fax: (219) 933-3525
www.midam-mail.com

Mystic Transport Services, Inc.
2187 New London Tpk
South Glastonbury, CT 06073
Phone: (800) 969-1566
Fax: (860) 659-1420
www.mystictransport.com

NCP Solutions
5200 E Lake Blvd
Birmingham, AL 35217
Phone: (205) 421-7004
Fax: (205) 421-7178
www.ncpsolutions.com

North Shore Agency, Inc.
751 Summa Ave
Westbury, NY 11590
Phone: (516) 370-9300
Fax: (516) 370-6510
www.northshoreagency.com

OCT Group
537 Newport Center Dr
Ste 309
Newport Beach, CA 92660
Phone: (949) 707-4509
Fax: (949) 707-4502

OPENFIRST- MidAtlantic
4333 Davenport Rd
Fredericksburg, VA 22401
Phone: (800) 336-3674
Fax: (540) 898-2612
www.openfirst.com

PostLinx Corp.
1100 Birchmount Rd
Scarborough, ON M1K 5H9
CANADA
Phone: (416) 752-8100
Fax: (416) 752-8239
www.postlinx.com

Precision Direct
68 Fairbanks
Irvine, CA 92618
Phone: (949) 470-4600
Fax: (949) 470-4602
www.pdirect.com

Prism Data Services Ltd.
1-435 Horner Ave
Etobicoke, ON M8W 4W3
CANADA
Phone: (416) 255-5556
Fax: (416) 255-1466
www.prism-data.com

Pro/Phase Marketing, Inc.
6550 Edenvale Blvd
Eden Prairie, MN 55346
Phone: (952) 974-1100
Fax: (952) 974-7874
www.repeatrewards.com

Rees Associates, Inc.
P.O. Box 831
Des Moines, IA 50304
Phone: (515) 243-2127
Fax: (515) 243-1026
www.reesassociates.com

REO Direct, Inc.
11601 S Central Ave
Alsip, IL 60803
Phone: (708) 686-3240
Fax: (708) 489-0516

Responsys.com
2225 E Bayshore Rd
Palo Alto, CA 94303
Phone: (800) 624-5356
Fax: (650) 565-8174
www.responsys.com

Royal Mail US Inc.
10 E 34th St
7th Fl
New York, NY 10016
Phone: (212) 725-5460
Fax: (212) 252-9950
www.royalmailus.com

SMR/Tytrek
201 Carlaw Ave
Ste 200
Toronto, ON M4M 2S3
CANADA
Phone: (416) 461-9271
Fax: (416) 461-9201
www.smrtytrek.com

Source Corporation
1211 Artesia Blvd
Carson, CA 90746
Phone: (310) 637-7100

SpeedGreetings
5272 River Rd
Bethesda, MD 20816
Phone: (240) 333-2211
Fax: (240) 333-2209
www.speedgreetings.com

Team Services
1047 Ardmore Ave
Itasca, IL 60143
Phone: (630) 227-3102
Fax: (630) 775-1570

Teraco, Inc.
2080 Commerce Dr
Midland, TX 79703
Phone: (915) 694-6941
Fax: (915) 697-0826
www.teraco.com

TNT International Mail
200 Garden City Plz
4th Fl
Garden City, NY 11530
Phone: (516) 535-5804
Fax: (516) 535-1383
www.tnt.com

Tucker Mailing and Distrtibution
3500 McCall Pl
Atlanta, GA 30340
Phone: (770) 454-1580
Fax: (770) 454-1592

U.S.A. Direct, Inc.
2901 Blackbridge Rd
York, PA 17402
Phone: (717) 852-1000
Fax: (717) 852-1030
www.usamailnow.com

Vestcom
5 Henderson Dr
West Caldwell, NJ 07006
Phone: (973) 882-7000
Fax: (973) 882-9523
www.vestcom.com

Watts Direct Marketing Services Ltd.
455 Horner Ave
Toronto, ON M8W 4W9
CANADA
Phone: (416) 252-7741
Fax: (416) 252-0037
www.wattsgroup.com

Webtrend Direct
1811 Riverview Dr
San Bernardino, CA 92408
Phone: (909) 799-5435
Fax: (909) 799-5449
www.webtrend.com

List Brokers & Compilers

A. Caldwell List Company
4350 Georgetown Sq
Ste 701
Atlanta, GA 30338
Phone: (800) 241-7425
Fax: (770) 458-4245
www.caldwell-list.com

AccuData America
1625 Cape Coral Pkwy
Cape Coral, FL 33904
Phone: (800) 732-3440
Fax: (941) 540-5372
www.accudata.com

Aldata
7000 W 151st St
Apple Valley, MN 55124
Phone: (952) 432-6900
Fax: (952) 432-7064
www.aldata.com

AllMedia, Inc.
17060 Dallas Pkwy
Ste 105
Dallas, TX 75248
Phone: (972) 818-4060
Fax: (972) 818-4061
www.allmedia.com

AZ Bertelsmann Direct GmbH
Carl-Bertelsmann Rd 161s
D-33311 Guetersloh
GERMANY
Phone: (0 52 41) 80-54 38
Fax: (0 52 41) 80-66 962
www.az.bertelsmann.de

Burnett Direct, Inc.
31700 W Thirteen Mile Rd
Ste 101
Farmington Hills, MI 48334
Phone: (248) 932-7100
Fax: (248) 932-7107

BDS BUSINESS DEVELOPMENT SOLUTIONS, INC.

139 Gaither Drive, Suite H
Mount Laurel, NJ 08054

Phone: **856.787.1500**
Fax: **856.787.1510**
E-mail: **clientservices@bdsdatabase.com**
Web: **www.bdsdatabase.com**

Specializing in Business-To-Business Lead Generation

● Target Market List Development
● Prospecting Programs
● Customer Relationship Management Software

Business Development Solutions, Inc.
133 Gaither Dr
Ste H
Mount Laurel, NJ 08054
Phone: (856) 787-1500
Fax: (856) 787-1510
www.bdsdatabase.com

Contact Solutions Marketing
11205 Wright Circle
Omaha, NE 68144
Phone: (402) 934-4081
Fax: (402) 934-4058
www.csmionline.com

Custom List Services
14440 Cherry Lane Ct
Ste 108
Laurel, MD 20707
Phone: (301) 497-1858
Fax: (301) 497-1687

Direct Media, Inc.
200 Pemberwick Rd
Greenwich, CT O6830
Phone: (914) 532-2447
Fax: (914) 934-9582
www.directmedia.com

Dun & Bradstreet Corporation
3 Sylvan Way
Parsippany, NJ 07054
Phone: (973) 605-6000
www.dnb.com

Focus USA
10 Metcalf St
Ashville, NC 28806
Phone: (828) 254-8266

HARRIS Marketing, Inc.
Janet I. Harris, President
In the List Business 20 Years
Lists & Mail = Direct Mail
Call **(317) 251-9729** in Indy
Authorized Reseller of **D&B** Business Lists and iMarket

Harris Marketing, Inc.
The Glendale Bldg
6100 N Keystone Ave
Ste 427
Indianapolis, IN 46220
Phone: (317) 251-9729
Fax: (317) 251-9733
www.listsandmail.com

Hogan Information Services
14000 Quail Springs Pkwy
Ste 4000
Oklahoma City, OK 73134
Phone: (405) 302-6954
Fax: (405) 302-6902
www.hoganinfo.com

Hugo Dunhill Mailing Lists, Inc.
30 E 33rd St
12th Fl
New York, NY 10016
Phone: (888) 274-5737
Fax: (212) 213-9245
www.hdml.com

I-Behavior Inc.
500 Mamaroneck Ave
Harrison, NY 10528
Phone: (914) 777-3777
Fax: (914) 777-7311
www.i-behavior.com

Infinite Media
190 E Post Rd
White Plains, NY 10601
Phone: (914) 949-1547
Fax: (914) 949-1605
www.infinite-media.com

Infocore, Inc.
626 Silas Deane Hwy
2nd Fl
Wethersfield, CT 06109
Phone: (860) 563-6360
Fax: (860) 563-6265
www.infocoreinc.com

InfoUSA/Donnelley Marketing
5711 S 86th Circle
Omaha, NE 68127
Phone: (402) 593-4653
Fax: (402) 596-0475
www.infousa.com

Integrated Marketing, Inc.
105 Walnut Branch Ln
Huntly, VA 22640
Phone: (540) 635-5413
Fax: (540) 635-1039

Intelitec
152 Taylor St
Granby, MA 01033
Phone: (413) 467-7420
Fax: (413) 467-9476

International Direct Response, Inc.
1125 Lancaster Ave
Berwyn, PA 19312
Phone: (610) 993-0500
Fax: (610) 993-9938
www.idronline.com

JF Direct Marketing, Inc.
73 Croton Ave
Ste 106
Ossining, NY 10562
Phone: (914) 762-8633
Fax: (914) 762-9247
www.bestweb.net

Kahn & Associates, Inc.
857 Bryn Mawr Ave
Penn Valley, PA 19072
Phone: (610) 668-8080
Fax: (610) 664-8202
www.cardweb.com

Kroll Direct Marketing
101 Morgan Ln
Ste 120
Plainsboro, NJ 08536
Phone: (609) 275-2900
Fax: (609) 275-6606
www.krolldirect.com

LeadMaster
P.O. BOX 678374
Orlando, FL 32867
Phone: (866) 568-9737
Fax: (407) 678-6360
www.leadmaster.com

Lenser, Inc.
630 Las Gallinas Ave
Ste 100
San Rafael, CA 94903
Phone: (415) 446-2500
Fax: (415) 479-2280
www.lenser.com

Lifestyle Change Communications
1000 Cobb Place Blvd
Ste 420
Kennesaw, GA 30144
Phone: (770) 218-8200
Fax: (770) 218-8211
www.lifestylechange.com

Lighthouse List Co.
6499 NW 9th Ave
Ste 301
Ft Lauderdale, FL 33309
Phone: (954) 489-3008
Fax: (954) 489-3040

List Advisor, Inc.
500 BI County Blvd
Ste 125
Farmingdale, NY 11735
Phone: (631) 777-2900
Fax: (631) 777-3050

The List Group, Inc.
1630 30th St
Ste 507
Boulder, CO 80301
Phone: (303) 448-0536
Fax: (303) 448-0537
www.thelistgroup.com

L.I.S.T. Inc.
320 Northern Blvd
Great Neck, NY 11021
Phone: (516) 482-2345
Fax: (516) 352 8021
www.lists-inc.com

List Services Corporation
6 Trowbridge Dr
Bethel, CT 06801
Phone: (203) 743-2600
Fax: (203) 778-4299
www.listservices.com

L.I.S.T.S. Inc.
8789 San Jose Blvd
Ste 104
Jacksonville, FL 32217
Phone: (904) 733-6106
Fax: (904) 730-7540
www.lists-inc.com

Manning Media International
3309 Westfield
Plano, TX 75093
Phone: (972) 473-2163
Fax: (972) 473-7449

MarketModels, Inc.
85 Brown St
Wickford, RI 02852
Phone: (401) 978 9508
Fax: (401) 294-3220
www.marketmodels.com

Midwest Direct Marketing, Inc.
501 North Webster
Spring Hill, KS 66083
Phone: (913) 686-2220
Fax: (913) 686-2320

MLA (Mailing Lists Asia Ltd)
6/F Seabird House
28 Wyndham St
Central Hong Kong
CHINA
Phone: +852 2526-1208
Fax: +852 2524-9177

PCS List & Information Technologies
39 Cross St
Peabody, MA 01960
Phone: (978) 532-7100
Fax: (978) 532-9181
www.pcslist.com

Phone Disc
5711 S 86th St
Omaha, NE 68127
Phone: (402) 537-6704
Fax: (402) 331-6681

PMM Marketing
1526 Sprice St
Ste 204
Boulder, CO 80302
Phone: (303) 928-2326
Fax: (303) 928-2351

RAD Marketing & RadioBase
167 Crary-On-The-Park
Mount Vernon, NY 10550
Phone: (914) 668-3563
Fax: (914) 668-4247

R.L. Polk & Co.
26955 Northwestern Hwy
Southfield, MI 48034
Phone: (800) 464-7655
Fax: (248) 728-6954
www.polk.com

Response Media Products, Inc.
3155 Medlock Bridge
Ste 220
Norcross, GA 30071
Phone: (770) 220-5041
Fax: (770) 451-4929
www.responsemedia.com

Response World Media
855 E Collins Blvd
Richardson, TX 75081
Phone: (972) 664-1115
Fax: (972) 664-1120

Rickard List Marketing
88 Duryea Rd
Melville, NY 11747
Phone: (631) 249-8710
Fax: (631) 249-9655
www.rickardlist.com

VentureDirect List Services Group
60 Madison Ave
New York, NY 10010
Phone: (212) 655-5160
Fax: (212) 576-1129
www.venturedirect.com

List Managers

Abacus Communications
4456 Corporation Ln
Virginia Beach, VA 23462
Phone: (757) 497-2004
Fax: (757) 497-8876
www.callabacus.com

Acacia Teleservices International
270 Oakway Center
Eugene, OR 97402
Phone: (541) 484-5545
Fax: (541) 465-9406
www.acaciaintl.com

ACP Interactive, LLC
150 Spear St
Ste 700
San Francisco, CA 94105
Phone: (415) 357-5123
Fax: (415) 357-5110
www.acpinteractive.com

Aggressive List Management, Inc.
18-5 E Dundee Rd
Ste 300
Barrington, IL 60010
Phone: (847) 304-4030
Fax: (847) 304-4032
www.aggressivelist.com

Baker Advertising & Mailing
4160 Wilshire Blvd
Los Angeles, CA 90010
Phone: (323) 964-4820
Fax: (323) 964-4843
www.bakeradvertising.com

No two are the same

Lists. No two are the same.
With the quality, deep demographic information
Cahners Business Lists can offer, our lists
make identifying your best prospects simple.

Case closed.

BUSINESS LISTS

Banta Corporation
225 Main St
Menasha, WI 54952
Phone: (920) 751-7777
Fax: (920) 751-7790
www.banta.com

Banta Direct Marketing Group
13 Salt Creek Ln
Ste 350
Hinsdale, IL 60521
Phone: (630) 323-9490
Fax: (920) 751-7790
www.banta.com

Byrum & Fleming
321 San Anselmo Ave
San Anselmo, CA 94960
Phone: (415) 457-1700
Fax: (415) 459-5162
www.byronfleming.com

Cahners Business Lists
1350 E Touhy Ave
Des Plaines, IL 60018
Phone: (800) 323-4958
Fax: (800) 390-2779
www.cahners.com

Conrad Direct, Inc.
300 Knickerbocker Rd
Cresskill, NJ 07626
Phone: (201) 567-3200
Fax: (201) 567-1530
www.conraddirect.com

Creative Automation
220 Fencl Ln
Hillside, IL 60162
Phone: (800) 773-1588
Fax: (708) 449-3283
www.cauto.com

Data Marketing Group
DMG Corporate Plz
60 E Industry Ct #5
Deer Park, NY 11729
Phone: (631) 586-5801
Fax: (631) 586-6081
www.dmglists.com

Focus USA
10 Metcalf St
Ashville, NC 28806
Phone: (828) 254-8266

The Hotlist
3858 Meadows Ln
Las Vegas, NV 89107
Phone: (702) 301-9050
Fax: (702) 320-3778

ICOM Information & Communications, Inc.
41 Metropolitan Rd
Toronto, ON M1R 2T5
CANADA
Phone: (416) 297-7887
Fax: (416) 297-7084
www.i-com.com

List Managers

The Information Refinery, Inc.
200 Route 17
Ste 5
Mahwah, NJ 07430
Phone: (201) 529-2600
Fax: (201) 512-0215
www.inforefinery.com

J. F. Glaser Incorporated
999 Main St
Ste 206
Glen Ellyn, IL 60137
Phone: (630) 790-5243
Fax: (630) 790-5244
www.glaserlists.com

The Kaplan Agency
700 Canal St
Stamford, CT 06902
Phone: (203) 968-8800
Fax: (203) 968-8871

Kroll Direct Marketing
101 Morgan Ln
Ste 120
Plainsboro, NJ 08536
Phone: (609) 275-2900
Fax: (609) 275-6606
www.krolldirect.com

Landscape Co., Inc.
Tokyo Opera City Tow
3-20-2 Nishishinjuku
Tokyo, JAPAN
Phone: 81 35388-7000
Fax: 81 35388-7300

The Leland Company
360 Hiatt Dr
Palm Beach Gardens, FL 33418
Phone: (561) 622-6520
Fax: (561) 622-0757
www.lelandlists.com

List Media, Inc.
251 W Garfield Rd
Ste 262
Aurora, OH 44202
Phone: (330) 995-0864
Fax: (330) 995-0873
www.dm1.com

Mal Dunn Associates, Inc.
2 Hardscrabble Rd
Croton Falls, NY 10519
Phone: (845) 278-1348
Fax: (914) 278-6681
www.dunndirect.com

Mardev New York
Two Rector St
New York, NY 10006
Phone: (212) 584-9370
Fax: (212) 584-9371

MarketTouch
1235 Old Alpharetta Rd
Alpharetta, GA 30005
Phone: (678) 942-2900
Fax: (678) 942-2955
www.markettouch.com

McCarthy Media Group, Inc.
1630 23rd Ave
Monroe, WI 53566
Phone: (608) 329-6097
Fax: (608) 329-4940

Medical Marketing Service
185 Hansen Ct
Ste 110
Wood Dale, IL 60191
Phone: (800) 633-5478
Fax: (630) 350-1896
www.mmslists.com

MeritDirect LLC
263 Tresser Blvd
One Stamford Plz
Stamford, CT 06901
Phone: (203) 541-2300
Fax: (203) 541-2350
www.meritdirect.com

Names In The News California, Inc.
1300 Clay St
Oakland, CA 94612
Phone: (415) 989-3350
Fax: (415) 433-7796
www.nincal.com

NCRI List Management
429 Sylvan Ave
Englewood Cliffs, NJ 07632
Phone: (201) 541-9500
Fax: (201) 541-1944

NCRI Ventures
1205 E Hermitage Rd
Bayside, WI 53217
Phone: (414) 540-1500
Fax: (414) 540-1200
www.ncrilists.com

Penton Media, Inc.
1300 E 9th St
Ste 316
Cleveland, OH 44114
Phone: (216) 696-7000
Fax: (216) 696-6662
www.penton.com

Peppermill Marketing, Inc.
8833 Sunset Blvd
Ste 408
Los Angeles, CA 90069
Phone: (310) 659-8900
Fax: (310) 659-8901
www.peppermillmktg.com

Prestige Mailing Lists Inc.
1539 Sawtelle Blvd
Ste 1
Los Angeles, CA 90025
Phone: (310) 473-7116
Fax: (310) 477-3217

Profile America List
429 Sylvan Ave
Englewood Cliffs, NJ 07632
Phone: (201) 569-7272
Fax: (201) 569-5552
www.profileamerica.com

Return Path, Inc.
56 W 22nd St
10th Fl
New York, NY 10010
Phone: (212) 905-5500
Fax: (212) 625-3597
www.returnpath.com

RMI Direct Marketing, Inc.
42 Old Ridgebury Rd
Danbury, CT 06810
Phone: (203) 532-3797
Fax: (203) 778-6130
www.rmidirect.com

RP Associates, Inc.
164 E Mt Gallant Rd
Rock Hill, SC 29730
Phone: (803) 329-0900
Fax: (803) 329-0958
www.rpassociates.com

Springhouse Corporation
1111 Bethlehem Pike
P.O. Box 908
Spring House, PA 19477
Phone: (215) 646-8700
Fax: (215) 646-8039
www.springnet.com

TCI Direct
10911 Riverside Dr
Toluca Lake, CA 91602
Phone: (818) 752-1800
Fax: (818) 752-1808
www.tcidirect.com

TFC List Services, Inc.
2 Eves Dr
Ste 104
Marlton, NJ 08053
Phone: (856) 810-2020
Fax: (856) 810-2021

ThinkDirectMarketing, Inc.
470 West Ave
Stamford, CT 06902
Phone: (203) 964-9411
Fax: (203) 978-5827
www.thinkdm.com

TransUnion LLC
120 S Riverside Plz
19th Fl
Chicago, IL 60606
Phone: (312) 466-7891
Fax: (312) 258-7751
www.transunion.com

TransUnion LLC
37 E 28th St
Ste 400B
New York, NY 10016
Phone: (212) 685-2705
Fax: (212) 685-2715
www.transunion.com

21stAZ Marketing
1750 New Hwy
Farmingdale, NY 11735
Phone: (631) 293-8550
Fax: (631) 293-8974
www.21staz.com

UtopiAds
11868 Sunrise Valley
Ste 101
Reston, VA 20191
Phone: (703) 654-9000
Fax: (703) 390-1339
www.utopiads.com

**VentureDirect List
Services Group**
60 Madison Ave
New York, NY 10010
Phone: (212) 655-5160
Fax: (212) 576-1129
www.venturedirect.com

VentureDirect Worldwide
60 Madison Ave
New York, NY 10010
Phone: (212) 684-4800
Fax: (212) 576-1129
www.venturedirect.com

Vision Marketing Inc.
429 Sylvan Ave
Englewood Cliffs, NJ 07632
Phone: (201) 816-1560
Fax: (201) 816-1610
www.visionmarketing.com

World Innovators, Inc.
72 Park St
New Canaan, CT 06840
Phone: (203) 966-7889
Fax: (203) 966-0926
www.worldinnovators.com

**The XactMail Opt-in Email
Network**
60 Madison Ave
New York, NY 10010
Phone: (212) 655-5231
Fax: (212) 576-1129
www.xactmail.com

Loyalty Marketing

**Customer Communications
Group**
12600 W Cedar Dr
Denver, CO 80228
Phone: (303) 986-3000
Fax: (303) 989-4805
www.customer.com

iSKY, Inc.
6100 Frost Pl
Ste 300
Laurel, MD 20707
Phone: (240) 456-4300
Fax: (240) 456-4338
www.isky.com

**Latham Synchronized
Relationship Marketing**
1400 W 16th St
Ste 300
Oak Brook, IL 60523
Phone: (630) 573-8787
Fax: (630) 573-0540
www.synchronicit-e.com

PreVision Marketing, Inc.
55 Old Bedford Rd
Lincoln, MA 01773
Phone: (781) 259-5100
Fax: (781) 259-1548
www.previsionmarketing.com

Pro/Phase Marketing, Inc.
6550 Edenvale Blvd
Eden Prairie, MN 55346
Phone: (952) 974-1100
Fax: (952) 974-7874
www.repeatrewards.com

Management Consultants

Consultants In Info. Management, Inc.
1520 S 70th St
Ste 101
Lincoln, NE 68506
Phone: (402) 484-5800
Fax: (402) 484-5810

Ernan Roman Direct Marketing Corporation
3 Melrose Ln
Douglas Manor, NY 11363
Phone: (718) 225-4151
Fax: (718) 225-4889

Jonah Gitlitz
3916 Highwood Ct NW
Washington, DC 20007
Phone: (202) 965-6185
Fax: (202) 337-4429

Ladd Associates, Inc
2527 Fillmore St
San Francisco, CA 94115
Phone: (415) 921-1001
Fax: (415) 921-2311
www.laddassociates.com

Liz Kislik Associates
99 W Hawthorne Ave
Ste 200
Valley Stream, NY 11580
Phone: (516) 568-2932
Fax: (516) 568-2936

Marketing Automation

FrontRange Solutions
1125 Kelly Johnson Blvd
Colorado Springs, CO 80920
Phone: (800) 776-7889
www.frontrange.com

GSP Group, Data Driven Marketing Resources
1343 Boswall Dr
Ste 200
Worthington, OH 43085
Phone: (614) 888-7502
Fax: (614) 885-1165

MarketSoft Corporation
10 Maguire Rd
Lexington, MA 02421
Phone: (781) 674-0015
Fax: (781) 674-0090
www.marketsoft.com

Salesforce.com
The Landmark @ One Market
Ste 300
San Francisco, CA 94105
Phone: (415) 901-7000
Fax: (415) 901-7040
www.salesforce.com

SalesLogic
8800 N Gainey Ctr
Ste 200
Scottsdale, AZ 85258
Phone: (480) 368-3700
Fax: (480) 368-3799

Siebel Systems
1855 S Grant St
San Mateo, CA 94049
Phone: (650) 295-5114
Fax: (650) 295-5477
www.siebel.com

Tri-Media Marketing
5309 Lincoln Ave
Ste 200
Skokie, IL 60077
www.tri-media.com

Marketing Consultants

Bel-Aire Associates
9 E 38th St
11th Fl
New York, NY 10016
Phone: (212) 696-5200
Fax: (212) 696-1112
www.bel-aire.com

Collinger & Associates
7751 Carondelet Ave
Ste 308
St. Louis, MO 63105
Phone: (314) 727-7488
Fax: (314) 727-0299

Conversant Relationship Marketing
50 Peabody Pl
Memphis, TN 38103
Phone: (901) 527-8000
Fax: (901) 527-3697
www.thompson-co.com

Customer Growth, Blau Moritz Partnership, Inc.
37 Franklin St
Ste 201
Westport, CT 06880
Phone: (203) 226-8795
Fax: (203) 227-8601
www.customer-growth.com

Frequency Marketing, Inc.
6101 Meijer Dr
Milford, OH 45150
Phone: (513) 248-2882
Fax: (513) 248-2672
www.frequencymarketing.com

Gruppo, Levey & Co.
60 E 42nd St
Ste 3810
New York, NY 10165
Phone: (212) 697-5753
Fax: (212) 949-7294
www.glconline.com

GSP Group, Data Driven Marketing Resources
1343 Boswall Dr
Ste 200
Worthington, OH 43085
Phone: (614) 888-7502
Fax: (614) 885-1165

Hallmark Capital Corporation
230 Park Ave
Ste 2430
New York, NY 10169
Phone: (212) 249-9634
Fax: (212) 249-9537
www.hallmarkcapital.com

Hanley-Wood Integrated Marketing
430 First Ave N
Ste 550
Minneapolis, MN 55401
Phone: (612) 338-8300
Fax: (612) 338-7044
www.hwcp.com

Harvey Associates - Direct Marketing Solutions
63 Hoover Dr
Cresskill, NJ 07626
Phone: (201) 816-1780
Fax: (201) 816-1781

Hauser List Services, NMIS
3 Commercial St
Hicksville, NY 11801
Phone: (516) 935-8603
Fax: (516) 935-8626
www.hausernet.com

Herbert Krug & Associates, Inc.
500 Davis Ctr
Ste 1010
Evanston, IL 60201
Phone: (847) 864-0550
Fax: (847) 864-0575

HispanAmérica
437 Madison Ave
7th Fl
New York, NY 10022
Phone: (212) 415-3054
Fax: (212) 415-3591

Hunter Business Group, LLC
4650 N Port Washington Rd
Milwaukee, WI 53212
Phone: (414) 203-8066
Fax: (414) 203-8225
www.hunterbusiness.com

Incite Marketing
100 Washington St
South Norwalk, CT 06854
Phone: (203) 855-9108
Fax: (203) 855-9164
www.incitemarketing.com

Interactive Marketing Group
50 Commerce Dr
Allendale, NJ 07401
Phone: (201) 327-0974
Fax: (201) 327-3596
www.imgusa.com

International Direct Marketing Consultants, Inc.
3419 Westminster
Lock Box 209
Dallas, TX 75205
Phone: (214) 443-9494
Fax: (214) 443-9512
www.dmtrademissions.com

International Marketing Solutions, Inc.
1930 San Marco Blvd
Ste 205
Jacksonville, FL 32207
Phone: (904) 346-3300
Fax: (904) 346-3303
www.ims-global.net

Invision Consulting Services, Inc.
100 Cummings Ctr
311H
Beverly, MA 01915
Phone: (978) 922-2540
Fax: (978) 927-3802
www.invisioncs.com

Jab Creative Inc.
124 Mount Auburn St
Cambridge, MA 02138
Phone: (866) 300-0090
Fax: (617) 254-0550
www.jabcreative.com

JK Associates, LLC
P.O. Box 61117
Palo Alto, CA 94306
Phone: (650) 838-9816
Fax: (650) 838-9867
www.jk-associates.com

John Condon & Associates
38 Angus Ln
Greenwich, CT 06831
Phone: (203) 869-7006
Fax: (203) 622-1488

Joseph Carlucci & Associates
481 W 22nd St
Ste 3
New York, NY 10011
Phone: (212) 924-8187
Fax: (212) 924-9914

J2S Marketing
6811 Melody Ln
Bethesda, MD 20817
Phone: (301) 365-7948
Fax: (301) 365-7949

Kannon Consulting, Inc.
208 S La Salle St
Ste 1240
Chicago, IL 60604
Phone: (312) 346-2244
Fax: (312) 346-3665
www.kannon.com

Kay Consulting
40 E 9th St #10-D
New York, NY 10003
Phone: (212) 254-3989

Kent Marketing Group, Inc.
1880 Williamette Falls Dr
Ste 200
West Linn, OR 97068
Phone: (503) 722-9080
Fax: (503) 722-1481
www.kentmarketinggroup.com

Kobs Strategic Consulting
205 N Michigan Ave
Ste 3900
Chicago, IL 60601
Phone: (312) 819-2300
Fax: (312) 819-2323
www.kgp.com

The Kornbluh Company
2636 Walnut Ave
Evanston, IL 60201
Phone: (847) 612-4205
Fax: (847) 248-8394
www.kornbluh.com

Lautman & Company
1730 Rhode Island Ave, NW
Ste 700
Washington, DC 20036
Phone: (202) 296-9660
Fax: (202) 466-2312
www.lautmandc.com

Lett Direct, Inc.
12933 Brighton Ct
Carmel, IN 46032
Phone: (317) 844-8228
Fax: (317) 844-1770
www.lettdirect.com

Lieber, Levett, Koenig, Farese, Babcock
299 W Houston St
New York, NY 10014
Phone: (212) 206-5800
Fax: (212) 206-5801
www.llkfb.com

Light Hill Partners
55 Light Hill Rd
Old Snowmass, CO 81654
Phone: (970) 927-4472
Fax: (970) 927-5153

Lists and Data Services Corp.
P.O. Box 200516
Arlington, TX 76006
Phone: (817) 277-1469
Fax: (817) 277-7580

Liz Taylor Marketing
1430 Park Circle
Tampa, FL 33604
Phone: (813) 237-8497
Fax: (813) 239-2175
www.liztaylormarketing.com

Madden Communications
115 Crawford Rd
Middletown, NJ 07748
Phone: (732) 462-4295
Fax: (732) 431-8162

The Mallett Group, Inc.
566 Danbury Rd
Ste 6
New Milford, CT 06776
Phone: (860) 350-0809
Fax: (860) 350-0853
www.mallettgroup.com

Market Response International
P.O. Box 387
293c Orleans Rd
North Chatham, MA 02650
Phone: (508) 945-4010
Fax: (508) 945-4011

Marketing Information & Technology
Three Riverside Dr
Andover, MA 01810
Phone: (978) 738-0544
Fax: (978) 738-0582

Marketing Solutions
39 Crestwood Ln
Milford, NH 03055
Phone: (603) 673-6786
Fax: (603) 673-0317

Marketrac, Inc.
131 Executive Dr
New Hyde Park, NY 11040
Phone: (516) 365-4330
Fax: (516) 365-5789

Markitecture
5 New St
Ste B
Norwalk, CT 06855
Phone: (203) 855-9050
Fax: (203) 855-9058
www.markitecture.com

McIntyre Direct
102 North Hayden Bay Dr
Portland, OR 97217
Phone: (503) 735-9515
Fax: (503) 286-7622

Medina Associates
12 Hilltop Rd
Wallingford, PA 19086
Phone: (610) 565-8836
Fax: (610) 565-8184

Michael I. Grant & Associates, Inc.
115 Carthage Rd
Scarsdale, NY 10583
Phone: (914) 722-4177
Fax: (914) 722-4179

Miglino Associates
210 Hamilton St
Harrisburg, PA 17102
Phone: (717) 234-7448
Fax: (717) 234-6229

Mission: Interactive, Inc.
409 N Pacific Coast Hwy
Ste 406
Redondo Beach, CA 90277
Phone: (310) 543-2733
Fax: (310) 540-5543
www.missioninteractive.com

MVC Associates International
3001 N Rocky Point Dr E
Ste 200
PMB 2034
Tampa, FL 33607
Phone: (813) 891-6641
Fax: (813) 855-5847
www.mvcinternational.com

NetCreations, Inc.
379 W Broadway
New York, NY 10010
Phone: (212) 625-1370
Fax: (212) 274-8835
www.netcreations.com

Oetting Company
1995 Broadway
New York, NY 10023
Phone: (212) 580-5470
Fax: (212) 873-3844
www.oetting.com

O'Keefe Henry Direct
600 Central Ave
Ste 322
Highland Park, IL 60035
Phone: (847) 681-9200
Fax: (847) 681-9299

Paradigm Direct, LLC
2 Executive Dr
9th Fl
Fort Lee, NJ 07024
Phone: (201) 461-5665
Fax: (201) 461-1963
www.paradigm.com

Peppers and Rogers Group
Merritt on the River
20 Glover Ave
Norwalk, CT 06850
Phone: (203) 642-5121
Fax: (203) 642-5126
www.ltol.com

Phoenix Marketing Group Ltd.
57 Danbury Rd
Wilton, CT 06897
Phone: (203) 355-8202
Fax: (203) 762-8285

Pilot Direct
150 W Brambleton Ave
Norfolk, VA 23510
Phone: (757) 446-2291
Fax: (757) 446-2534

PLEXUS International
17 W 695 Butterfield Rd
Ste C
Oakbrook Terrace, IL 60181
Phone: (630) 889-0871
Fax: (630) 792-0984

Quinetix
300 State St
Ste 302
Rochester, NY 14614
Phone: (716) 546-1860
Fax: (716) 546-1887
www.quinetix.com

R & R
3790 Kings Way
Boca Raton, FL 33434
Phone: (561) 883-3530
Fax: (561) 883-3280
www.lowrisk-highreward.co

The Response Shop, Inc.
7910 Ivanhoe Ave
Ste 519
La Jolla, CA 92037
Phone: (858) 456-6180
Fax: (858) 456-5803

Retail Strategy Center, Inc.
6 Parkins Lake Ct
Greenville, SC 29607
Phone: (864) 458-8277
Fax: (864) 458-8144
www.brianwoolf.com

Right Coast Marketing
25 First Ave
East Greenwich, RI 02818
Phone: (401) 884-0500
Fax: (401) 884-0529

ROCKINGHAM*JUTKINS* marketing
Rockingham Ranch
Roll, AZ 85347
Phone: (810) 785-9400
Fax: (810) 815-2520
www.rayjutkins.com

Ron Perrella DRS
29632 Seriana
Ste 1000
Laguna Niguel, CA 92677
Phone: (949) 495-7661
Fax: (949) 495-7660

Ron Weber & Associates, Inc.
185 Plains Rd
Milford, CT 06460
Phone: (203) 799-0000
Fax: (203) 882-9998
www.telethinking.com

Saboia Campos
One W 85th St
New York, NY 10024
Phone: (416) 925-3003
Fax: (416) 925-3605

Sargeant House
1433 Johnny's Way
P.O. Box 299
Westtown, PA 19395
Phone: (610) 399-1983
Fax: (610) 399-8953

The Schmidt Group International, Inc.
1535 Harvest Ln
Manasquan, NJ 08376
Phone: (732) 223-8186
Fax: (732) 223-7931
www.the-schmidt-group.com

SIBO, Inc.
10813 Indian Trail
Cooper City, FL 33328
Phone: (954) 680-4580
Fax: (954) 680-8231

Spaulder & Associates, Inc.
8231 Ranchview Dr
Ste 2048
Irving, TX 75063
Phone: (214) 574-4660
Fax: (214) 574-4661

Stanton Direct Marketing, Inc.
1009 W Water St
Elmira, NY 14905
Phone: (607) 734-1665
Fax: (607) 734-3708

Strand Marketing
55 New Montgomery
Ste 601
San Francisco, CA 94105
Phone: (415) 777-5070
Fax: (415) 777-5340
www.strandm.com

Sutton & Associates, Inc.
7355 Garden Ct
River Forest, IL 60305
Phone: (708) 771-0400
Fax: (708) 771-0436
www.suttondirect.com

TeleDevelopment Services
4816 Brecksville Rd
Ste 2
Richfield, OH 44286
Phone: (330) 659-4441
Fax: (330) 659-4442
www.teledevelopment.com

TeleStrategy Group International, Inc.
4321 Downtowner Loop N
Ste 201
Mobile, AL 36609
Phone: (334) 344-8787
Fax: (334) 344-6364
www.telestrategy.net

Three AM
3961 NE 13th Ave
Fort Lauderdale, FL 33334
Phone: (954) 390-7004
Fax: (954) 565-6856
www.threeam.com

Transactional Marketing Partners
3340 Ocean Park Blvd
Ste 3050
Santa Monica, CA 90405
Phone: (310) 392-4042
Fax: (310) 392-4052
www.transactionalmarketing.com

Trilogy Consulting
202 Carnegie Ctr
Princeton, NJ 08540
Phone: (609) 520-0779
Fax: (609) 520-0730
www.trilogyusa.com

TSP - TeleServices Partners, Inc.
14217 Dayton Circle
Omaha, NE 68137
Phone: (402) 445-4100
Fax: (402) 445-9186

Urban Science Applications
200 Renaissance Ctr
Detroit, MI 48243
Phone: (313) 259-9900
Fax: (313) 259-1362
www.urbanscience.com

USY Consulting
710 Cathy Ln
Mount Prospect, IL 60056
Phone: (847) 259-6140
Fax: (847) 259-6180

Van Groesbeck & Company
506 Libbie Ave
Richmond, VA 23226
Phone: (804) 288-8000
Fax: (804) 288-3901

The Verdi Group, Inc.
400 Andrews St
Ste 300
Rochester, NY 14604
Phone: (716) 325-6304
Fax: (716) 325-5571
www.theverdigroup.com

Voting Direct
38 E 85th St
Apt #5A
New York, NY 10028
Phone: (212) 790-1451
Fax: (212) 719-5106

Web Direct Marketing, Inc.
401 S Milwaukee Ave
Wheeling, IL 60090
Phone: (847) 459-0800
Fax: (847) 459-7378

Wesley R. Weber & Associates
901 Messner Rd
Chester Springs, PA 19425
Phone: (610) 827-7202
Fax: (610) 827-7249

W-R Marketing Resources, Inc.
7810 Millicent Circle
Shreveport, LA 71105
Phone: (318) 798-3039
Fax: (318) 798-8105

Quaero, LLC
5275 Parkway Plz Blvd
Charlotte, NC 28217
Phone: (704) 414-2189
Fax: (704) 414-2195
www.quaero-corp.com

Marketing Research Firms

BAIGlobal Inc.
580 White Plains Rd
Tarrytown, NY 10591
Phone: (914) 332-5300
Fax: (914) 631-8300
www.baiglobal.com

Beta Research Corporation
6400 Jericho Tpk
Syosset, NY 11791
Phone: (516) 935-3800
Fax: (516) 935-4092
www.nybeta.com

Customer Affinity, Inc.
2827 Calhoun Ave
Chattanooga, TN 37407
Phone: (423) 629-6030
Fax: (423) 629-7145

David Ganz Marketing, Inc.
566 Westchester Ave
Rye Brook, NY 10573
Phone: (914) 937-1680
Fax: (914) 937-1968

Digital Marketing Services, Inc.
1305 S State Hwy 121
Ste 190
Lewisville, TX 75067
Phone: (972) 874-5080
Fax: (972) 353-9750
www.dmsdallas.com

FIND/SVP, Inc.
625 Avenue of the Americas
2nd Fl
New York, NY 10011
Phone: (212) 645-4500
Fax: (212) 645-7681
www.findsvp.com

Harris Interactive
201 N Charles St
Baltimore, MD 21201
Phone: (585) 214-7949
Fax: (585) 272-7258
www.harrisinteractive.com

Harte-Hanks Market Intelligence
3344 N Torrey Pines Ct
La Jolla, CA 92037
Phone: (800) 456-9748
Fax: (858) 587-8169
www.hartehanksmi.com

Information Resources, Inc.
150 N Clinton St
Chicago, IL 60661
Phone: (312) 726-1221
Fax: (312) 474-8465
www.infores.com

Ipsos - NPD, Inc.
100 Charles Lindberg Blvd
Uniondale, NY 11553
Phone: (516) 507-3000
Fax: (516) 507-3200
www.ipsos.npd.com

iVOX, LLC
3541 Investment Blvd
Ste 3
Hayward, CA 94545
Phone: (800) 747-8271
Fax: (510) 732-5070
www.ivoxllc.com

Kubas Consultants

2300 Yonge St
Ste 2002
Toronto, ON M4P 1E4
CANADA
Phone: (416) 487-7040
Fax: (416) 487-0816
www.kubas.com

Moskowitz Jacobs Inc.

1025 Westchester Ave
White Plains, NY 10604
Phone: (914) 421-7400
Fax: (914) 428-8364
www.mji-designlab.com

ORC ProTel, Inc.

17253 Continental Dr
Lansing, IL 60438
Phone: (708) 418-7413
Fax: (708) 418-7457
www.orcprotel.com

Phoenix Group, Inc.

34115 W Twelve Mile Rd
Farmington Hills, MI 48331
Phone: (800) 832-1935
Fax: (248) 324-3186
www.phoenixgroup.com

SmartDM, Inc.

1437 Donelson Pike
Nashville, TN 37217
Phone: (615) 850-3000
Fax: (615) 399-9867
www.smartdm.com

Paper Mills and Distributors

Bowater

11440 Carmel Commons
Charlotte, NC 28226
Phone: (704) 540-2671
Fax: (704) 540-7532
www.bowater.com

Roosevelt Paper Company

One Roosevelt Dr
Mount Laurel, NJ 08054
Phone: (856) 303-4100
Fax: (856) 642-1950
www.rooseveltpaper.com

St. Marys Paper Ltd.

1 Westbrook Corporate Ctr
Westchester, IL 60154
Phone: (708) 562-5500
Fax: (708) 562-5574
www.stmaryspaper.com

Payment Processing Services

EPX Electronic Payment Exchange

100 W Commons Blvd
Ste 100
New Castle, DE 19720
Phone: (302) 326-0700
Fax: (302) 326-0664
www.epx.com

NPC (National Processing Company)
1231 Durrett Ln
Louisville, KY 40213
Phone: (800) 255-1157
Fax: (502) 315-3535
www.npc.net

Pacific Network Services Ltd.
405-595 Howe St
Vancouver, BC V6C 2T5
CANADA
Phone: (604) 689-0399
Fax: (604) 689-0311
www.pacnetservices.com

Paymentech
1601 Elm St
Dallas, TX 75201
Phone: (214) 849-3000
Fax: (214) 849-3596
www.paymentech.com

Planet Payment
950 Third Avenue
18th Fl
New York, NY 10022
Phone: (212) 980-5100
Fax: (212) 319-4880
www.planetpayment.com

Printers - Sheet Fed, Web, Print Services

American Print Solutions
561 President St
Brooklyn, NY 11215
Phone: (718) 246-7800
Fax: (718) 246-7830
www.aps-net.com

Arandell Corporation
N 82 W 13118 Leon Rd
Menomonee Falls, WI 53051
Phone: (262) 253-3177
Fax: (262) 253-3162
www.arandell.com

Barton-Cotton, Inc.
1405 Parker Rd
Baltimore, MD 21230
Phone: (410) 204-7575
Fax: (410) 247-7224
www.bartoncotton.com

Bernadette Business Forms Inc.
8950 Pershall Rd
Hazelwood, MO 63042
Phone: (314) 522-1700
Fax: (314) 524-6161
www.bbf.com

Cadmus
2750 Whitehall Park Dr
Charlotte, NC 28273
Phone: (704) 583-6543
Fax: (704) 583-6787
www.cadmus.com

Capitol Communications
2505 Silver Dr
Columbus, OH 43211
Phone: (614) 419-0485
Fax: (614) 268-9329
www.capitolcommunications.com

CommuniMax Direct
25 Claude St
Beaconsfield, QC H9W 4E9
CANADA
Phone: (888) 644-6062
Fax: (888) 644-6117
www.communimax.ca

Dixonweb/Sleepeck Printing Co.
815 S 25th Ave
Bellwood, IL 60104
Phone: (708) 544-8900
Fax: (708) 544-8928
www.sleepeck.com

Essex Printing Co., Inc.
240 E 48th St
New York, NY 10017
Phone: (212) 688-4720
Fax: (212) 308-2764
www.essex-printing.com

Harty Integrated Solutions
25 James St
P.O. Box 324
New Haven, CT 06513
Phone: (203) 562-5112
Fax: (203) 782-9168
www.hartynet.com

High Tech Printing Systems
138 N Federal Hwy
Deerfield Beach, FL 33441
Phone: (954) 480-6000
Fax: (954) 480-6088

ImageNow
98 W Main St
Victor, NY 14564
Phone: (716) 924-3974
Fax: (716) 924-3880
www.imagenowonline.com

International Business Systems
431 Yerkes Rd
King of Prussia, PA 19406
Phone: (610) 265-8210
Fax: (610) 265-7997
www.ibs4cmyk.com

Japs-Olson Company
7500 Excelsior Blvd
St. Louis Park, MN 55426
Phone: (800) 548-2897
Fax: (612) 912-1900
www.japsolson.com

Kael Direct
6020 Richmond Hwy
Ste 201
Alexandria, VA 22303
Phone: (703) 960-7220
Fax: (703) 960-6760
www.kaeldirect.com

Lehigh Cadillac Direct
1900 S 25th St
Broadview, IL 60155
Phone: (708) 681-2828
Fax: (708) 681-9604

Lone Star Web, Inc.
6730 Oakbrook Blvd
Dallas, TX 75235
Phone: (214) 443-2200
Fax: (214) 630-4364
www.lonestarweb.com

L.P. Thebault Company
249 Pomeroy Rd
Parsippany, NJ 07054
Phone: (973) 884-1300
Fax: (973) 952-8296
www.thebault.com

Moody Direct
4900 Augusta Dr
Fort Worth, TX 76106
Phone: (817) 429-9393
Fax: (817) 429-9472
www.moodydirect.com

Moore Response Marketing
1200 Lakeside Dr
Bannockburn, IL 60015
Phone: (847) 607-6000
Fax: (847) 607-7205
www.moore.com

Moore Response Marketing Services
300 Lang Blvd
Grand Island, NY 14072
Phone: (716) 773-0512
Fax: (716) 773-0208
www.rms.com

Nahan Printing, Inc.
7000 Saukview Dr
P.O. Box 697
St. Cloud, MN 56302
Phone: (320) 654-5715
Fax: (320) 259-1378
www.nahan.com

Official Offset Corporation
8600 New Horizons Blvd
Amityville, NY 11701
Phone: (631) 957-8500
Fax: (631) 957-4606

Packaging Printing Specialists
3915 Stern
St. Charles, IL 60174
Phone: (630) 513-8060
Fax: (630) 513-8062

Phenix Label Company
371 Main St
Wakefield, MA 01880
Phone: (781) 246-7450
Fax: (781) 246-5805
www.phenixlabel.com

Plastag
1800 Greenleaf
Elk Grove Village, IL 60007
Phone: (847) 258-1000
Fax: (847) 258-1012
www.plastag.com

Print Technologies & Services, Inc.

290 Gerzevske Ln
Carol Stream, IL 60188
Phone: (630) 752-1600
Fax: (630) 752-8642

Redfield & Co., Inc.

1901 Howard St
Omaha, NE 68102
Phone: (402) 341-0364
Fax: (402) 341-1454
www.redfieldandcompany.com

Private Delivery Services

Directory Distributing Associates, Inc.

P.O. Box 116
Somerville, MA 02143
Phone: (617) 623-1685
Fax: (617) 623-2136
www.ddai.com

Drop Ship Express

2725 Wayzata Blvd W
Long Lake, MN 55356
Phone: (800) 650-8826
Fax: (952) 476-7488
www.dropshipexpress.com

OCS America, Inc.

49-27 31st St
Long Island City, NY 11101
Phone: (718) 784-6080
Fax: (718) 433-1881
www.shipocs.com

Publications/Professional Journals

BtoB Magazine

711 Third Ave
New York, NY 10017
Phone: (212) 210-0402
Fax: (212) 649-5326
www.btobonline.com

Ziff-Davis Media Inc.

28 E 28th St
New York, NY 10016
Phone: (212) 503-3500
Fax: (212) 503-5317
www.ziffdavis.com

Public Relations

Internet Wire, Inc.

5757 W. Century Blvd
Ste 391, 2nd Fl
Los Angeles, CA 90045
Phone: (310) 846-3602
Fax: (310) 846-3707
www.internetwire.com

Sales Promotional Agencies

The Cullinan Group

1128 Harmon Pl
Minneapolis, MN 55403
Phone: (612) 338-7636
Fax: (612) 338-8173
www.cullinangroup.com

›› The breakfast of marketing champions

Join this power breakfast today. Subscribe to BtoB Magazine.
Visit BtoBonline.com. Or, register for BtoB's free daily e-mail alerts.
No matter how you slice it, you'll get a hearty serving of
what you need to build a better integrated marketing strategy.
From direct marketing to advertising to CRM to online marketing,
top marketers know they can depend on BtoB. You can too.

THE MAGAZINE FOR MARKETING AND E-COMMERCE STRATEGISTS

To Advertise in BtoB: 212-210-0782 • To Subscribe: 888-288-5900

D'Arcy Masius Benton & Bowles
1675 Broadway
4th Fl
New York, NY 10019
Phone: (212) 468-3403
Fax: (212) 468-3600
www.dmbb.com

Frank Mayer & Associates, Inc.
1975 Wisconsin Ave
Grafton, WI 53024
Phone: (262) 834-1467
Fax: (262) 377-3449
www.frankmayer.com

Frankel Convergence 121
111 E Wacker Dr
Chicago, IL 60601
Phone: (312) 552-3910
Fax: (312) 552-5425

Intelligent Direct Marketing
1520 Eureka Rd
Ste 101
Roseville, CA 95661
Phone: (916) 784-3887
Fax: (916) 784-1306

KCSA PR Worldwide
800 Second Ave
5th Fl
New York, NY 10017
Phone: (212) 896-1210
Fax: (212) 697-0910
www.kcsa.com

Marden-Kane, Inc.
36 Maple Pl
Manhasset, NY 11030
Phone: (516) 365-3999
Fax: (516) 365-5250
www.mardencane.com

Wunderman
675 Avenue of the Americas
4th Fl
New York, NY 10010
Phone: (212) 941-3000
Fax: (212) 627-8521
www.wunderman.com

Seminars/Webinars

Centra Marketing & Communicaiton
1400 Old Country Rd
Westbury, NY 11590
Phone: (516) 997-3147
Fax: (516) 334-7798

eInterCall
18201 Von Karman Ave
Ste 220
Irvine, CA 92612
Phone: (800) 605-9277
Fax: (801) 640-8537
www.intercall.com

PlaceWare, Inc.
295 N Bernado Ave
Mountain View, CA 94043
Phone: (888) 526-6170
Fax: (650) 526-6199
www.placeware.com

Raindance Communications
1157 Century Dr
Louisville, CO 80027
Phone: (800) 878-7326
Fax: (303) 928-2832
www.raindance.com

WebEx
1035 Breezewood Ln
Neenah, WI 54956
Phone: (920) 729-6666
www.webex.com

SFA Software

Business Development Solutions, Inc.
133 Gaither Dr
Ste H
Mount Laurel, NJ 08054
Phone: (856) 787-1500
Fax: (856) 787-1510
www.bdsdatabase.com

Specialized Information Services

Accenture
234 Kennedy Dr
Horseheads, NY 14846
Phone: (607) 796-2445
Fax: (607) 796-0655
www.accenture.com

ActiveNames, Inc.
20 Exchange Pl
41st Fl
New York, NY 10005
Phone: (212) 785-5960
Fax: (212) 785-5958
www.activenames.com

Audit Bureau of Circulations
405 Lexington Ave
48th Fl
New York, NY 10174
Phone: (212) 867-8992
Fax: (212) 867-8947
www.accessabc.com

CommercialWare, Inc.
24 Prime Park Way
Natick, MA 01760
Phone: (508) 655-7500
Fax: (508) 647-9495
www.commercialware.com

Inside Direct Mail
401 N Broad St
Philadephia, PA 19108
Phone: (215) 238-5437
Fax: (215) 238-5284
www.insidedirectmail.com

ProofreadNOW.com
447 Boston St
Topsfield, MA 01983
Phone: (978) 887-6675
Fax: (978) 887-3680
www.proofreadnow.com

RealNames Corporation
Two Circle Star Way
San Carlos, CA 94070
Phone: (650) 298-8080
Fax: (650) 298-8085
www.realnames.com

Solutionary, Inc.
9420 Underwood Ave
Omaha, NE 68112
Phone: (402) 361 3000
Fax: (402) 361-3100
www.solutionary.com

360 Group
700 Fifth Ave
San Rafael, CA 94901
Phone: (800) 947 9299
Fax: (415) 258-2715
www.360Group.com

Specialized Media

Ernex Marketing Technologies, Inc.
4259 Canada Way
Burnaby, BC V5G 1H1
CANADA
Phone: (604) 415-1513
Fax: (604) 415-1591
www.ernexinc.com

Imagitas Inc.
48 Woerd Ave
Waltham, MA 02453
Phone: (781) 906-4800
Fax: (781) 906-4848
www.imagitas.com

Supermarket of Savings
75 Chestnut Ridge Rd
Montvale, NJ 07646
Phone: (201) 307-8888
Fax: (201) 307-1200
www.supermarketofsavings.com

Telephone Marketing Consultants

Direct Response Enhancements
12772 E Sunnyside Dr
Scottsdale, AZ 85259
Phone: (480) 451-7384
Fax: (480) 661-8460
www.dreteleconsultants.com

Holldon Telemanagement Group
8428 Kings Trail Dr
Cordova, TN 38016
Phone: (800) 760-9091
Fax: (901) 754-7503
www.holldon.com

Oetting Company
1995 Broadway
New York, NY 10023
Phone: (212) 580-5470
Fax: (212) 873-3844
www.oetting.com

Paramount Lists, Inc
3126 Peach St
Erie, PA 16508
Phone: (814) 459-8787
Fax: (814) 459-1398
www.paramountlists.com

Telephone Marketing Services

Access Direct Telemarketing
4515 20th Ave SW
Ste B
Cedar Rapids, IA 52404
Phone: (800) 892-8276
Fax: (319) 390-8901
www.accdir.com

ACI Telecentrics
3100 W Lake St
Ste 300
Minneapolis, MN 55416
Phone: (612) 928-4700
Fax: (612) 928-4701
www.acitel.com

Business Development Solutions, Inc.
133 Gaither Dr
Ste H
Mount Laurel, NJ 08054
Phone: (856) 787-1500
Fax: (856) 787-1510
www.bdsdatabase.com

Calling Solutions, Inc.
2200 McCullough
San Antonio, TX 78212
Phone: (210) 822-7400
Fax: (210) 491-1777

The Connection - Call Center
11351 Rupp Dr
Burnsville, MN 55337
Phone: (800) 883-5777
Fax: (952) 948-5498

CONVERGYS Corporation
201 E Fourth St
P.O. Box 1638
Cincinnati, OH 45202
Phone: (801) 629-6204
Fax: (801) 629-6272
www.convergys.com

Core Communications
2400 N Lincoln Ave
Fremont, NE 68025
Phone: (402) 727-1100
Fax: (402) 753-6211
www.corecc.com

CSC
777 South State Rd 7
Margate, FL 33068
Phone: (954) 969-2304
Fax: (954) 969-2407
www.globalresponse.com

CTC Teleservices, Inc.
2021 Midwest Rd
Ste 205
Oak Brook, IL 60523
Phone: (630) 953-2827
Fax: (630) 953-6186
www.ctcteleservices.com

Dial America Marketing
960 Macarthur Blvd
Mahwah, NJ 07495
Phone: (201) 327-0200
Fax: (201) 327-5101
www.dialamerica.com

e-Commerce Support Centers, Inc.
1650 A Gum Branch Rd
Jacksonville, NC 28540
Phone: (888) 773-3501
Fax: (910) 455-1937
www.e-comsupport.com

Hamilton Telecommunications
1006 12th St
Aurora, NE 68818
Phone: (402) 694-4343
Fax: (402) 694-4433
www.hamilton.net

Harte-Hanks CRM Services
2800 Wells Branch Pkwy
Austin, TX 78728
Phone: (800) 333-3383
Fax: (512) 244-9222
www.harte-hanks.com

HCS Marketing, Inc.
2000 First Dr
Ste 320
Marietta, GA 30062
Phone: (770) 977-8467
Fax: (770) 509-0898
www.hcsmarketing.com

Henry M. Greene & Associates
28457 N Ballard Dr
Ste A1
Lake Forest, IL 60045
Phone: (800) 356-1300
Fax: (847) 816-0576
www.greeneassoc.com

Holden Direct Marketing Group
4900 Augusta Dr
Ft Worth, TX 76106
Phone: (817) 429-9393
Fax: (817) 429-9472
www.holdendirect.com

Holldon Telemanagement Group
8428 Kings Trail Dr
Cordova, TN 38016
Phone: (800) 760-9091
Fax: (901) 754-7503
www.holldon.com

ICT Group, Inc.
800 Town Center Dr
Langhorne, PA 19047
Phone: (215) 702-2002
Fax: (215) 757-7877
www.ictgroup.com

Incept Corporation
4150 Belden Village
Canton, OH 44718
Phone: (330) 649-8000
Fax: (330) 649-8007
www.inceptcorp.com

InfoCision Management Corporation
325 Springside Dr
Akron, OH 44333
Phone: (330) 668-1400
Fax: (330) 668-1401
www.infocision.com

Infotel
8300 NW 53rd St
Ste 310
Miami, FL 33166
Phone: (305) 470-7511
Fax: (305) 591-2129
www.infotel.com.do

InService America
129 Vista Centre Dr
Forest, VA 24551
Phone: (804) 316-7444
Fax: (804) 316-7418
www.inserviceamerica.com

Intelogistics Corporation
8411 W Oakland Park Blvd
Ste 300
Fort Lauderdale, FL 33351
Phone: (800) 715-9990
Fax: (877) 453-5700
www.intelogistics.net

Interactive Teleservices Corporation
21 E State St
18th Fl
Columbus, OH 43215
Phone: (614) 280-1600
Fax: (614) 280-1610
www.intertel.org

IRT
4500 N State Rd 7
Ste 200
Ft Lauderdale, FL 33319
Phone: (800) 700-3033
Fax: (954) 484-0818
www.callcenter.com

iVOX LLC
3541 Investment Blvd
Ste 3
Hayward, CA 94545
Phone: (800) 747-8271
Fax: (510) 732-5070
www.ivoxllc.com

Judson Enterprises, Inc. dba K-Designers
11261 Sunrise Park Dr
Rancho Cordova, CA 95742
Phone: (916) 631-9300
Fax: (916) 631-8471
www.k-designers.com

Meyer Associates Teleservices
14 N 17th Ave
St. Cloud, MN 56303
Phone: (320) 259-4000
Fax: (320) 259-4064
www.callmeyer.com

New Medium Direct
7 Sunshine Blvd
Ormond Beach, FL 32174
Phone: (386) 471-1818
www.newmediumdirect.com

Omega Direct Response, Inc.
4800 Sugar Grove Blvd
Ste 290
Stafford, TX 77479
Phone: (281) 243-9058
Fax: (281) 243-9059

PeopleSoft
4411 People Soft Pkwy
Pleasanton, CA 94588
Phone: (925) 468-2150
Fax: (925) 468-2199
www.peoplesoft.com

Periodical Publishers' Service Bureau
1 N Superior St
Sandusky, OH 44870
Phone: (419) 626-0623
Fax: (419) 621-4300
www.ppsb.com

PriceInteractive
11800 Sunrise Valley Dr
8th Fl
Reston, VA 20191
Phone: (703) 620-4700
Fax: (703) 758-7108
www.priceinteractive.com

Proxy Communications
2200 Ave K
Ste 300
Plano, TX 75074
Phone: (800) 967-7997
Fax: (214) 969-7311
www.proxycom.com

PTM Communications International
352 Seventh Ave
New York, NY 10001
Phone: (212) 643-5458
Fax: (212) 643-5486

Quality Telemarketing Inc.
13434 A St
Omaha, NE 68144
Phone: (402) 697-1661
Fax: (402) 697-1611

Index to Advertisers

Index to Supplier Categories

Company Alpha Index